African American Literature

Politics of Marginal Space in the Fiction of Gloria Naylor

Anurag Kumar

ATLANTIC
PUBLISHERS & DISTRIBUTORS (P) LTD

Published by
ATLANTIC
PUBLISHERS & DISTRIBUTORS (P) LTD
7/22, Ansari Road, Darya Ganj, New Delhi-110002
Phones : +91-11-40775252, 23273880, 23275880, 23280451
Fax: +91-11-23285873
Web: www.atlanticbooks.com
E-mail: orders@atlanticbooks.com

Branch Office
5, Nallathambi Street, Wallajah Road, Chennai-600002
Phones : +91-44-64611085, 32413319
E-mail: chennai@atlanticbooks.com

Printed in India at Nice Printing Press, A-33/3A, Site-IV, Industrial Area, Sahibabad, Ghaziabad, U.P.

Preface

The book clearly conveys its central argument in the opening paragraphs and makes the assertion that novels of Gloria Naylor give literary expression to a marginal spatial reality that sustains a dialectic of repression and resistance. Referencing Hegelian dialectics, Kantian antimonies and Foucauldian agonism, the introduction of this book delineates the complexities of identity, ideology and consciousness in the marginal space and identifies female bonding as a central, recurring mechanism of resistance in Naylor's novels. Her novels are then discussed chronologically by date of publication with consistent attention to the ways in which each novel defines the marginal space, not only as a site of gender and racial oppression, but also as a site of celebration and potential resistance. The second last chapter of the book, in its analysis of the liminal position of African American men, offers a useful and insightful theorizing of gender as dialectical opposition and continuum in *The Men of Brewster Place*. The last chapter highlights an interesting phenomenon, where the persona (Naylor) undergoes the surveillance that has no limit, and even the most private space of the mind is monitored by the state agencies.

The depth and breadth of the research conducted for this book are impressive. In the review of literature, the foundational works of black feminist critics like Frances Beale and bell hooks offer a solid theoretical and methodological grounding. At the same time, the study is attentive to the work of Naylor scholars like Virginia Fowler, Maxine Montgomery and Charles Wilson. Using relevant scholarly sources from a number of other disciplines and theorists, the book clarifies the role, nature and function of politics and history in the construction of the marginal space.

Clearly written and formatted, the book makes complex theoretical concepts accessible, skilfully includes quoted material and is accurate and careful in its documentation. It makes a substantive contribution, not only to the critical corpus on Gloria Naylor and to African American studies, but contributes as well to the growing scholarship on the modern, postmodern and postcolonial conditions, informing the global structural inequities which expel the dispossessed and the powerful to marginal space.

Anurag Kumar

Acknowledgements

I must acknowledge the indispensible and unforgettable assistance of those who have overtly or covertly been able to extend some help in shaping, rationalizing and reshaping the book. I must begin with acknowledging Almighty for enabling me through His blessings to complete this work. I owe a sincere and venerable indebtness to my Ph.D. supervisors Prof. Nagendra Kumar and Dr. Smita Jha, IIT Roorkee for their suggestions and encouragements. I am indeed fortunate to have a mentor like Prof. G. Neelkantan, IIT Kanpur, who has always motivated me to work with sincerity, vigor and honesty. I feel blessed to express my sense of gratitude to Prof. Madhu Mehrotra, University of Lucknow, who has introduced me to the uncanny and unfathomable writings of Gloria Naylor. I further place on record my thanks to Prof. Pashupati Jha and Dr. Binod Mishra, IIT Roorkee, for their valuable inputs and enthusiastic support.

I feel a deep sense of gratitude for my parents, Smt. Meera and Munendra Pandey and my siblings who have formed my vision, shaped my consciousness and infused in me the sense and value of filial relationship.

I warmly thank Dr. Veerendra Mishra, my fellow, brother and above all, a wonderful human being who has always offered me, with his critical acumen, deep penetrating insight and theoretical understanding over a cup of tea and beyond. Yet another scholar, Sudhir Pandey, whose feedback of my work has indeed been encouraging requires my heartfelt gratitude. A word of acknowledgement may seem incomplete without acknowledging the venerable thanks to Ms. Monika who has always supported and encouraged me in my endeavors.

Anurag Kumar

Contents

Preface ..... *iii*

Acknowledgements ..... *v*

1. Introduction 1

2. Marginal Space and Female Bonding: Resistance in Gloria Naylor's *The Women of Brewster Place* 38

3. Dialectics of the Location: Resistance through Female Bonding in Gloria Naylor's *Linden Hills* 72

4. Locating Resistance in Willow Springs through Cultural Practices and Female Bonding in Gloria Naylor's *Mama Day* 105

5. Transforming the Subject through Female Bonding in the Marginal Space: Resistance in Gloria Naylor's *Bailey's Café* 135

6. Dialectical Opposition and Continuum: Resistance in Gloria Naylor's *The Men of Brewster Place* 170

7. Writing from the Margin: Reading Gloria Naylor's *1996* 202

8. Conclusion 216

Works Cited 223

Chapter 1

Introduction

A systematic study of the complete array of literary discourse, theory and criticism divulges the fact that they explicitly or implicitly refer to the arguments related to epistemology and ontology of consciousness, identity, and ideology on the one hand and the metaphysics of existence and presence on the other. The philosophical underpinnings of Feminism, Marxism, Psychoanalysis, Postcolonialism, Structuralism, Poststructuralism, New-historicism, and Deconstruction light upon the complex process of subjectivization which finally, acculturate an individual through the complex web of social constructionism which gradually turn one into a subject. Similarly, all forms of literary genre particularly novel expounds the historical realities of the formation of subject in which the individual is conditioned by all social and ideological apparatuses and finally, gets interpellated by experiencing the hegemonic and homologic order of the oppressive, imperialist and capitalist power structure. If novel, on the one hand, represents the socio-historical realities of subject formation and oppression, it, as a literary genre, also manifests the historical condition of diglossia or heteroglossia, carnivalesque tendency, and maximum contact zone which allows the subject to get disillusioned in the entire process of subject formation. Further, literature from the firmament of postcolonial or colonial experiences adumbrates the complex processes of subject formation and also certain ways of liberation in which the primary focus is laid upon socio-historical realties, cultural-materialistic condition and linguistic determinism. The literature, from the domain where the aforementioned cardinal elements play a significant role in the realization of the self and the process of subjectivization, may here be dealt with great perspicacity. In addition, with the growth of cultural and economic liberalism the significant changes have been registered and debated with regard to the formation of identity, ideology and consciousness. A gradual shift from structuralism, modernism, poststructuralism to postmodernism has also paved a path where multiple realities may exist by questioning the grand narrative. They represent the contingent universality which is fleeting and always welcoming the condition of hyperreal and simulacra. The advent of post-colonialism also encapsulates the basic principles of modernism, post-structuralism, and postmodernism which bring an apposite focus on the ideas of identity formation, construction of consciousness, and the politics of marginal space. Literatures particularly of the world which experienced the oppressive rule of colonial masters reflect upon some remarkable elements which are ambivalently employed for the construction of the self and which also in turn allows itself for liberation or anti-thesis. The literature, for instance, which emanates from African American realities, is indeed an outcome of modern, postmodern, and postcolonial conditions which creates some space where the marginal and the unspeakable voices can be heard.

A close examination of the synchronic and diachronic literary taxonomy on African American literature propagates the fact that the whole poetics of it is based upon the inexorable and relentless nexus between repression and resistance. The present research presents this nexus as an ever existing phenomenon in the lives of African American people in general and African American women in particular. Repression as a phenomenon is viewed as a process of subjectivization of the people of African descent triggered by the politics of patriarchy, racial discrimination, and hegemonic power structure of the ruling class. The study also attempts to locate and define the role of marginal space in the formation of subject in the process of resistance. It further examines the condition of the people who are controlled and repressed by the machinery of power structure within their own community and family. The recognition or the awareness of this repression leads to resistance which further fosters a bond among the repressive communities. The literature of resistance not only voices the repression inflicted on the people of African descent but also entails hope for the possibility of being liberated from the practices of what Foucault calls 'intolerable' (Pickett 462). The intention of the resistance is to liberate the people of African descent from the "oppressive external force" (Armstrong 22) and "to show inequalities among races and socio-economic groups in America and to encourage a transformation in society that engenders such inequalities" (Harris).

The present study confines itself to the analysis of the novels of Gloria Naylor "a self avowed feminist and black cultural nationalist" who "has produced a body of work that resists easy classifications" (Fowler 01) because it is "enormously diverse in its literary appeal and extensive in its vision" (Felton and Loris 01). The novelist has "a keen eye for moral and emotional dilemmas, a keen sympathy for the trials and triumphs of her characters, a vibrant response to the challenges of her own self-authorization and a compelling prose style that is gritty and sensuous, incantatory and apocalyptic..." (Smith 267). The geographical location of Naylor's novels represents the nature and function of marginal space. They conspicuously explicate the possibility of dialectics that is inbuilt into marginal space. As it is evident that her novels establish that 'marginal space' on the one hand, is the precarious consequence of the power structure, but on the other, it is a desired choice of a few because it allows them to question the authoritative nature of power, and further it also allows them to resist in order to identify their consciousness, identity, and ideology. In addition, the resistance in her novels is achieved through the bonding among the women which reflects through support, care, love, nurture, and sharing. It is an overt consequence of their important phenomenon of equally sharing the marginal space. The bonding among subjects helps them not only to resist the oppression of power structure but it also provides them with the sanctuaries of comfort, security and healing. An odyssey into the literary, cultural, political, and economic history of African American community may allow one to explore and to locate the viable reasons of their repression and resistance against the white, capitalist and hegemonic world order of the power structure.

The literature of the African Americans is deeply rooted in their history which has been an appropriate example of the worst kind of inequality, subjugation, oppression, and dehumanization. The repression and denigration of the blacks as human beings may be traced back to their arrival on the American continent in seventeenth century, in order to serve the plantation economy of the American South. They were deprived of every basic attribute of a human being and converted into a bestial figure. Even their reproductive, sexual, and material prerogatives were appropriated for the benefit of their white masters, as Joel Kovel has beautifully explained the process of dehumanization of black people in the following paragraph:

> [F]irst reduced the human self of his black slave to a body and then reduced the body to a *thing*; he dehumanized his slave, made him quantifiable, and thereby absorbed him into a rising world market of productive exchange.... Thus, in the new culture of the West, the black human was reduced to a black thing, virtually the same in certain key respects as the rest of non-human nature—all of which could become property. (18)

The aforementioned extract expounds the fact that the white masters signify blackness as a sign of negativity, ugliness, uncontrolled irrational behavior, and violent sexuality. The power structure owned and controlled by the whites has forced the African Americans to lead a mean, degrading, and traumatically torturous life. The signification of the black underlies their relevance as a labor force for the whites and they exist only as a beast of burden in an inhuman condition. By associating such negative meanings to the black color as burden of evil, fear and ugliness, the discourse of race has degraded the black to the level of a devil and a new incarnation of Satan. Furthermore, the aboriginal and essential values of African Americans such as self-respect, self-love, dignity and pride in their race have been erased by the inextricable association of negativity with blackness. The perpetuation of their inhuman predicament has aptly been delineated by A.K. Shukla who notes that during slavery "a black was lynched, degraded, condemned and looked down upon leading to the bruising of his ego and distortion of his self image" (64). It portrays the candid representation of the narrative of the blacks who have been devalued and have been forced to lead a dehumanized life. Further, the study may light upon the predicament of African American women who are predominantly controlled and subjectivised by the patriarchal and the capitalist society.

The condition of African American women has been more pathetic and miserable as they have to work both in the house and in the field; and they have been used as "an object of sexual exploitation. They have been viewed as an over-sexed, immoral, loose women who were always available for instant sexual gratification, as well as for the procreation of the race" (Plakkoottam 12-13). Megha Bharati and L.M. Joshi reiterate that the same phenomenon when they point out that "[b]lack Community had to face atrocities like racism and exploitation, irrespective of sex. However, black women were more oppressed physically and mentally and their cause of grievances was greater. Pushed to the periphery on account of their gender, a black woman's life was full of horrors" (37). They have been assigned a number of stereotypical images which have deeply been rooted in American slavery. The stereotypical images have denied them the status of a civilized human being. Thus, they did not have any claim to respect and dignity they deserved as human beings. They are defined as if they belong to the animal species and therefore, they must be denied the respect which is assigned to a human being. Further, the lack of the support of black men in their lives complicates their corporeal and psychological predicament. Since the black male has himself been mistreated, tormented and under a great weight of helplessness pressing on him, he has found himself unable to help his woman. Gerda Lerner views it remarkably when she finds two reasons for black woman's repression "[t]hat black woman was degraded by the sexual attack (by white men) and more profoundly, by being deprived of a strong black man on whom she could rely for protection" (xxiii). In a similar fashion, Francis Beal has viewed the condition of black woman in the patriarchal white society:

> By reducing the black man in America to such abject oppression, the black woman had no protector and was used, and is still being used in some cases, as the scapegoat for the evils that this horrendous system has perpetrated on black men. Her physical image has been maliciously maligned; she has been sexually molested and abused by the white colonizer; she has suffered the worst kind of economic exploitation, having been forced to serve as the white woman's maid and wet nurse for white offspring while her own children were, more often than not, starving and neglected. It is the depth of degradation to be socially manipulated, physically raped, used to undermine your own household, and to be powerless to reverse this syndrome. (343)

The foregone discourse has explained the condition of the black women in an oppressive and exploitative air of the white patriarchal society. The society in context has always exercised different agencies and apparatuses to control and to subjectivize the ideology and identity of the black women—the political, economic, and social. One of the apparatuses of the power structures to control the African Americans is their confinement in the marginal spaces of ghettoes which have further prompted the black women to resist the hegemonic world order of the power structure. This brings out the historical reality of resistance which emanates from the literary history of the black women. Black women's literary history is the history of resistance against all possible kinds of forces that have constantly been trying to suppress their voices historically, textually, and culturally. However, their odyssey of resistance against the power structure has not been easy one as it implies a resistance against a lethal combination of both racial and patriarchal repression. Bell hooks, an eminent African American critic and theorist, observes that black women have been caught between the polarities of race and gender repression as they have been subjected to "racial polarity in the form of white supremacy and sexual polarity in the form of male dominance" (*Ain't I a Woman* 120). The polarity is quite visible in that the black women have been disillusioned by the white women's movement of 1960s. This mainstream feminism is identified with the movement defined by the white, middle-class, college-educated women. Betty Friedan's *Feminist Mystique* (1963) expresses the frustration and exclusion of white middle-class women from the positions of power and privilege occupied by white males in American society. The book has earned sympathy of the women who are the victims of sexism within their family and personal lives. The agenda that Friedan has proposed is to eliminate sexist oppression imposed by the patriarchal society which would, in turn, end the discrimination against women on the job, in the home, and in all areas of women's lives.

The form of feminism which has emanated from Betty Friedan's *Feminist Mystique* and which is occupied only by white, middle-class, college-educated women, does not address the concern of the African American women. Though black feminism is a part of mainstream feminist discourse, it has been pushed into the margins because of its peculiar but crucial issues of race and class. Black female writers have contributed to the separation of black feminism from the mainstream white feminism by portraying such characters that are constantly used to question the issues and strategies of white feminism by putting them into a context of racial and class conflict in order to assert the importance of margin to the centre. Consequently, a number of critics have reacted against it, for instance, Francis Beal in her essay, "Double Jeopardy: To Be Black and Female" (1970) criticizes white women's movement for its limited focus. She says, "[a]ny white group that does not have an anti-imperialist and anti-racist ideology has absolutely nothing in common with the Black Women's struggle" (351). Bell hooks has pointed out that black feminists are concerned about economic survival, ethnic and racial discrimination along with sexism, and she interrogates the mainstream white women's movement for failing to speak on these issues. Speaking of the movement, hooks says "[w]hite women who dominate feminist discourse, who for the most part make and articulate feminist theory, have little or no understanding of white supremacy as a racial politics, of the psychological impact of class, of their political status within a racist, sexist, capitalist state" (*From Margin to Center* 04). Hooks further comments that white women may be victimized by sexism, but racism enables them to act as exploiters and oppressors of black women:

> Black women are in an unusual position for not only are we collectively at the bottom of the occupational ladder, but the overall social status is lower than that of any other group. Occupying such a position we bear the brunt of sexist, racist and classist oppression. Racist stereotypes of the strong, superhuman black woman are operative myths in the minds of many white women, allowing them to ignore the extent to which black women are likely to be victimized in this society, and the role white women play in the maintenance and perpetuation of that victimization. (14)

Thus, black women's experiences of oppression in social and patriarchal space cannot be equated with those of the white middle-class women because the white middle-class women represent an inherent dialectics with regard to the situation of being the oppressor and the oppressed. On the one hand, their condition in the patriarchal society is that of an oppressed whereas the same white women function as oppressor when they are among the black women. This socio-economic, political, and racial phenomenon portrays the condition of the white women through the place of pharmakon. Evelyn Brooks Higginbotham in "African American Women's History and the Metalanguage of Race" points out that despite all efforts by the black and third world feminist scholars' emphasis on "homogeneous womanhood," "woman's culture," and "patriarchal oppression of women," the "[w]hite feminist scholars pay hardly lip service to race as they continue to analyze their experience in even more sophisticated form" (251-52). However, Higginbotham emphasizes the "[f]eminist scholars, especially those of African-American women's history, must accept the challenge to bring race more prominently into their analysis of power" (252). The historical realities of the black with regard to their racial conditions may veritably explicate their possibilities of oppression and resistance. Hence, a proper deliberation of their racial identities may represent their realities in the complex web of capitalist world in which social, economic, political, and cultural realities are inextricably intertwined. Henderson in his article "Speaking in Tongues: Dialogics, Dialectics, and the Black Woman Writer's Literary Tradition" also finds the reason for black women's resistance which reads as "black women have been discounted or unaccounted for in the 'traditions' of black, women's, and American literature as well as in the contemporary literary-critical dialogue" (02). These movements have cardinally focused upon several elements of repression, resistance and emancipation, and they further try to kindle a kind of self-respect in the black people but ignore the contribution of black women. Harlem Renaissance, for instance, is said to have been considered as the beginning of the resistance as it paves the way for African American voices which is quite evident in its revisionary mode that revives all the forgotten texts written by blacks, with the intention of putting them in a literary tradition rooted in the time of slavery. Black Power movement is also a reaction against the ideology and consciousness of integration which is "based on the assumption that there is nothing of value in the black community and that little of value could be created among black people" (Carmichael 05). The Black Power movement intends that "[t]he racial and cultural personality of the black community must be preserved and that community must win its freedom while preserving its cultural integrity" (06). Unfortunately, they have undermined or rather rejected the contribution of women in African American tradition. Bell hooks explains the reason behind such an exclusion as "[u]nderlying...is the assumption that the experience of men are more important than those of women and that what matters most among the experience of men is their ability to assert themselves patriarchally" (*Ain't I a Woman* 22).

Tapan Basu brilliantly exposes the indifference of these movements towards women by quoting a witty observation of Frederick Douglass about Martin Delaney, a separatist African American leader. The statement reads "[e]very morning

I [Douglass] am satisfied to thank god for making me a man simply; but he [Delaney] always thanks him for making him a black man" (quoted in Basu 378). He observes that this "piece of witticism would bring to notice the remarkable sidelining of women from the strategic discourse of both the primary schools of thought in African American dissent (Separatist and integrationist)" (378). In addition, Basu finds that the leaders of the movement of African American resistance were patriarchal in their thought and approach as they "...shared the view that racism was the foremost evil confronting African American men, most agreed, needed to assert their masculinity..." (382). The notorious Moynihan Report further acted to create this void between African American male and African American female. It popularized that "African American man was victimized more than the African American woman and that the time had come for him to step forward and for her to step backward. Some African American men even claimed to have been victimized by African American women—grandmothers, mothers, sisters and wives" (382).

The primary reason for the "insufficient participation of African American women in African American protest movements" has been chauvinism that is brought about by the Moynihan Report (382). Another explicable reason has been the patriarchal attitude of the leaders of the movement. Basu further points out that Malcolm X's attitude, for instance, has been influenced by Islamic teachings and he has openly blamed African American women "for the miserable condition of African American men" (382). Further, quoting Malcolm's "grossly offensive utterance," Basu makes Malcolm's approach towards women more transparent (382). He quotes "I'd had too much experience that women were only tricky, deceitful, untrustworthy flesh. I had seen too many men ruined, or at least tied down, or in some other way messed up by women" (quoted in Basu 382). It is because of the aforementioned attitude of the leaders, "[d]uring 1970s and after, the African American movement has got repeatedly fractured over the issue of gender, an inevitable consequence of its patriarchal orientation" (382). He suggests that the contribution and relevance of women in the movements should have been recognized and the leaders of the movement must feel that "African American women exist at the intersection of all forms of oppression in American society—sexual, racial, economic—and their struggle for equality forms a window through which the liberatory potential of the African American movement at large may be glimpsed" (382).

The aforementioned discussion represents the marginal, repressed, subjugated, subjectivised, exploited, and devalued condition of the black women in the entire trajectory of historical realities of the African Americans in a dominant society. The black women have been pushed into the margin and have been exploited by the capitalist power structure which is not only reflected in the literary discussion but also in integrationist and separatist movements led and controlled by the African American political leaders. The recognition of the marginalized status and the identification of the location of marginal space of the blacks in general, and the black women in particular, has confabulated their consciousness to resist the knotty knots of marginality which is not necessarily "imposed by oppressive structure" (hooks *Yearning* 148) rather it is:

> One chooses as site of resistance—as location of radical openness and possibility. This site of resistance is continually formed in that segregated culture of opposition that is our critical response to domination. We come to this space through suffering and pain, through struggle to be that which pleasures, delights, and fulfils desire. We are transformed, individually, collectively, as we make radical creative space which affirms and sustains our subjectivity, which gives us a new location from which to articulate our sense of the world. (*Yearning* 148)

The critical discourse in the context explains that the marginal space is a critical and political response to domination. In continuation, bell hooks proposes that the marginal space to which the black women belong in a society provides them with the space for resistance against the dominant ideology. She also makes it clear that representing marginality as a site of resistance is an act of being political that may help in overcoming the brutal act of silencing those who are disposed and powerless. She adumbrates that:

> Understanding marginality as position and place of resistance is crucial for oppressed, exploited, colonized people. If we only view the margin as a sign, marking the condition of our pain and deprivation, then certain hopelessness and despair, a deep nihilism penetrates in a destructive way the very ground of our being. It is there in that space of collective despair that one's creativity, one's imagination is at risk, there that one's mind is fully colonized, there that the freedom one longs for as lost.... So I want to note that I am not trying to romantically re-inscribe the notion of that space of marginality where the oppressed live apart from their oppressor as 'pure'. I want to say that these margins have been both sites of repression and sites of resistance. And since we are well able to name the nature of that repression we know better the margin as a site of deprivation. We are more silent when it comes to speaking of the margin as site of resistance. We are more silenced when it comes to speaking of the margin as site of resistance. (149-51)

Marginal discourse further produces the counter-hegemonic identities and fosters a bond among the communities of resistance. Bell hooks inchoates the preface of her benchmark book, *Feminist Theory: From Margin to Center* as "[t]o be in the margin is to be part of the whole but outside the main body" (ix). The statement comprises the whole matrix of black women's position which bears marginal location in the mainstream American society. It implicitly connotes that the black women's experiences of oppression in social and patriarchal space cannot be equated with that of the white middle-class women. This is the margin which exists in opposition to the centre and which could be used to produce the 'counter-hegemonic' discourse to use hooks' terminology. Further she says "[i]t was this marginality that I was having as a central location of a counter-hegemonic discourse that is not just found in words but in habits of being and the way one lives. As such, I was not speaking of a marginalized one wishes to lose, to give up, but rather as a site one stays in, clings to even, because it nourishes one's capacity to resist..." (*Yearning* 153). Hooks sends an invitation proclaiming that "[m]arginality is the space of resistance. Enter that space. Let us meet there. Enter that space. We greet you as liberators" (152). This space of marginality ensures the survival of the oppressed, nurtures resistance, and provides openings "on the edge" in the chosen context of marginality, to build larger communities of survival and resistance (152). Thus, according to hooks, marginality not only stands for voicing the concerns of underprivileged but it is also an opportunity for the people on the margin to question the established order and to fight discrimination against them by forming a bond among themselves. Similarly, Surya Nath Pandey in his edited volume, *Writing in a Post-Colonial Space* (1999) proposes that the post-colonial space is the ongoing project of analyzing and combating unequal power-structures that addresses to the multiple intricacies of the post-colonial resistance. He further expounds that the very discourse of post-colonial literature "demonstrates 'resistance' and 'subversion' of the imperial 'centre' (the 'colonizer', the 'dominant' or the 'hegemonic' power)" (vii). Thus, post-colonial space that has been a site of all possible kinds of repressions—cultural, literary, and linguistic, now writes back to the centre to resist the sovereignty of the empire. He broods upon "several assumptions of the discourse of resistance in respect of the text, the author, and the social order" (viii). He also holds that some of the "major Indian writers appropriate the post-colonial space to manifest their strong animus against the erstwhile hegemonic power and its assumption" (vii). It propels the dwellers of the marginal space to identify and to locate their identity, consciousness and ideology which may allow them to survive even in the oppressive power structure.

The search and the location of marginal spaces have been necessary for the survival of African American women in America. These spaces are also important because of their counter-hegemonic attributes as they provide a chance to make significant changes in black female consciousness which is otherwise not possible. The world outside the domestic space, for instance, never allows black women to realize their consciousness.

Consequently, it becomes viable to construct such spaces where black women could identify and realize their consciousness. This indeed has a significant influence on the writers of color, for instance, the significance of the marginal spaces is quite viable to understand the novels of Gloria Naylor as they are not only important to African American women's survival, but also they exhibit black female emancipation and empowerment. Barbara Christian remarks in her essay "Naylor's Geography: Community, Class and Patriarchy in *The Women of Brewster Place* and *Linden Hills*" that "[be]cause of the consistency of forced displacement in our collective experience, we know how critical where we are is to the character of our social creations, of how place helps to tell us a great deal about who we are and who we can become" (106).

The seasonable phenomenon of becoming from the being or substance to the condition of subject has aptly been adumbrated by Gloria Naylor. Her novels are interconnected and have a strong sense of the place which signifies the site of power structure that is really dominating. Barbara Christian emphasizes the role of location on characters and how location defines their personality, identity, and status of life. It is because of the location that Brewster Place, though inhabited by working class poor blacks appears to be a "community held together primarily by women, while Linden Hills is characterized as a group of houses that never becomes a community, a showplace precariously kept in place by the machination of one wealthy black patriarchal family" (106). The role of location is quite evident in Naylor's novels as the location of space provides characters with an opportunity to create an unsurpassable bonding to galvanize their relationship which further allows them to combat the condition of exploitation and repression. Margot Anne Kelley in "Framing the Possibilities: Collective Agency and the Novels of Gloria Naylor" demonstrates that Naylor in her *Baileys Café* makes "the marginal become centre" by using different frames for the representation of different women "that had previously been unrepresentable" (135). She puts her characters in a natural environment of Eve's boarding house and empowers them without uprooting them from their non-privileged position or marginal location, making true what Culler says, "...the marginal becomes central by virtue of its own marginality" (quoted in Kelley). Similarly, in "Spiritual and Moral Sanctuary in Gloria Naylor's Fiction," Virginia C. Fowler illustrates how Naylor's fictional space provides a safe place from the tyrannical world. This trajectory is symbolically representative of the survival strategies of the black Americans to survive in a racist and sexist society. This sanctuary created by Naylor fosters human bonds which "generate hope and provides healing, enabling her characters, in the words of Mama Day's father, to 'just live on' (*Mama Day* 266)" (142). Thus, it is seemingly clear that the marginal space, which is on the one hand a result of political, economic, and racial and social repression of the black by the white capitalist dominant class but it is also an alternative choice of the dispossessed and marginals because it provides them with an opportunity to resist dominant and hegemonic power structure. It may not be an exaggeration to say that the place if cannot design, it can at least affect the construction of the subject in the process of subjectivization or in the journey from being to becoming. The marginal space does not only provide the hegemonic, homologic and heterologic experiences to its dwellers but it also allows them to search a new space 'home' which may allow them to form a cohesive bond among themselves and also an emancipatory consciousness or ideology.

The home space provides the African American women not only the location to resist the hegemonic white world order but also an opportunity to form a bond among them which may necessitate their survival in a hostile world. Bell hooks along with Maxine Lavon Montgomery, Patricia Hill Collins and Paul Marshall present home as an important construct in resisting the harmful and negative images of the black, a creation by the hegemonic white world. Bell hooks, for instance, in the following lines deliberates upon the appropriation and expansion of home space by the black women which resists its sexist or patriarchal construction:

> Historically, black women have resisted white supremacist domination by working to establish homeplace. It does not matter that sexism assigned them this role. It is more

> important that they took this conventional role and expanded it to include caring for one another, for children, for black men, in ways that elevated our spirits, that kept us from despair, that taught some of us to be revolutionaries able to struggle for freedom. (*Yearning* 44)

Hooks, further, observes that homeplace, more than a domestic service or the necessity for everyday survival, has been an important source of resistance. Hooks also observes in the following paragraph that home space offers the African Americans a safe sanctuary. The world outside of home has always been hostile to them and has denigrated them into objects; home is the only space where they control their subjectivity:

> Historically, African American people believed that the construction of a homeplace, however, fragile and tenuous (the slave hut, the wooden shack), had a radical political dimension. Despite the brutal reality of racial apartheid, of domination, one's homeplace was the one site where one could freely confront the issue of humanization, where one could resist. Black women resisted by making homes where all black people could strive to be subjects, not objects, where we could be affirmed in our minds and hearts despite poverty, hardship, and deprivation, where we could restore to ourselves the dignity denied us on the outside in the public world. (43)

In addition, Maxine Lavon Montgomery also ruminates on the subject of home as a site of resistance in her book, *The Fiction of Gloria Naylor: Houses and Spaces of Resistance* (2010). Lavon presents "home and home space to be more conducive to black self-actualization, thus providing a stark contrast to a dominant white patriarchy evident in a broader public sphere" (flap). She employs "a postcolonial and feminist theoretical framework to analyze Naylor's evolving body of work" (xv). Maxine Lavon "offer[s] an interrogation of representations of home as Naylor reinscribes a history involving black resistance and the adoptive strategies that have allowed African Americans to achieve an autonomous existence apart from white society and its killing definitions of the self" (xviii). Further, in "Good Housekeeping: Domestic Ritual in Gloria Naylor's Fiction," Maxine Lavon

Montgomery explores a connection among the first four novels of Gloria Naylor based on "representations of the housewife, beleaguered by an endless round of cooking, cleaning, and mothering" (55). Naylor, unlike other black women writers, presents the gendered and cultural aspect of domesticity and home space. She extends the location of home to the domain of domestic activities which provides the characters with an opportunity to interrogate the oppressive order, and also to resist it. It can viably be viewed in *The Women of Brewster Place,* which highlights the relentless and triggered endeavors of marginalized women in establishing and maintaining the domestic order.

Unlike white women, these black women have to work outside the home else they have to depend upon social welfare, a gift of the dominant to the marginalized, as in the case of Cora Lee which is one of the aspects of black women's domesticity. The domestic construction of Brewster Place of which Mattie acts as a spiritual mother results in communal bond. Contrary to *The Women of Brewster Place* (1982) where domesticity is controlled by black women, in *Linden Hills* (1985), 'Home' becomes a place which is dominated by patriarchy and is used to confine and subjugate women "[t]he Nedeed home is a locale where the hierarchical socio-political structure responsible for the marginalization of the black women is replicated" (60). *Linden Hills* also reinstates the danger that may emanate from domesticity, if, divorced from community empowerment. This is followed by a discussion of *Mama Day* (1988) which is set in a total matrilineal context inhabited by "semi-divine women" (63). These women figures appear to be the "guardians of indigenous culture" which is African in nature (63). They are also involved in maintaining a home, the history of which could be traced back to Sapphira Wade, the island matriarch. The next novel, *Bailey's Café* (1992) suggests that black women in America are not left with much options; house work is generally the only job available to a black woman which is exemplary in the case of Sadie who "is socialize to believe that her self-worth is predicated upon her success as a homemaker, so she tries to become the ideal housekeeper, first, in order to win her mother's approval and, later, that of her elderly husband, Daniel" (65). The novel has created a "woman centered cosmology" which has faith in "family of choice", rather than the nuclear family system (67). Miss Maple, in the text offers "an alternative to the burdened housewife" that challenges the gendered construction of the home space (66).

Similarly, in "The Social Construction of Black Feminist Thought," Patricia Hill Collins articulates that the African American women activists are supported by numerous "countless, ordinary African American women who, through strategies of everyday resistance (dynamics of home), created a powerful foundation for this more visible Black feminist activist tradition" which further contributes to the construction of black feminist thought (745-46). In another article titled "Shifting the Center: Race, Class, and Feminist Theorizing about Motherhood," Collins contextualizes and outlines the practice of using the home as a site of resistance. In this connection, the power of maternal resistance (which is a construct of home space) has been elucidated in Paul Marshall's short essay "From the Poets in the Kitchen". She proposes that the kitchen provides the women a space which allows them to construct around them to be themselves and which in turn resists the stereotypes of menial labor. Marci Bounds Littlefield in "Black Women, Mothering, and Protest in 19th Century American Society" studies how black Americans have been subjected to "oppression, bondage, and capitalism" (53). Black motherhood, for instance, which operates from home, "was connected and rooted in a racial system of bondage" (54). She puts black motherhood in the context of slavery and reads "black women's response to motherhood; the importance of motherhood for black family life; and finds that black motherhood challenged hegemonic construction of race, gender, and class in 19th century American society" (53).

Furthermore, Naylor's whole oeuvre of writing marks a resistance to the objectification of black women in white as well as black male literature only to make them as the subject of discourse to establish them as a respected human being in the domain of hegemonic power of the capitalist society. This resistance is performed through the construction or formation of a bond among the women in her works. This female supportiveness provides them with an opportunity to question the oppressive system and may allow them to resist such repressive orders by strengthening their cumulative voice as a result of their filial bonding. Larry R. Andrews in "Black Sisterhood in Naylor's Novels" explores the bond of sisterhood among the realities of African American women. She observes that the female characters of Naylor's novels mark a distinguishable difference from the characters of previous writers in which the women characters do not have inter-generational bond which can be seen in her fictional world. Andrews finds that the bond in Naylor's first two novels, *The Women of Brewster Place* and *Linden Hills*, is based on "the women's previous sense of isolation, from their mistreatment by men, and from their regenerative discovery, through suffering, of the saving grace of shared experiences" (285) while her third novel, *Mama Day*, represents the filial bond among the women as something which:

> [D]oes not arise as a refuge from isolation, mistreatment by men, or loss of identity in the white and black bourgeois worlds. It predates and transcends these modern conditions. Most important is the historical connection that runs from the legendary free spirit who founded the community, Sapphira Wade, through Miranda (Mama Day) to Miranda's great-niece Ophelia. (286)

Further, Andrews observes that Naylor's *The Women of Brewster Place* is the most powerful example of black sisterhood as "despite numerous conflicts, she unites the women in Mattie's dream of the block party (which may come true). They join in an act of protest against the power of men over women (the gang-rape of the lesbian Lorraine) and, more broadly, against the barriers of racist and class oppression (the bloodstained wall) that distort relations between the sexes" (286).

The female bonding may also be based on the collective memory of the women; this is what Sarah Katherine Foust Vinson has explored in her thesis *Storied Memories: Memory as Resistance in Contemporary Women's Literature* (2010) where she locates memory as a site of resistance. She delves deeper into the fact that the collective memory of the community may help the characters to form a bond and devise "new ways of understanding and overcoming the horrors of their own personal pasts, while also generating the strength to resist the communal patriarchal and racist traumas that oppress them as a group" (255). Similarly, women's screams and laughter may also serve the motif of shared bonding among them. Jenny Brantley in her article "Women's Screams and Women's Laughter," for instance, suggests that the sounds of screams and laughter could be read as the sounds of resistance, celebration of bonding and are "instrumental to the narratives, to the creation of the new—to the creation of a community that carries in it the potential for salvation" (37). Screams have been used by Naylor to whenever there is a narrative shift "be they births, deaths, moves, or losses" (22). Laughter, on the other hand is viewed in opposition to screams which "opens a place to begin the healing, and healing leads to salvation" (22). Brantley identifies these screams and laughter as "what Kristeva would identify as preverbal sounds" (22). These screams and laughter become the whole narrative, for instance, in *The Women of Brewster Place* as the novel begins with the laughter of the black girls; and they play almost a very important role in each story. Though in *Linden Hills* also the scream has been used as a narrative, this is different, for instance, from Ciel's that represents the inner hurt as Willa's screams are used as a narrative of resistance against her husband's cruelty and a desire to reconnect to the outside world. Willie is the only character in the novel who could hear and interpret the screams of Willa and acts as a "gendered female and holds the traditional female role of silence" (30). Naylor's *Mama Day* is full of so many losses and the only way out that Naylor seems to suggest in the novel is through screams, "[t]he recovery from these losses, signaled by the screams, can only occur through the generation of still more screams, from the merging of the preverbal with the verbal text" (32). Laughter, on the other hand, works as a reunion much like between Etta Mae and Mattie in *The Women of Brewster Place*, as when George arrives Willow Springs the women are waiting with their laughter and call him "Child" which was a strange word for him so far. Naylor's fourth novel *Bailey's Café* has mixed gentry of characters; some of them like Sadie, a 25 cents whore, who despite her condition manages to laugh. Her "laughter is countered by the screams of Mariam", a virgin mother (36) who also represents the shared bonding of the women at Eve's house.

It is often observed that the bonding among the African American women is constrained due to their different sexual orientation and that further results in the women's conformation to heterosexual hegemonic patriarchal control. Barbara Christian in one of her chapters from *Black Feminist Criticism* "No More Buried Lives: The Theme of Lesbianism in Audre Lorde's *Zami*, Gloria Naylor's *The Women of Brewster Place*, Ntozake Shange's *Sassafras, Cypress and Indigo*, and Alice Walker's *Color Purple*" explores that the 1980s is remarkable for the exploration of the experiences of lesbians in the fictional works by black writers who "include overtly lesbian characters among their presentation of the varieties of black womanhood" (187). While exploring the oppression of the lesbians in American society, Christian finds that the lesbians in *The Women of Brewster Place* are "oppressed because they are black and women and lesbians" (195).

What Naylor puts forth through these lesbian characters in the novel is that despite the nature of their sexual relationship, they are essentially women and thus have to be allowed to be an integral part of the female coalescence of Brewster community. Mattie echoes the same when she answers to Etta when she says that they are not different from us, "[m]aybe it's not so different.... Maybe that's why some women get so riled up 'bout it 'cause they know deep down it's not so different at all" (141). In Naylor's *Linden Hills*, Jesse Bell is yet another character who is a lesbian; she is a victim of isolation and marginality at her husband's home which has further pushed her into a lesbian relationship. Her engagement in a lesbian relationship is an act of defiance against the male control over female sexuality. Similarly, Kimberly A. Costino in her paper "'Weapons Against Women': Compulsory Heterosexuality and Capitalism in *Linden Hills*" explores that the mandatory heterosexual norms in the society may constrain the possibility of female bonding, for instance, in *The Women of Brewster Place* Theresa and Lorraine are not accepted in any communities "like Linden Hills and Park Heights...because of their homosexual identities" (43). She explicates that Gloria Naylor's novels "examine compulsory heterosexuality as a political institution" (41) which, for instance, is evident in the suffering of Laurel who could not "completely conform to heterosexual norms by producing heirs" (45) and which further constrains her acceptance in Linden community. Naylor interrogates sexuality in a variety of ways and produces "a spectrum of sexual identities" which is evident in Mattie and Etta's relationship, and Willie and Lester's relationship for instance (41). What she makes clear is that Naylor finds "heterosexuality as a strategy...not an innate or inevitable, then it is not necessarily fixed and stable" (46) and which further constrains the possibilities of female bonding. In "Dream, Deferral, and Closure in *The Women of Brewster Place*", Jill L. Matus locates female bonding in the last scene of the novel despite the fact that the dreams of the characters are constantly shattered and even the ending of the novel is deferred because it only takes place in Mattie's dream. In his opinion, "there are many readers who feel cheated and betrayed to discover that the apocalyptic destruction of Brewster's wall never takes place" (52). The novel refers to Langston Hughes' poem "Dream Deferral" which shows the nature of dream as unachieved one. Matus also refers to the dreams of the inhabitants of Brewster who keep on having a dream despite all odds so is Mattie's dream of destruction of the wall. Also, for him Mattie's dream marks a significant resistance to the authorial social setup that controls everything around but cannot stop, the seed of resistance that lies within and spurts in the dream reality. Mattie seems hopeful, however, that the dream will come true.

Female bonding is innate and inherent in the lives of African American women which further depend on their shared repressive experience in the hegemonic world. Though the women may appear different in their thoughts and actions, they are united beneath the superfluous confrontation. This is explored by Ebele Eko in "Beyond the Myth of Confrontation: A Comparative Study of African and African-American Female Protagonists." She expounds the bonding between mother and daughter in *The Women of Brewster Place* despite the initial confrontation on each other's location. The writings by Black women across geography since 1960s have given "creative birth to a new breed of female protagonists" who are used by these writers "to show the crucial importance of female determination to stand for equity and choice" (13). These protagonists, because of their age and times, are radical in their nature and approach which makes them confront their mothers against the 'totems' of that tradition (13). Another reason for their confrontation is that "their mothers too experienced similar frustrations in their youth but lacked a voice and silently conformed" (13). But the point is that unlike their mothers the young protagonists do not want to conform to the repressive orders and just want to be themselves for which they go to any extent; for instance, Kiswana denounces her mother as she cries out "I'd rather be dead than be like you—a white man's nigger who's ashamed of being black" (*WBP* 85). Ebele explores that there is something beyond existing this superfluous confrontation as "each (of the protagonist) discovers in herself a mere extension of her mother's personality" (14) and "each mother…somehow glimpses in her daughter "the girl she had once been" (16). What Ebele wants to point out is that the source of these young protagonists' dynamism and radicalism is none other than their mothers as when Kiswana listens to "her mother's theatrical recounting of her proud heritage and commitment to the black cause, suddenly, she comes to understand and appreciate the source of her own dynamism, idealism, and radicalism: her mother" (17).

The determination shown by these young protagonists forces people like her mother and others to "reevaluate their lives, to see what they have lost and gained, to come to grip with crucial issues of unity and cooperation in the black community" (18) and "[t]he cultural symbols of Kiswana's African name, hairdo, dress, and artifacts are her way of warning the upward-moving blacks not to forget their roots nor the bridge over which they have passed, that human bond and link to mother Africa that makes them a people. Nothing could be more practical" (18-19). Ebele concludes that "[t]heir sacrificial engagement to a vision of a better world order is, in the final analysis, the only valid measuring rod of their effectiveness as social, cultural and political missiles within fiction" (21) and which connects them with each other. Michael Awkward in the article "Authorial Dreams of Wholeness: (Dis) Unity, (Literary) Parentage, and *The Women of Brewster Place*" explores that Naylor in *The Women of Brewster Place* has demonstrated a different approach "by exhibiting essential psychological and circumstantial affinities between the women and by offering significant evidence of these women's recognition of such affinities—that the protagonists of the individual texts actually form, at the novel's conclusion, a community of women" (37-38) which emerges from "the redemptive possibilities of female coalescence" (37). This may have been influenced by "[b]lack cultures insistence on unity, even in the face of powerfully divisive opposition" (37).

If marginal space and home along with the strategy of female bonding has provided African Americans with an opportunity to register their voices of resistance against the supremacist, capitalist world order, the act of representation may allow them to identify their ideology and consciousness. Henderson regards the process of representation quite necessary for black women's self-inscription. He writes "[t]he self-inscription of black women requires disruption, rereading and rewriting the conventional and canonical stories, as well as revising the conventional generic forms that convey these stories" (11). In "'Shakespeare's Black?': The Role of Shakespeare in Naylor's Novels," Peter Erickson demonstrates that there has been four revisions of Renaissance which for black women is the most powerful among all eras as it provides a tendency of revising the canon which includes "another avenue for considering Shakespeare's work in relation to questions of race" (231). The author here explores that though Naylor's novels have reference to Shakespeare, Shakespeare has been diminished because of his cultural reach and "the absence and restriction imposed" on women (232). This is exemplary in *The Women of Brewster Place* where "Shakespeare's rendering of the dream motif" is followed by that of Langston Hughes' "What happens to a dream deferred?" (235). In *Mama Day,* "Naylor's subversive strategy is to create a black female equivalent to Prospero" and in naming characters "with double names," for example, Miranda has double name—"Miranda and Mama Day",—"...the former suggests the tie to Shakespeare, the latter breaks it by indicating the possibility of escaping from Shakespearean entrapment in the subservient daughter role" (243). Erickson finds Naylor's work defying Shakespearean position as "...the all-defining center of things", and belonging to "a separate tradition of black women writers" (246).

In a similar fashion, Karen Schneider in "Gloria Naylor's Poetics of Emancipation" explores that in her revision of Judeo-Christian mythic discourse, Naylor modifies the contents and scope, "infusing it with feminist and African American significance" (10). Her *Bailey's Café*, for instance, "destabilize[s] absolute ontological boundaries defined by genre, gender politics, class, and cultural/literary tradition" (03). Thus, she transcends from what Henry Louis Gates, Jr., has called "discursive indenture" (Quoted in Schneider 25). She gives an example of the character of Esther "...whose beauty gains her permission to speak and to act, Naylor's "Tar. Coal. Ugly" (*BC* 95), Esther finds herself in a dark, silent paralysis, sealed by betrayal and complicity" (Karen 10). She also foregrounds such characters as Bailey who is the central narrative in Bailey's Café and the story of Stanley (Miss Maple) who suffers the worst treatment in a racial society of America in spite of the best education he receives, in order to counter argue the charges on Naylor that she makes a "disparaging representations of black male characters" (02).

Similarly, Celeste Fraser rewrites the myth of the black matriarch against the power of the state which believes "in breaking the power of the black matriarchy" by creating "the monolithic image" in the article "Stealing B(l)ack Voices: The Myth of the Black Matriarch and *The Women of Brewster Place*" with reference to Moynihan report which locates the cause of poverty within the black family structure where the head of the family is a woman (95). He also points that Murray puts black women and children in one chapter and man in another and blames black women for "moral fecundity...which drains federal funds" (94). In order to dismantle the images of black women, Naylor portrays a number of characters that deny easy classification. Naylor shows that the cause of poverty does not lie in the matriarchal powers of black women rather the "illicit partnership between government and commerce that creates the ghetto(es)" (95). The last part of Naylor's novel in which the women dismantle the wall, in fact, "tear(s) down the definition of the African American family erected by Murray, Moyers, and Moynihan" (103). He concludes that "Naylor registers a profound protest against the robbery of the voice of African-American women attempted by makers of the myth of the black matriarchy" (103). Margaret Homans' essay "The Woman in the Cave" may also be as an act of protest against "the canonical erasure of women" (153) with an aim of "restoration and revaluation of lost women's experience" (153) in the face of the negative images of the black women being circulated in the society. She explores how, for instance, in Naylor's *Linden Hills* "Willa Nedeed's story of resistance and rebirth resonates not only with classical and later Western accounts of the successful effacement of women but also with feminist critique of and resistance to such effacements" (152).

After a close analysis, Homans reaches the conclusion that despite limitation of their "narrations as constructed by, as well as subversive of, androcentric culture," Naylor has been able "to expose to view the underworld of male domination, letting its horror speak for themselves" (177). Amy K. Levin in "Metaphor and Maternity in *Mama Day*" reconstructs the concept of mothering by offering "a model...based not on biological kinship or the Freudian reading of the nuclear family, but on female solidarity and a vision of women's leadership that can be traced to West African women's tradition" (70). This tradition of female leadership has existed for hundreds of years, and though altered, yet, not been completely wiped out by the slave trade. It exists to a great extent in Naylor's *Mama Day* where the whole community turns out to be a family and Mama Day acts as the mother figure. Drawing heavily upon this model and comparison between *Sowei* and Mama Day and *Gonde* and Ruby, Naylor through this metaphor of mothering taken from West African Women's tradition, subverts the Eurocentric theoretical framework and further takes the novel "beyond surface allusions to canonical works such as *The Tempest, Hamlet,* and *Clarissa*" (73). She also explores how the other works of Naylor "reinforce the importance of connections to an African model of female leadership, both directly and indirectly" (86). Similarly in "Authority, Multivocality, and the New World order in Gloria Naylor's *Bailey's Café*", Maxine Lavon Montgomery attempts to redefine Naylor's *Bailey's Café* as a novel that revises "the myriad forms of authority patriarchy legitimizes" in order to "construct(ing) a new world order among partially dispossessed women world-wide" (187). Naylor has portrayed each woman character emerging empowered even after almost crushed under patriarchal authority. Eve, for instance, "forced to provide for herself amidst dire economic circumstances" soon emerges as a powerful matriarch once she reaches the pilot town by establishing a boarding house (189). She further points "Eve encourages a creative revisioning of the spaces that traditionally have defined women's lives" (189). She concludes that *Bailey's Café* "reveals her attempt to revise codes of power, domination, and assertion present in a male text" (193).

In "Africana Womanist Revision in Gloria Naylor's *Mama Day* and *Bailey's Café*", Dorothy Thomson explores Gloria Naylor's revisionist acumen which has emerged from her academic pursuit that has enabled her in the discourses like "deconstruction and the tenets of feminism as well as...the Eurocentric canon" that validates the feminist exploration of Naylor's work having "dense symbology for delineations of oppressed women prevalent in the texts, especially *Linden Hills* and *Bailey's Café*" (89). Naylor's revisionary efforts or "the discursive practices of an 'Other' culture" (89) are at best in her novels, *Mama Day* and *Bailey's Café* as both of them align with "Africana womanism" (90) with a purpose "to liberate its subjects from oppressive histories through recursion and destabilization" (92). Gloria Naylor uses Africana womanist strategy that "successfully revises/deconstructs Judeo-Christian myth by stripping it of male-centred power" (92). Further, Dorothy notes that Naylor "establishes the collective voice of Willow Springs as having discursive authority" (93). She further comments that *Mama Day* belongs to "the tradition of the speakerly text, which recalls African oral tradition, the reader becomes a listener, a participant in the discourse community" (93). She continuously seeks similarity between the matriarchs of the island as the revision of Africana womanism. Naylor's *Bailey's Café* "roots each female's story in biblical history" that enables them to "make a place for African-descendent women in the central myth of western tradition; and...her rewriting of that myth purges women of thousands of years of blame and shame" (99). For instance, "Naylor's revision of the expulsion myth juxtaposes the logic of Eve's natural urges with the illogical wrath of God. Additionally, she highlights Adam's complicity: he may have been an idiot, but he, too, enjoyed the game" (99). Naylor falls into the category of the black women writers who "are constructing texts that pointedly call for a reversal of "the contemporary "Western scholarship" by "ask(ing) them (critics) to consider the Africana womanist as subtext, as negotiator of meaning in her own work" (108). Asked by Virginia C. Fowler about the use of Biblical allusions and revision, Naylor explains "I know there are times when I consciously will use biblical allusions, from *Brewster Place* on—that business about rain for forty days is a Biblical allusion. This last book [*Bailey's Café*], I did nothing but rewrite Biblical women, rewrite their lives. I've used it because I think it's a part of me" ("A Conversation" 127). Adriane L. Ivey in her article, "Beyond Sacrifice: Gloria Naylor Rewrites the Passion" writes about the Biblical influence on Naylor as, "[e]ach woman in *Bailey's Café* represents a Biblical figure as part of Naylor's grand critique of the Christian narrative. And each also offers a glimpse of the conflict between a feminine spirituality and the traditional masculine Christianity" (88). Fowler has further explained that, "Naylor commands knowledge of the Bible equal to that of many Biblical scholars. Her membership in the Jehovah's witness during her teens and early twenties rendered Biblical texts the language with which she apprehended the world and through which, as a writer, she shapes fictional worlds" (*Gloria Naylor: In Search of Sanctuary* 153).

The above discourse exemplifies that African American women writers have registered resistance to their negative representation or non-representation in the media and other literary art. This resistance of the African American women to the negative representation is perpetuated "through…recognition of how a contemporary critique of racist and sexist representation marginalizes women of color" (Crenshaw 1283). hooks observes that the very exposure of black people to film and television has been marked with the awareness that "mass-media was a system of knowledge and power reproducing and maintaining white supremacy. To stare at the television, or mainstream movies, to engage its images, was to engage its negation of black representation" (*Black Looks* 117). Elucidating Foucault, hooks emphasizes that all "relations of power" incorporate "...necessarily the possibility of resistance" (quoted in hooks 116), therefore, it is required "...to search those margins, gaps, and locations on, and through the body where agency can be found" (116). Similarly, Brooks and Hebert, too, necessitate the revisionist tendency when he points that "contemporary academic writing has criticized mainstream media for their negative depiction of African American women" (299). Quoting the critics such as hooks, Hudson and Collins, they assert that the African American women are trapped in media representation and it "distort(s) both the ways in which black women view themselves (individually and collectively) and the ways in which they are viewed by others" (Hudson 249 quoted in Brooks and Hebert). They also expound that "Black feminist thought also challenges the way some media outlets run by black men engage in misogynistic depiction of black women" (299). Further, they elucidate their proposition with a quote from Burks, "black independent cinema is not necessarily free of the dominant white, male, heterosexual hegemony that has succeeded, at one point or another, in colonizing us all" (Quoted in Brooks and Hebert 299). Jacqueline Bobo and Ellen Seiter in "Black Feminism and Media Criticism: *The Women of Brewster Place*" explore that the true representation of black women by black women through the media adaptations of black women's text meets with cold critical response from the critics despite the fact that they enjoy a wide acclaim from the audience. They further reiterate that this is high time for black women that there is "the aggressive move towards adapting black women's literature for film and television" but there is a lacuna of serious criticism directed towards them, and it is precisely triggered by racial and feminist cultural politics (27). The lack of media criticism is also motivated and controlled by the fact that "much of the creative and theoretical work written by black women is available only through alternative outlets, some mainstream critics remain ignorant of, and uneducated in black feminist thought" (29). However, the television adaptation of the novel, *The Women of Brewster Place* reconstructs and revises the mainstream Hollywood movies in many ways. Though the novel or film does not present "a utopian image of the community" however, it raises different points which "deeply held values that are starkly opposed to the values of mainstream white culture and economy" and "a scrutiny of sexism and of violence against black women by black men", along with "an exploration of a range of relationships between women: as friends, room-mates, lovers, mothers and daughters" (34-35). She further concludes that keeping in mind the contribution *The Women of Brewster Place* has made to the black feminist thought and its popularity among audience, much has to be done by the feminist critics concerning the works of women of color because "the creative work of black women writers, and the success of that work when adapted to small and large screens, can revitalize an interest among feminists in identifying and producing television and film which is both popular and politically challenging" (39).

In addition, Tanner appropriately notes how Naylor has represented the process of subjectivization and the condition of subjectivised black women in American society. His article, "Reading Rape" begins with a discussion of Duchamp's room-size art work which portrays "a life size model of a woman's naked body" (71), in an artificial landscape. Her body "announces as its most prominent feature a hairless vagina that is cut into the woman like a wound" (71) which indicates that the woman is lying abandoned after an act of rape, but the violence that has been perpetrated against this woman does not arouse any kind of sympathy, rather his work of art has perpetuated the crime by allowing the viewer to gaze, and thus, reduce the woman merely to the miserable state of object. Another text that the writer takes before discussing Naylor's *The Women of Brewster Place* is Faulkner's *Sanctuary* where the reader not only remains an observer, as in the case of Duchamp's art work, rather he also participates in the act of violence of rape. Faulkner does not present the rape but creates a gaping hole that the reader fills in. Further, the writer puts both these works into the category devised by Mulvey first being "the erotic identity of the viewing subject is clearly separated from the object (usually a woman) on the screen" and the second "viewing allows the spectator to identify with the object on the screen (usually a male hero)" (81). Further the writer has explored that Naylor's *The Women of Brewster Place* "upsets Mulvey's model of patriarchal viewing" (86). In Naylor's representation of Lorraine's rape, the victim does not appear to be an erotic object. She does not alienate the reader from the literary experience, rather she allows the reader to be the viewer and to be the participant in the pain Lorraine goes through while being raped by C.C. Baker.

The preceding discourse and the mentioned datum have appropriately delineated the forms and processes of resistance. They have also explained some plausible methods and methodologies which are employed for inculcating and maintaining resistance by fundamentally focusing upon the nature and function of resistance. Margin of space, Home, Female bonding, Revision and Representation have been discussed as some viable and yet remarkable methods and forms of resistance. All afore-mentioned principles of resistance surreptitiously bring the entire discourse into the magnetic field of power where the Hegelian 'dialectics', Kantian 'antinomies' and Foucauldian 'agonism' are at play. It represents the fact that there is an imperceptible yet inevitable continuum among all principles of resistance. Similarly, Tapan Kumar Basu in his article "Beyond the National Question: Shifting Agendas of African American Resistance" surveys the whole trajectory of the African American Resistance since its very inception till the 1992 riots in Los Angeles. He concludes that despite many leaders and organizations that took to resist the racism in the United States, because of the division "along lines of class, gender and ideology" all efforts seem to have outlived, thus, making space for an altogether different agenda for African American resistance (377). A close observation of the whole genealogy of African American resistance makes it evident that it is always confined to either integrationist or separatist discourse. If it moves from there, it is gripped by different movements like Black Panthers and Black Power movements, thus, limiting the scope and method of resistance. A solution or what Basu calls a different agenda of African American resistance could be traced to Foucault's idea of resistance which should be free from any limits "since any limits will be derived from ideals supported from modern power" (Pickett 447). Seeing a binary opposition between power and resistance, Foucault suggests that "[s]ince power is spread throughout society, and not localized in any particular place, the struggle against power must also be diffused" (458). Foucault is alleged by some critics as he "presents a bleak view of disciplinary society" because he finds every social agency should be resisted (445). For example, Foucault is of the opinion that "[h]umanism is also the legitimating force behind liberal democracy. It tells people that although they do not have power, they are still the rulers", and thus creates an illusionary power to trap the people (452). As a result:

> Foucault argues that it is necessary to undermine the categories and central concepts of humanism.... At the heart of humanism, according to Foucault, is the theory of the subject...who is subjected to the laws of society, nature, truth, and God.... That is, the very desire for power is to be eradicated from the individual in the name of truth, nature and society. (452-53)

Foucault's concern compels to observe the agenda of the writers of color who are intrinsically involved in resisting the white hegemonic world view through different methods and sites that could be assumed to be a new agenda of African American resistance. This is quite evident in the works of the black women writers like Maya Angelou, Toni Morrison, Zora Neale Hurston, Paule Marshall, Gloria Naylor, Ntozake Shange, Alice Walker, and Shirley Anne Williams. Gloria Naylor; whose writing is the prime concern of this study, resists the hegemonic, racist world-view as she exclusively focuses upon creating a sanctuary for black women in her novels. One of the major concerns of her fiction is that it depicts resistant colored women, and their resistance is nurtured in their positionality in the marginal spaces. This marks a shift from and resistance to the portrayal of the women in mainstream literature as well as black male literature, and even some of her counterparts.

The foregone discourse on the African American resistance necessitates the subjectivity of African American people to ideological repression in American society. Various scholars and critics have encountered this issue from the front and have devised their own ways, methods, and sites of resistance. Critics like bell hooks, Surya Nath Pandey, Barbara Christian, and Margot Anne Kelley have emphasized and located the marginal space as the site and opportunity for resistance as it provides the marginal an outsider's view to the power structure. Again authors like hooks, Collins, and Marshall along with Lavon present 'Home' as a site of resistance against the hegemonic worldview that controls and defines women outside the home space. In addition, there are critics who reiterate that the female bonding is quite instrumental in resisting the patriarchal and racial repression. Andrews, Brantley, Matus, and Awkward, etc. have supported the female bonding. The other methods of resistance discussed above are revision and representation. The methods of revision and representation provide an opportunity to review the state of black people in classical and contemporary literature and media which consequently resist and reconstruct the same. The discussion is concluded with the proposition of a gap for further resistance as has been proposed by Tapan Kumar Basu and Pickett.

The present study on one hand proposes to explore the marginal space in the novels of Gloria Naylor, and on the other, it also aims at looking into the constructs that influence the process of subjectivization. Further, it delineates the location of marginal space and the marginalized status of characters which provide them with an opportunity to critically examine their position in society and how they resist the racial and gender repressions. The special emphasis has also been laid upon the role of female bonding which incepts, and maintains the process of resistance. The thesis hypothesizes that the marginal positionality of the characters leads them to form a bond among them to shield and to immune as well as to resist the tyranny of the hegemonic world order. In order to achieve the proposed objective, the thesis relies heavily upon textual analysis and has also extensively drawn upon the critics and theorists like Foucault, hooks,

Fanon, Cixous, Beauvoir, Lacan, Spivak, Zizek, Collins, etc. to support and to prove its proposition of marginality, repression and resistance along with the phenomenon of bonding to analyse the first five novels of Naylor. The thesis has been divided into seven chapters including introduction and conclusion. A brief preamble of each proposed chapter may prove to be a lighthouse through which the thesis can be viewed.

The first chapter titled 'Introduction' traces the whole trajectory of African American resistance, and it explores how different methods of resistance have been adopted and appropriated. The major methods on which the chapter delineates are marginal space, home, female bonding, revision and representation/reconstruction. The chapter further proposes the objective that is based upon the gap which is located after the close examination of the synchronic literary corpus which is appropriately related to African American novels with a special focus on historical realities of resistance and repression with regard to the novels of Gloria Naylor. Finally, it gives a graphic adumbration of each chapter which may underline the overt or covert content of the chapter.

The second chapter, '*The Women of Brewster Place*' explores the underlying condition in which the women of Brewster place, a marginal space in a North American city, have succeeded in forming a bond among themselves in order to survive and to resist the patriarchal and racial subjugation by the dominant power structure. Further, the chapter highlights upon the significance of wall, which separates the blacks from the mainstream American world and provides them with an opportunity to resist what bell hooks calls "imperialist white-supremacist capitalist patriarchy". The wall stands as chimera in its nature and function. On the one hand, the wall has been constructed by the power structure to exercise different apparatuses of power machinery which may control the consciousness, ideology and identity of the marginal, but on the other, it also provides the marginals with an opportunity to resist oppressive power structure. It has also traced the journey of the women of Brewster Place which is replete with racial and gender repression in hegemonic patriarchal world. The repressive condition of the women is located into the process of subjectivization which is controlled by the socio-economic and political realities. Further, it has also elaborated upon the condition in which the women of Brewster Place come forward to resist the power of the patriarch. The resistance that emanates from their positionality at the marginal space to the Foucauldian power has been made possible by forming a bond among the women of Brewster Place on the basis of their shared common experiences of patriarchal repression and racial stranding. The chapter also adds that this marginal space is acquired or allotted to the women of Brewster Place because of the inherent rebellious tendency in them which defies the societal norms of gender, class, and racial definitions.

The third chapter makes an attempt to untie the knotty and significant rubric of Naylor's *Linden Hills* that traces the repression of the females of the Nedeed Family through the historical construction of the place. It also describes that these Nedeed women lodge some sort of repression in their own ways and methods, however, the insufficiency of their resistance emanates from their lack of bonding among themselves and also among other women of the place. When the last Nedeed woman, Willa, establishes the correspondence with her ancestral women, their resistance strengthens her, and further, she resists by bringing down the patriarchal empire of the Nedeeds. Moreover, the chapter presents a comparison of the Luther House with that of Anderson House which celebrates love and happiness. Finally, the chapter also explains the catastrophic ruin of Laurel under the tyrannical and deadly weight of patriarchy which reiterates the lack of female bonding among the women. Furthermore, the chapter also delineates how patriarchy uses compulsory heterosexuality to perpetuate its domination and control.

Chapter four once again emphasizes on Naylor's strategy on constructing a marginal space of Willow Spring in order to preserve the cultural and mythical practices which are deeply embedded into African American mythos to resist the mainstream world view. The location of marginal space through historical realities since its very inception defies the principle of bell hooks' configuration about the construction of marginal space through suffering, pain, and struggle and the notion of segregation of the subalterns by the power structure. Practices of the island—conjuring, healing, hoodoo, and candle walk protest against the consciousness and ideology of the dominant class. These cultural practices not only act as apparatus to preserve the identity but also prove to be the potential sites of resistance to the dominant or hegemonic power structure of American mainstream. These archetypes and motives hold the identity and the subjectivity; for instance, Cocoa, the protagonist defies the processes of subjectivization through her roots in the community and practices of the island, however, the character who is bereft of the above- mentioned mythical practices is easily subjectivised by the dominant ideology of the dominant class.

The fifth chapter makes an attempt to unravel the uncanny structure of power which seems to be omnipresent with its roots in knowledge and in the process of subject formation. It explains the basic philosophy of power and its structure, which through its nature, expels the dispossessed, powerless, isolated, and destitute to the brink of margin by confining them into a marginal space. The marginal space in Naylor's *Bailey's Café* contains a Hegelian dialectics in itself with the perpetuation of the subalterns who dwell there and its potentiality of resistance. The antinomy of power does not only allow the characters to explore their space in the world but also allows the characters to be trapped into the eminence of power. This entrapment of the characters into the vortex of power at the marginal place inculcates a rebellious tendency in them. Gloria Naylor through her subaltern and marginalized characters in the novel explicates and delineates the entire process of objectification and subjetification in which her characters experience the odour of repressive, oppressive and exploitative nature of power. This allows the characters of the novel to play with the aporatic nature of marginal space. Further, the novel also proposes the fact that female subjectivity may find full play at Eve's boarding house, the marginal space in the mainstream world. The place provides ample space for female bonding where the female may share common experiences and the world view. However, Naylor provides her characters with the place of Eve, only as sojourn where they may recollect enough energy so that they may fight against the power of patriarch and may continue their search into the dismal yet eliminating space where they may find their subjectivity, ideology, or the world view.

Chapter six makes an attempt to explore the mechanism of repression that runs its course equally on African American men and women. The chapter also locates how African American men perpetuate oppression on their women on the one hand, and they themselves are subjected by the power structure, on the other. They fall into the category of both oppressor and the oppressed. Further, it also explains the fact that the men at Brewster Place share the same marginal space as the women of Brewster have shared at the same place which reiterates the fact that the men, despite their sexist behavior, are their compatriot in their struggle against the hegemonic power structure which subjects the African Americans alike, irrespective of their gender.

Chapter six traces the process of subjectivity and subjectivization of the protagonist in Naylor's recently published novella *1996* (2005) where she has fictionalized her own story. The chapter once again enters in a socio-political discourse of marginality and marginal space as it tends to expose the dominant hegemonic power structure which has relegated Naylor's (persona) life to the brink or margin and continually reminds her that "my life no longer was mine; it belonged to the strangers in dark glasses. It was invasion in its crudest form and it robbed me of my sense of peace. It also robbed me of my privacy for reasons that were still hidden to me" (49-50). In particular her home space has been under surveillance snatching away the only space she had where she could gather herself against the hegemonic forces outside. In addition, Naylor's consciousness has also been targeted making her crippled to the extent where she gets almost insane.

Finally, 'Conclusion' summarizes the whole discourse carried on the repression and resistance of African American men and women in the novels of Gloria Naylor along with their mechanism of bonding against repression and the role of marginal positionality in enabling and offering them with the opportunity to resist.

Chapter 2

Marginal Space and Female Bonding: Resistance in Gloria Naylor's *The Women of Brewster Place*

The present chapter explores the underlying condition in which the women of Brewster Place, a marginal space in an anonymous North American city, have succeeded in forming a bond among themselves in order to survive and to resist the patriarchal and racial subjugation in American society. It evinces the historical condition and avers them to be united and to include all women, despite sexual and class differences in their assemblage, failing which they shall meet the gravest consequences, thus, necessitating the chimera of resistance and bonding in their daily lifestyle. Moreover, it is reiterated through the rape case of Lorraine, one of the inhabitants of the marginal space of Brewster Place. Bobo too, peeps into Naylor's intention through Lorraine's rape case: "her intent was to demonstrate how black people's survival depends on mutual support and when this fails, the community can collapse" (36). This temporal and spatial phenomenon of resistance arises from their positionality in the marginal space, 'Brewster Place' which imbibes in them the vision of the world, that is different from that of the racist and patriarchal world outside, which helps them realize the injustices carried out against them in the hegemonic patriarchal capitalist world. Thus, the resistance that the women of Brewster Place exhibit is constructive as it strengthens the bond among them and the sense of community and cooperation. In other words, the chapter aims at contextualizing the marginal women's individual experiences within the larger world of gender inequality, racial oppression and center/margin dichotomy, which on the one side, may help them to find the root cause of gender and racial repression, and on the other, may serve to create a sense of female solidarity and communal identity among them to resist the injustices inflicted upon them.

The condition of racial oppression and female solidarity along with communal identity which is embedded in the marginal space and is astutely dealt in here, has also been expounded and explained by Jewell, who adumbrates, "the privileged classes use 'images and ideologies' to keep African American women on the periphery of society, consequently limiting their access to societal resources and institutions" (4). He seems to believe that the privileged class assigns the marginal space to the African Americans women in the United States in order to control, define, and marginalize their location in geopolitics. However, he might sound relevant and authentic; he has not been able to locate the potentiality of the marginal space as he highlights only the bleak side of it. Bell hooks seems to depart from his notion of marginality when she differentiates between "...marginality which is imposed by oppressive structure and that marginality one chooses as a site of resistance—as location of radical openness and possibility" (*Yearning* 148). This radical space is not assigned by the privileged class rather achieved "through suffering and pain, through struggle", which could be used as a "radical creative space which affirms and sustains our subjectivity, which gives us a new location from which to articulate our sense of the world" (148). The afore-mentioned *discorsum* and *datum* affirms that the creative and literary firmament of Gloria Naylor exemplifies the dialectical nature of oppression and marginality. It is evident through the literary corpus of Gloria Naylor that marginality is the creation of the mainstream power structure; however, it also imperceptibly establishes the fact that marginality is a labored choice of the dispossessed which may allow the marginals to maintain and to continue with the antinomies or pharmakon of marginality. Gloria Naylor in her novel, *The Women of Brewster Place* oscillates between these two kinds of geopolitics of marginality; for example, 'Brewster Place' as a periphery or marginal space assigned by the dominant class and a deliberate choice of the subjects from the upper middle class who find it as a space of "radical creative[ity]" (148). Consequently, Brewster Place inhabits some characters who are marginal as they have been subjectivised by all apparatuses of power structure and ideology and hence are left with no choice but to be there. However, some other characters, like Kiswana, who choose to habitat in Brewster Place are in fact those who choose the status of marginality in order to act and question the hegemonic power-structure.

However, the incubation of Brewster Place, 'the bastard child' itself seems to be inextricably and inexorably intertwined into the complex rubric of power politics involved in its construction, "on some worthless land in the badly crowded district" (*WBP* 01). Naylor uses the term 'bastard' to refer to Brewster Place in order to highlight political illegitimacy and marginality of the place. Further it emphasizes that because of its illegitimacy, the place cannot claim legacy from American mainstream. In addition, Maxine Lavon Montgomery finds 'bastard' to be an apposite adjective to describe the origin of the street as she points "[b]astardy serves as an apt metaphor for the exclusion owing to race that the residents of the community experience. From their (women's) perspective, linear history is an oppressive cycle that perpetuates their exclusion in a world that is characteristically white and therefore off-limits" (Fathomless Dream 42). The Brewster Place comes into existence due to the negotiation "between the alderman of the sixth district and the managing director of Unico Realty Company", which does not bear the testimony of any legal documentation and affirmation and it further marks its geopolitical stand as marginal (*WBP* 01). The location of Brewster Place in the political marginality makes it devoid of any authentic version of powerful voice or representation which further leads to the construction of a wall between the Brewster Place and the mainstream world turning it into "a dead-end street" which exemplifies the marginal condition of Brewster Place (02). Sarah Katherine Foust Vinson identifies that the wall in Gloria Naylor's *The Women of Brewster Place* "becomes a public representation of the women's histories and storied memories and also a symbol of collective memory" (259) and "representative of their collective identity, emphasizing their shared community, while constantly reminding them of their oppressed histories and haunting memories of racism and sexism" (260). She further illustrates that the wall necessitates a coactive memory at Brewster Place which binds the women together.

The people who initially live at Brewster place are the have-nots and subaltern as they "had no political influence; people were dark-haired and mellow-skinned—Mediterraneans—who spoke to each other in rounded guttural sounds, and who brought strange foods to the neighborhood stores" (*WBP* 02). These Mediterraneans are replaced by the African Americans on the street and "Brewster Place rejoiced in these multi-colored "Afric" children of its old age. They worked as hard as the children of its youth, and were as passionate and different in their smells, foods, and codes from the rest of the town as the children of its middle years" (04). The portrayal and comparison of the African Americans in the above reflection authenticates the difference that these people bear with that of the mainstream town in terms of their smell, food, etc.; which once again assign the marginality to the Brewster Place. More so, the women became a special feature as:

> Brewster Place became especially fond of its colored daughters as they milled like determined spirits among its decay, trying to make it a home. Nutmeg arms leaned over windowsills, gnarled ebony legs carried groceries up double flights of steps, and saffron hands strung out wet laundry on back-yard lines.... They were hard-edged, soft-centered, brutally demanding, and easily pleased, these women of Brewster Place. (04-05)

However, despite staunch deprivation of mainstream participation, the place paved the way for the construction of an alternate world away from the influences of the modern agencies of power structure "[c]ut off from the central activities of the city, the street developed a personality of its own. The people had their own language and music and codes" (02). Another reason of these people's embracement of the place has been that "they had no choice and would remain [there] for the same reason" (04). The gradual habitation of the people in Brewster place with a sense of carnival attracts many inhabitants towards it. The Brewster Place offers a safe sanctuary to its inhabitants as it is "better than the starving southern climates they had fled from" (04). These residents have "come to this space through suffering and pain, through struggle to be that which pleasures, delights, and fulfils desire" (hooks 148) as "[e]ach of these women doubly affected by their racial and gender status" (Christian, "Naylor's Geography," 110) "in her own time and with her own season had a story (of suffering and pain)" (*WBP* 05). In addition, these subaltern and marginalized women of Brewster Place are pushed into this space because of their rebellious attitude as they do not conform to the social and patriarchal apparatuses. A close observation of the journey of the women may indicate another reason of their confinement into this marginal place which is the patriarchal, authoritative, and insensitive behavior of the men in their lives along with the racial orientation of the society. In other words, the most common problem in the lives of the Brewster women is patriarchy; for instance, Mattie leaves her house for controlling her sexuality and giving it to Butch Fuller whom her father always hated; Etta is used by Reverend Woods as nothing more than a sexual object; Ciel becomes the victim of a disloyal and insensitive husband who leaves her in such a situation where she almost collapses, had Mattie not been there; Cora Lee has visitors who show her "the thing that felt good in the dark" and leave her with babies; Lorraine's father throws her out of the home once he discovers the letters of her girlfriend. Later she gets raped brutally by C.C. Baker (*WBP* 113).

The women of Brewster place exemplify the phenomenon of patriarchal repression by implicitly defying its deadly weight. The act of resistance and defiance, in Mattie's life, for instance, makes her rebellious against her loving father, an epitome of patriarchal control. Fowler points out that "Mattie's life before her encounter with Butch has been led within strict and conventional guidelines. Her future and her sexuality are in the control of her father" (Gloria Naylor: *In Search of a Sanctuary* 28). Her father has always provided her with every kind of need and expects in turn that Mattie should look towards him for approval for everything in her life. Her father allows her to see only Fred Watson who "was the only man in the church that her father thought good enough for her" (*WBP* 14). However, when her father discovers that it is not Fred Watson who is the corporeal reason of Mattie's pregnancy, he "grabbed her by the back of the hair, and yanked her face upward to confront the blanket of rage in his eyes" (22). He wants to know the name of the person who has "sneaked into his house and distorted the faith and trust he had in his child" (23). However, going against her patriarchal father, Mattie does not disclose the name of Butch "and in a fury, he tried to stamp out what had hurt him the most and was now brazenly taunting him—her disobedience" (23). Mattie's disobedience is an avid act of defiance of patriarchal power and a serious threat and challenge to its perpetuation. The resolute act of not disclosing the name of Butch Fuller, the violator, exhibits her rebellious nature and that propels her for the odyssey towards Brewster Place, a 'marginal space'.

Mattie's narrative of repression in her family in the novel, *The Women of Brewster Place* echoes the Althusserian concept of institutions being oppressive in order to construct an ideology through the constant process of interpellation. Institution like family, which is profoundly controlled by the patriarch, is the most powerful tool which constructs the ideology, identity and the consciousness of the character. Similarly, Suranjita Ray espouses the same epistemic construction as she articulates that "[p]atriarchy is based on a system of power relations which are hierarchical and unequal where men control women's production, reproduction and sexuality. It imposes masculinity and femininity character stereotypes in society which strengthen the iniquitous power relations between men and women" (01). Further, bell hooks defines patriarchy as "...a political-social system that insists that males are inherently dominating, superior to everything and everyone deemed weak, especially females, and endowed with the right to dominate and rule over the weak and to maintain that dominance through various forms of psychological terrorism and violence" (Understanding Patriarchy 02). However, Mattie's case reiterates the fact that the men in the novel are patriarchal in their thought and approach and want to exercise a control over their women. Generally, the novel is a presentation of a community of women "men are mostly absent or itinerant, drifting in and out of their women's lives, and leaving behind them pregnancies and unpaid bills" (Matus 61). Mattie, for instance, is punished and consequently forced to leave her house simply because she has acted outside the norms of sexuality prescribed by the patriarchy which is being practiced by her father here. Mattie's father acts as a Puritan in case of Mattie's control of sexuality and thus conforms to, what Cheryl Clarke, an African American cultural critic puts in relation to African American sexual politics which he discovers exists at par with that of the mainstream American sexual politics:

> Like all Americans, black Americans live in a sexually repressive culture. And we have made all manner of compromise regarding our sexuality in order to live here. We have expanded much energy trying to debunk the racist mythology which says our sexuality is depraved. Unfortunately, many of us have overcompensated and assimilated the Puritan values that sex is for procreation, occurs only between men and women, and is only valid within the confines of heterosexual marriage.... Like everyone else in America who is ambivalent in these respects, black folk have to live with the contradictions of this limited sexual system by repressing or closeting any other sexual/erotic urges, feelings, or desires. (199)

Similarly, Virginia C. Fowler observes the patriarchal power structure embedded in Mattie's father when she explicates that "Samuel Michael is the only member of the household for whom Mattie's pregnancy represents dishonor and shame; as the patriarch of the family, he and only he has the power to decide to whom Mattie's sexuality will belong" (Gloria Naylor: *In Search of a Sanctuary*, 28). And perhaps for not abiding by the rules of patriarchal patterns, Mattie Michael is beaten by her loving but strict patriarchal father. However, Mattie seems to be aware of the patriarchal attitude of her father because when Mattie is drawn in conversation with Butch Fuller, she soon realizes that "her father would kill her if he heard she had been seen with

Butch Fuller" (*WBP* 10) because he was a man "her father had repeatedly warned her against" (09). This reiterates that Mattie has consciously defied the patriarchal control of her father. As a result of holding her consciousness against the patriarchal power structure, Mattie's father forces her out of the paternal house. Mattie's forced journey to the Brewster Place from her father's house is quite certainly the result of the gender situation. The gender situation, along with racial discrimination, proves to be a lethal combination in her life, which pushes her towards Brewster Place. In addition, when Mattie walks out, with her son, in search of a safer accommodation, she once again experiences the patriarchal and racial discrimination in the society. After countless attempts she discovers that "there was no need in wasting energy to climb to steps in the white neighborhoods that displayed the vacancies signs" (30). It is because of her color that she could not get a house in the white neighborhood, and since she does not have a legal husband, she does not get accommodation at a black "respectable place" (30). At the end of the day, it is an old woman, the kind Miss Eva who "rescues her and her young son from the streets and offers them the warmth, comfort, and security they need" (Montgomery, *The Apocalypse* 90).

Miss Eva is a woman whose story in the novel sets "a repeated pattern of concern, generosity, and love between and among women" (Branzburg 118). Eva indeed shares the same syntagmatic and paradigmatic experiences as far as the oppressive role of power structure in general and patriarchy in particular is concerned. It is quite explicable in the case of Eva when she says "[m]y daddy was just like that, too. I remember the night I run off with my first husband, who was a singer. My daddy hunted us down for three months and then drag me home and kept me locked in my room for weeks with the windows all nailed up" (*WBP* 34).

The shared experiences of Mattie and Eva divulge the gruesome reality about the oppressive system of patriarchy which not only controls the consciousness, identity, and ideology but also the body and sexuality through which a woman writes her history as has rightly been expounded by Simone de Beauvoir in her *The Second Sex* (1952). Mattie's story reveals that patriarchy governs the sexuality, and if someone tries to go beyond to defy the sexual norms of the society, he or she is looked down upon and faces severe punishments. Mattie bears the apodosis of being marginalized and oppressed when, she is pushed out of her loving father's house for controlling her sexuality, after "becoming sexually active and pregnant as a teenager" (Harris 119-20). Similarly, Lorraine and Theresa, 'the two' lesbian couple who share the same marginal space of Brewster Place with Mattie, also experience the same oppressive and explosive air of patriarchy. They "have come to Brewster Place not because they are economically deprived, but because they are socially scorned" for controlling their sexuality (*WBP* 47). The patriarchal world wants them to channel their energy to the opposite sex. Lorraine's subjectivization to patriarchy along with her rebellion marks her journey towards Brewster Place. The difference she has with Mattie is that unlike Mattie she loves a girl and not a boy and she is thrown out of her house for the same patriarchal disobedience.

Naylor has portrayed in Lorraine a stronger and more radical character than Mattie because unlike her, she has gone far to challenge male control of sexuality by trespassing into Lesbianism "[m]y father...Kicked me out of the house when I was seventeen years old. He found a letter, one of my girlfriends had written me, and when I wouldn't lie about what it meant, he told me to get out and leave behind everything that he had ever bought me. He said he wanted to burn them...so I walked out of his home with only the clothes on my back" (148). Through Lorraine, Naylor also resists the lesbian stereotyping as Barbara Christian notes by presenting one as wishing 'good morning' that may be interpreted to be Lorraine's desire to mix with people and the other is pretty. By ascribing one of the lesbians as pretty, Christian makes a point to shatter the reason of the physical appearance "for the lesbian's sexual preference: she was too ugly to get a woman" (*Black Feminist Criticism* 191). Theresa, however, also shares the marginal space and the experiences of marginality along with oppressive order of patriarchy while living with her lesbian compatriot, Lorraine. Through Lorraine and Theresa's episode, Naylor has articulated her concern for all the women across sexual preferences defying all kinds of difference through a sense of true female bonding.

The repressive experiences and odyssey of the two lesbians—Lorraine and Theresa propose the fact that both of them have been pushed into the marginal space of Brewster Place by '*they*', the patriarchs. On the contrary, there is a character in the novel, Kiswana who defies hooks' idea of coming to marginal space "through suffering and pain, through struggle"; it is her rebellious attitude that has motivated her to come to Brewster Place (hooks, *Yearning* 148). Kiswana Browne has come to live at Brewster Place by choice, for she has a genuine desire to serve her people and assert her African identity. The purpose of her life, she claims, is to be "with my people, fighting for equality and a better community" (*WBP* 83). She is radical in her thought and approach and is in full control of her consciousness. She rebukes her own mother when she says that she is "trying to be what you're (she's) not" (85) which implies that she is pretending to be a social activist working for the poor blacks. Kiswana gets infuriated and shouts at her mother asserting her conviction, "trying to be something I am not, Mama! Trying to be proud of my heritage and the fact that I'm from African descent. If that's being what I'm not, then I say fine. But I'd rather be dead than be like you—a white man's nigger who's ashamed of being black!" (85). However, this does not mean that these two women do not share the compassion and love between each other. Her mother is concerned about her, for she counsels Kiswana not to be afraid of anybody in her life, not even her mother. She also leaves seventy-five dollars for her when she leaves the house which articulates her economic concerns towards Kiswana. Apart from all this, both of them agree on the point of the exploitation of black people in the United States, "a country still full of obstacles for black people to fight their way over—just because they're black" (84) which implies the emotional bond that both of them share with their people.

Kiswana Browne replicates what Ebele Eko articulates in her article on Gloria Naylor "Beyond the Myth of Confrontation: A Comparative Study of African and African American Female Protagonists" that the contemporary African and African

American Female writers have given "creative birth to a new breed of female protagonists" in order to "help destroy degrading images and myths and recreate for black women images that liberate and build up self-identity" (13). Kiswana Browne seems to have applied Collins's proposition of rebellious youth with her vision, commitment and sincerity, "[r]ebellious youth who are armed with a vision and the knowledge and skills needed to build a movement can work wonders. When it comes to issues of gender and sexuality, Black youth must lead the way in the next phase of antiracist struggle because failing to do so virtually guarantees them an impoverished future" (*Black Sexual Politics*, 307). Further, Kiswana tries to bring all women of Brewster Place under the banner of Tenants' Association where they may come up with their problems and fight together for their cause. She knows that it is not an easy task, but she is not willing to give up. She does this as part of her agenda to fight "...for equality and a better community..." for her own people (*WBP* 83).

Naylor indicates that the resistance in this novel exists between these women and capitalist patriarchal society of the United States through Kiswana and her mother. Kiswana Brown resists her mother because of their different orientation towards society, culture, race, and gender. Since Kiswana's mother lives in Linden Hills, a place marked by its 'colored whites' inhabitants as they have symbolically sold their souls in order to secure a place in Linden Hills, where the black culture is missing, she thinks like a white woman or her mind has been tuned like a white woman who hardly dares to think to question racial and gender repression prevailing in society. Whereas, Kiswana thinks otherwise and "feels repressed, both communally and sexually, in her natal home, Linden Hills. She sees her sojourn to Brewster Place for bonding with her true people, black people" (Christian, "Naylor's Geography" 112). Answering her mother's worries about her that "anything could happen—especially live among these people", Kiswana tries to remind her mother about these people saying, "[t]hey're my people and yours, too, Mama—we're all black. But maybe you've forgotten that over in Linden Hills" (*WBP* 83). Her mother can also not be able to feel herself with or even sympathize with 'her own people' while

Kiswana leaves her comfort and luxuries to live with her 'own people' as she possesses the internal urge to work for them and identifies herself with them "[m]y place was in the streets with my people," and the purpose of her life is "fighting for equality and a better community" (83). Kiswana also changes her name from Melanie to Kiswana which is one of the steps in the larger process of cultural revisioning and her assertion of "[t]rying to be proud of my heritage and the fact that I'm from African descent" (85). She rebukes her mother for accepting slavery in her soul and giving up fighting "I'd rather be dead than be like you—a white man's nigger who's ashamed of being black!" (85). This is not completely true of her mother who defends herself by the argument that "I am alive because of the blood of proud people who never scraped, or begged or apologized for what they were. They lived asking only one thing of this world—to be allowed to be. And I learned through the blood of these people that black isn't beautiful and it isn't ugly—black is! It's not kinky hair and it's not straight hair—it just is" (86).

Ebele Eko observes that "the cultural symbols of Kiswana's African name, hairdo, dress, and artifacts are her way of warning the upward-moving blacks not to forget their roots nor the bridge over which they have passed, that human bond and link to mother Africa that makes them a people" (18-19). Later on she rebukes Kiswana for changing her name even without knowing the meaning of it. She tells her that she is named after her mother's grandmother's name "who bore nine children and educated them all, who held off six white men with a shotgun when they tried to drag one of her sons to jail for 'not knowing the place'" (*WBP* 86). She also tells that though she resided in Linden Hills she always wanted "...to see that my children were prepared to meet this world on its own terms, so that no one could sell them short and make them ashamed of what they were or how they looked" (86). Further, Ebele Eko points that by listening "...to her mother's theatrical recounting of her proud heritage and commitment to the black cause..., she comes to understand and appreciate the source of her own dynamism, idealism, and dedication: her mother" (18). Mrs. Kiswana's visit to her daughter is marked by her concerns towards her daughter and a sense of well-being and what Barbara Christian says "... the fact she is concerned about her daughter's welfare despite their disagreements that is an indication of the strength of their bond" ("Naylor's Geography" 113). Larry Andrews finds this conflict between Kiswana and her mother 'healing' as she puts, "Kiswana Browne is 'healed' in her conflict with her mother by coming to identify herself with her mother as a woman" (288). Her mother's disapproval of Kiswana's ways of dealing with the racial conflict and her support of her people comes from her experiences which she seems to share in the following paragraph:

> It was damned important to stand up and say that you were proud of what you were and to get the vote and other social opportunities for every person in this country who had it due. But you kids thought you were going to turn the world upside down, and it just wasn't so. When all the smoke had cleared, you found yourself with a fistful of new federal laws and a country still full of obstacles for black people to fight their ways over—just because they're black. There was no revolution, Melanie, and there will be no revolution. (*WBP* 84)

Though both of these women are quite sympathetic towards black people, they think differently to resist the white Americans, her mother wants to penetrate into the system and wants Kiswana to "become an assembly woman or a civil liberties, lawyer or open a freedom school in this very neighborhood" (84) while Kiswana wants to live among these people and let the revolution start from the inside and one of the steps towards that is to form tenants' Association. "Kiswana Browne", as observed by Charles Wilson, "emerges as the representative of this (Black Art) movement" which "challenged white mainstream notions of good, normal, and standard..." (56). Asked by her mother to join school again, Kiswana shows her disbelief in modern American school "[w]hat good would I be after four or five years of a lot of white brainwashing in some phony, prestige institution, huh? I'd be like you and Daddy and those other educated sitting over there in Linden Hills with a terminal case of middle-class amnesia" (*WBP* 85). Naylor echoes here what Gramsci calls 'hegemony' of the white people which is executed to control the blacks in America through the education system. These people are given such an education that they become the victim of servitude and hence cannot question the power structure and finally find white people's ideologies justified and do not raise their voice against the white hegemony. It also sounds the Hegelian dialectics of master-slave power structure and Raymond William's concepts of oppressed, residual and emergent. Hegemonic power, as explained by Mark C.J. Stoddart, "works to convince individuals and social classes to subscribe to the social values and norms of a inherently exploitative system.... Hegemony appears as the 'common sense' that guides our everyday, mundane understanding of the world" (11).

However, Etta Mae Johnson, another compatriot in the saga of female bonding who comes to live Brewster Place once she experiences betrayal from everywhere, is in full possession of herself. She defies all controls of patriarchal and racial power structure or hegemony. She, like Kiswana Browne, experiences and exhibits the same rebellious tendency which allows her to stand and to negotiate against the power structure of patriarchy. She is the only woman in the novel who celebrates female sexuality to the fullest and is in full control of her sexuality. Her defiant attitude during her teen age reflects in the following paragraph:

> There ain't nothing I ever do
> Or nothing I ever say
> That folk don't criticize me
> But I'm going to do
> Just what I want to, anyway
> And don't care just what people say
> If I should take a notion
> To jump into the ocean
> Ain't nobody's business if I do.... (*WBP* 57)

However, her attitude is not approved by the racist and patriarchal society which has translated her teen age years into the era of troublesome and languishing psychological unrest as she says "Rock Vale had no place for a black woman who was not only unwilling to play by the rules, but whose spirit challenged the very right of the game to exist" (59). Etta's resistance against the racial authority of the whites in Rock Vale is legendary in its own terms. Her behavior is especially indigestible for the whites of Rock Vale, a place marked by "the strange fruits... Black bodies...hanging.... From the popular tress" (60):

> The whites of Rock Vale were painfully reminded of this rebellion when she looked them straight in the face while putting in her father's order at the dry goods store, when she reserved her sirs and mams for those she thought deserving, and when she smiled only if she pleased, regardless of whose presence she was in. That Johnson gal wasn't being an uppity nigger, as talk had it; she was just being herself. (60)

Naylor universalizes Etta's experiences when she exemplifies that Rock Vale is not the only place that suppresses women and curtails freedom but the places like Memphis, Detroit, Chicago, and even New York have been the same for Etta Mae simply because she "claims the right to her own sexuality" (Fowler, *Gloria Naylor: In Search of a Sanctuary* 50). She "soon found out that America wasn't ready for her" which implies that the control of female sexuality is exercised by the patriarchal power structure which does not allow the females to exercise or own their sexuality (*WBP* 60). Wheresoever she goes, she found the same attitude of the people which reflects in the poem that is quoted in the beginning of the section, entitled 'Etta Mae Johnson' and she very well identifies herself with "The music, the woman, the words" (55):

> I love my man
> I'm a lie if I say I don't
> I love my man
> I'm a lie if I say I don't
> But I'll quit my man
> I'm a lie if I say I won't
>
> My man wouldn't give me no breakfast
> Wouldn't give me no dinner
> Squawked about me out of doors
> Had the nerve to lay

A matchbox to my clothes
I didn't have so many
But I had a long, long way to go. (56)

Etta undergoes the similar experience that the woman who sings experiences when she consummates with Reverend Woods, who is "a streetwise preacher, a charlatan who is concerned only about his material gain and carnal lusts" (Montgomery, *The Apocalypse* 95). Though throughout her life Etta has encountered a number of men like Reverend Woods, this is the first time that she realizes that a wall of gender exists in the society. She "stood looking at the wall that closed off Brewster from the avenues farther north and found it hard to believe that it had been just this afternoon when she had seen it" (*WBP* 73). This exemplifies that somebody who has not undergone the experiences of suffering and pain may not realize demarcation existing between the margin and center. Through her episode with Reverend Woods she ultimately realizes that men simply view her or any woman for that reason as an object of instant sexual gratification only. Consequently, when Etta is through her momentarily sexual relation with Moreland, she goes to Mattie and "noticed there was a light under the shade at Mattie's window.... Someone was waiting up for her" (74) which is an epitome of the only and ultimate sanctuary for Etta as "[s]he breathed deeply of the freedom she found in Mattie's presence. Here she had no choice but to be herself" (58).

The condition of repression in the marginal space exists in the novel not only in the lives of the characters who are either pushed into the margin by oppressive power structure or make a labored choice to live in the marginal space as is evident in the above instances, rather the condition of repression and the marginal experience continue. The marginal space in its temporal and spatial reality perpetuates the oppressive machinery of power structure equally on whosoever is associated with the position of marginality. The women of Brewster Place reach to this marginal space "through suffering and pain" and their suffering and victimization continues even after reaching the marginal space too (hooks, *Yearning* 148). Ciel, for instance, has been the most tragic victim of male insensitivity and patriarchal mode in Brewster Place. She is drawn to the extent where she almost dies had Mattie not shown her extraordinary healing abilities. Since the very inception of her married life, the perpetuation of the patriarchal repression has been exercised on her and she has always been trying to figure out the reason of the behavior of her husband, Eugene who constantly complains of everything associated with Ciel. She always thinks new job or paint or Serena, their daughter to be the reason of his behavior "[y]et the real truth went beyond her scope of understanding" (*WBP* 92). She is a woman who has gone to the extent of getting aborted to retain him but still could not hold him. However, Eugene's real self may be traced though their discussion about caring of Serena. He is against Mattie caring and nurturing Serena as he fears "fat bitch'll turn the kid against me" (94). This statement of Eugene points out two things he considers a woman a bitch who may turn the kid against its father. Another point that is noticeable about his character is that he wants to see women subdued like Ciel and not to be self-assertive like Mattie. This is the only reason why he hates Mattie's presence. However, Ciel comes to realize the real Eugene but it is quite late as she has already lost everything—the child to be born and Serena, the existing one.

The uncanny and the knotty texture of oppression are not only exercised by the patriarchy but by matriarchy also, which is another model of perpetuating patriarchal subjugation in the marginal space. It is presented through the case of the two girls, Lorraine and Theresa. This subjectivization is carried out equally by the women and men of Brewster Place. This patriarchal control is exemplary in what leaves C.C. Baker "greatly disturbed by the thought of a Lorraine. He knew of only one way to deal with women other than his mother...he knew how to please or punish or extract favors from them by the execution of what lay curled behind his fly.... And thought of any woman who lay beyond the length of its power was a threat" (*WBP* 161-62). Naylor, then, presents a unified view of males and how dangerous can they be if any woman ever acts outside the prescribed patriarchal norms of sexuality which is exemplary in Lorraine's case who is lesbian which is a definition that exists outside the patriarchal definition of sexuality and which is why

C.C. Baker carries out the sexual assault against Lorraine who "found herself, on her knees, surrounded by the most dangerous species in existence—human males with an erection to validate in a world that was six feet wide" (170). Srirupa Chatterjee and G. Neelkantan in "Woman as Survivor in Oates' *Rape: A Love Story*" too have located the female sexuality and sexual identity in the capitalist patriarchal order, "Oates' contemporary Gothic conjures up a behemoth of capitalist consumption that preys on the vulnerable" (04). Like Lorraine in *The Women of Brewster Place,* Oates' Teen is raped by "a pack of dogs (boys)" which further stresses the immanence of women's vulnerability in the capitalist patriarchal social order (*Rape* 3). The authors also explore that the setting of the rape scene is a deliberate site in the park replete with the figure of "nude male warriors with swords and shields, females with blank faces and hair to their waist... [and] a mermaid with a ridiculous curving fish tail instead of legs" (*Rape* 25) which "connotes female sexual subordination" (Srirupa and Neelkantan 04). They conclude the article with a critique of the power structure when they deliberate that "the novella goes beyond sensationalizing the grotesque in depicting the horror inhering in the might of phallocentric societies that victimize defiant subjects" (06). Barbara Christian points that Lorraine's rape is the result of the "fear and anger powerless men feel against women who reject their only visible sign of manhood—their penis" (*Black Feminist Criticism* 196). Another reason of Lorraine's rape that Naylor seems to indicate is women's psychological vulnerability to be attacked. Had Lorraine been as strong as Theresa, she could have not been raped. However, the only protest that Lorraine could make to resist her rape is the articulation of the word "Please" (*WBP* 170):

> ...she worked her sore mouth, trying to form the one word that had been clawing inside of her—"Please". It squeezed through her paralyzed vocal cards and fell lifelessly at their feet. Lorraine clamped her eyes shut and, using all of the strength left within her, willed it to rise again.
>
> "Please". (170)

Further, Theresa screams on Cora Lee when Cora says "Please, Please" asking Theresa to hold the brick that she has snatched from the wall (188). Theresa says "[d]on't ever say that!" she takes the brick and further says "[n]ow, you go back up there and bring me some more, but don't ever say that again—to anyone!" (188) simply because "[t]he nicety of the polite word of social discourse that Lorraine frantically attempts to articulate—"Please"—emphasis the brute terrorism of the boys' act of rape and expose the desperate means by which they rule" (Tanner 84). Tanner further "...proclaims that Naylor has represented the rape of Lorraine in such a way that it "ceases to be an object of erotic pleasure" (83) which is performed by locking the reader "into the victim's body, positioned *behind* Lorraine's corneas along with the screams that try to break out into the air" (84). Naylor's portrayal of rape makes a shift from the previous representation of the violence against women where the reader/audience, is generally, allowed being a violator as he imaginatively participates in the act of violence. In *The Women of Brewster Place*, the reader is pinned into "...the victim's body and communicating an experience of rape that genders the reader—whatever sex he or she may be—female" (87). Rape is simply a phenomenon which is used to perpetuate an atmosphere of fear which helps the patriarchal authority to control women and confine them to the domestic space. Tanner summarizes Susan Brownmiller's ideas:

> ...the phenomenon of rape strips not only rape victims but all women of their freedom to act as autonomous persons. The ever-present vulnerability of women's bodies makes the possibility of rape a constant threat; by virtue of their physiology, women may be forced into a position of curtailed activity and physiological vulnerability that Brownmiller likens to enslavement. (86)

The physiological vulnerability makes the women feel 'Other' in male's world where by the virtue of their penis and its function men are able to think freely and control the women. Further, women are devoid of free thinking and free movement in a society where their sexuality and body can be controlled and consumed by sexual monsters. The realization of physiological vulnerability and the locus of their sexuality in the body of the women unite all the women of Brewster Place, "...there is a vital oneness created among all the women of Brewster Place as a result of the vulnerability of black womanhood" (Montgomery, *The Apocalypse* 95). Every woman apprehends this kind of brutal rape "[a]lthough only a few admitted it, every woman on Brewster Place had dreamed that rainy week of the tall yellow woman in the bloody green and black dress.... Even Mattie's sleep was fitful, her dreams troubling" (*WBP* 175-76). For instance, Ciel had a dream about it, and something in it told her that she should be there as she is needed. Ciel even goes further to identify herself with Lorraine; she utters "there was a woman who was supposed to be me, I guess. She didn't look exactly like me, but inside I felt it was me.... And something bad had happened to me by the wall—I mean to her—something bad had happened to her" (179). Ciel's dream identifies that there exists some bond or she shares some communion at least with Lorraine that's why she is able to identify herself with Lorraine "...whom she has never met and of whose rape she knows nothing" (Matus 53) which reveals what Maxine Montgomery calls "the suppressed conflicts underlying the women's troubled lives. Each of the women dreams that she is Lorraine, the final victim who is impossibly separated from the community" ("The Fathomless Dream" 47).

The oppressive machinery and methodology of the patriarchy function not only outside the margin but also at the locus of margin, which is clearly explicated by the novelist in the case of Lorraine and Ciel. Similarly, Cora Lee too exemplifies the continuation of the patriarchal machine in the marginal space where she is objectified as commodity and used as a fashionable object and is constantly consumed by power structure which leaves nothing unturned to make her life unlivable and miserable. The gruesome and oppressive act of patriarchy and their monstrous sexuality compels her to produce around a dozen children, however, without one to be called as husband and to lend a supporting hand. The men in her life visit her "only [as] the shadows—who came in the night and showed her the thing that felt good in the dark, and often left before the children awakened..." (*WBP* 113). These shadows often times leave her with pregnancy and which further causes these shadows to torture her "[a] pot of burnt rice would mean a fractured jaw, or a wet bathroom floor a loose tooth, but that had been their fault for keeping her so tied up she could not keep the house straight. But she still carried the scar under her left eye because of a baby's crying, and you couldn't stop a baby from crying" (113).

It is conspicuously clear from the aforementioned discussion that the marginal space is not only the perpetuation and the construction of the oppressive power structure but in some cases it is also a desired and a labored choice of the marginal. In the former, the power structure propels the ideological apparatuses which push the common at the brink of the margin; however, in the later the marginal deliberately chooses to be at the margin or to share the marginal space precisely because it may allow the marginal to negotiate discernibly with the power structure. The narrative of the characters who dwell at the marginal space, however, represents a different tale of power antinomies or the dialectics of power. In other words, the female characters at the marginal space continue to be exploited, oppressed and subjectivised. It is indeed a gargantuan and Herculean task for them to survive in such a demonic power structure, however, the role of their female bonding proves vital which brings them together and gives them a sense of community where they may share their common experiences. Female bonding may also be understood as the essentialisation of female value, solidarity and community which may be read as a resistance against "the Western patriarchal emphasis on the individual...competition, conquest and power" (Christian "Naylor's Geography" 118). One of the French feminists, Julia Kristeva in her "Women's Time" avers that the condition of female bonding is possible because they share the same symbolic order. Living in the same world exhibits inheriting the same symbolic situation, says Kristeva (29). Similarly, in Naylor's *Mama Day* (1988) the bond among the women exists on the basis of shared history, culture and familial roots; however, in *The Women of Brewster Place* the female-bonding is based on the idea of common sexist oppression. In *The Women of Brewster Place*, Naylor creates an image of a liberated black woman who gets ardent support from her black female compatriots which emerges from the shared experiences of racial and sexist oppression not only by the white world but from their own people alike. As bell hooks puts it rightly when she says that "sexist ideology teaches women that to be female is to be a victim...women's liberationists embraced it, making shared victimization the basis of woman bonding" (*From Margin to Center* 45). Naylor further emboldens these women to have faith in their culture, rituals and traditions; "...so great is the wealth of our experience, culture, and ideas we have to share with one another. We can be sisters united by shared interests and beliefs, united in our struggle to end sexist oppression" (hooks, *From Margin to Center* 65). Montgomery, too, asserts that when these women discover that the legitimized patriarchal social set up has denied them the due attention, "...they turn inward, look to each other, and find strength" in one another's company (*The Apocalypse* 96). The women remain stranded in the novel for two reasons: first, they are women, and, second, they are black.

The wall which is symbolic of repressive racial and patriarchal artifact is also a *stoa* of female bonding. The wall encapsulates Hegelian dialectics in it because on one hand it is an artifact of oppression but on the other an illuminating force of female bonding. Henderson points out the same when he articulates, "[t]he wall, the image that separates its inhabitants from the city and each other becomes, in the end, a source of communal strength as each woman faces her own personal demons and forms a powerful cultural link that enables them to dismantle this wall one brick at a time" (103). However, resilient character of the women in the novel is evinced through their narratives and their experiences that they share at Brewster Place. The survival of these women of Brewster Place depends upon their resistance to the hegemonic power structure through female bonding. Living in a world that has always been hostile and antagonistic, they develop a sense of bonding among themselves that proves the only reason for their survival in this street. This bond could be understood as a mutual, supportive feeling of attachment and loyalty to one another, which grows out of a shared experience of oppression. It is this sense of female-bonding that enables them to deal with the everyday pressures they face in the male dominated society in which they live. Montgomery explicates the same when she says that "[o]nly by forming bonds among themselves do the women overcome life's difficulties and find the necessary strength to survive in a changing world" (*The Apocalypse* 89). Female bonding is relevant and essential in building and preparing confidence in black women for survival in indifferent circumstances. Barbara Christian is of the opinion that "because of the nature of American slavery, Afro-American women had to bond with each other in order to survive" ("Naylor's Geography" 118). In order to resist, the women of the Brewster Place rely upon "female friendship, lesbian relationships, and self-affirmation through sisterhood" (Matus 62). Naylor creates in her novel female characters with bonding between them who question the existing sexist oppressions "bound by a sense of community and sisterhood that enables them to deal with the everyday pressures they face in the male-dominated society in which they live" (Khay NP). Further, Dill notes that female bonding, "has been a binding force in the struggle against male chauvinism and patriarchy" (131).

The discussion in the context has elaborately explicated the fact that female bonding is one of the major means through which the female characters in the novel are able to co-exist in a community. The female bonding in *The Women of Brewster Place* is suitably presented through more than one character, initially; it is Mattie who acts like a binding force among all the women and their narratives. Since the novel is centered on dispossessed women, Naylor seems to pay a tribute to the community of women, "of which Mattie is hub" (Whitt 24). Whitt further goes to call Mattie, "the willing surrogate mother for each of Brewster Place's woman in need" (52). Mattie's role is inevitable in Brewster Place as she is "...the life force at Brewster Place", and "puts her dearly bought wisdom at their service, becoming mentor, mother, nurse, and confidante" (Smith 269). She has her first encounter of female support and care with her mother who rescues her being brutally beaten up by her father by opening fire on him and thus saving Mattie from being tortured for committing the sin of disobedience of the patriarchal norms of having sex with somebody else other than her father wanted her to do with. Her mother "jumped on his (Mattie's father's) back and tried to wrestle the stick from him" with which he has been beating Mattie (*WBP* 24). And when she is thrown away by Samuel, she looks here and there and:

> She finally found the shotgun pegged over the front door. She struggled with the heavy gun, and her hand was trembling so much it was difficult to load the bulky shells.... She wrapped her fingers around the trigger, aimed, and pulled... The edge of the fireplace exploded and sent flying bits of bricks into Mattie's back and cut up the right side of her father's face. (24)

Mattie's mother's empathetic action to save Mattie from her husband is indeed an assertion of some sort of bond existing between both of them; it is because of which that Mattie's mother may not see her suffering through the tyranny of the patriarch. Perhaps, such kind of empathetic values have been inculcated in Mattie too, through her such experiences which she later displays when she heals Ciel, consoles Etta and favors Lorraine at Brewster Place. Though Mattie loses the care and love of her mother, she gets the alternative mother in Miss Eva. This mother-daughter relationship generates the bond between the women more strongly. Gradually, both of them become part and parcel of each other's life. Whenever during the mock fight Miss Eva speaks of her death, Mattie becomes restless as she "...did not want to imagine facing the loss of another mother" (39). Even on their first meeting, both of them start sharing with each other their experiences as if they were known to each other for years:

> Miss Eva unfolded her own life and secret exploits to Mattie, and without realizing she was being questioned, Mattie found herself talking about things that she had buried within her. The young black woman and the old yellow woman sat in the kitchen for hours, blending their lives so that what lay behind one and ahead of the other became indistinguishable. (34)

The patriarchal and repressive experiences that both of the women seem to share strengthens the bond between them.

They also share the same rebellious temperament of controlling their sexuality and challenging the established patriarchal order. However, the bond between these women reinforces the proposition of the commonality of repressive experiences that the individual share in order to share the bond which is what is exemplary when Miss Eva tells Mattie the story of her life; it's almost the same as that of Mattie's:

> Child, I know what you talkin' about. My daddy was just like that, too. I remember the night I ran off with my first husband, who was a singer. My daddy hunted us down for three months and then drag me home and kept me lock in my room for weeks with the windows all nailed up. But soon as he let me out, Virgil came back and got me, and we was off again. (34)

Mattie's bond with Miss Eva is not only a mother-daughter relationship; it is also that of a mentor, and a guide. Miss Eva offers Mattie the accommodation without any conditions or any material reasons. Eva does not accept even the money that Mattie is ready to pay as the rent of the house. However, Mattie feels at home in at Miss Eva's place. Bobo Jacqueline and Ellen Seiter remark on their relationship positively and find that it is something unlikely to be found in the white culture:

> Miss Eva rejects the money that Mattie offers her for board, refusing to translate into market relations her gesture of help to a woman in need.... Miss Eva shares all her material wealth and comfort with Mattie—literally strangers off the street—without hesitation. It is almost impossible to conceive this kind of act towards a person unrelated by blood in the universe of the white family melodrama. Miss Eva also shares her home with her granddaughter Ciel, and cares for and raises Mattie's son Basil just as though he were a member of her own family. (34)

She cares for Mattie like her own daughter who in turn finds herself at Eva's place "settling like fine dust on her surroundings and accepting the unexplained kindness of the woman (Miss Eva) with a hunger of which she had been unaware" (*WBP* 34).

Mattie lives in the house for thirty years and is compelled to leave by nobody than her own son, Basil who has jumped the bail. Though, Miss Eva appears for only a short period in the novel, her influence on Mattie and her sense of resiliency lasts for around thirty years, she lives in there. The relationship between Miss Eva and Mattie exemplifies the unconditional love and care that the women may feel for each other, based on their requirement of survival in the hegemonic world of power structure. Miss Eva's home may also be identified as the workshop for Mattie who learns to impart the same unconditional love, support and care that she receives there. This is evident in her relationship with Etta Mae Johnson. There exists a friendship between Etta and Mattie too, which "exhibits the powerful and preserving quality of female friendship" (Khay NP). These two women have been friends since the days of their struggle and rely upon each other for their survival. Mattie and Etta discover a sisterly bond between themselves because of their common experiences, for both of them have experienced disappointment in love. It is natural that in each other's company they acquire the strength they need "Etta laughed soft to herself as she climbed the steps towards the light, and love and the comfort that awaited her" (*WBP* 79). Etta knows that she may be disowned everywhere, but there is someone who is "waiting for her. It is Mattie who has always been constant and the comfort" (Whitt 32). Another commonality that both of them share is their final arrival. In spite of their moving in directions different, they have ultimately reached Brewster Place because of the existing racial and gender condition in American society which is not ready to accept their "blooming independence" (*WBP* 60). Mattie's presence invigorates Etta with a deep sense of freedom and self-confidence. Both the women share everything that has happened in their lives. When Etta comes to Brewster Place, they move "back, a singular turn that claimed co-knowledge of all the important events and almost all of the unimportant ones" (58). The bond between Etta and Mattie may be viewed as both sisterly and friendly.

Similarly, the female bonding between Mattie and Ciel is deeply and profoundly rooted, it goes back to the time when both of them were happily living in Miss Eva's home. Though they belong to different generations, they rely upon each other. Ciel is portrayed as a child who "looks at Mattie for knowledge and wisdom about how to handle situations in her life. She values Mattie's experience and often looks to her for motherly approval" (Khay NP). For instance, when Serena's death comes as a blow in Ciel's life, it is Mattie who rescues her exhibiting extraordinary example of female bonding, nurturing and caring. She breaks down completely with pain and grief, and gives up the desire to live anymore. At this time when she is in such a critical condition and needs motherly care and support, Mattie moves with a strong impulse to protect her, "like a Black Brahman cow desperate to protect her young, she surged into the room, pushing the neighboring woman and others out of her way" (*WBP* 103). Her love for Ciel manifests itself when she brings Ciel literally back to life and persuades her to release the pain that she has been holding inside:

> [S]he rocked.... Ciel moaned. Mattie rocked. Propelled by the sound, Mattie rocked her out of bed, out of that room, into a blue vastness just underneath the sun and above time.... She rocked her into childhood and let her see murdered dreams. And she rocked her back, back into the womb, to the nadir of her hurt, and they found it—a slight silver splinter, embedded just below the surface of the skin. And Mattie rocked and pulled—and the splinter gave way, but its roots were deep, gigantic, ragged and they tore up flesh with bits of fat and muscle tissue clinging to them. They left a huge hole, which has already starting to pus over, but Mattie was satisfied. It would heal. (103-04)

Mattie gives her a healing bath which breaks her into tears in Ciel's eyes "[t]he tears were flowing so freely now Ciel could not see and she allowed herself to be led as if blind" and "Ciel lay down and cried. But Mattie knew the tears would end. And she would sleep. And morning would come" (105). Barbara Christian goes on to compare Mattie's bath of "the numb grief-stricken Ciel" to "Rosalee's bathing of Avey Johnson in Marshall's *Praising for the Widow*, a ritual still practised in voodoo and derived from African religions" which are in fact the larger part of the ritual of shared womanhood that reawakens the senses (*Black Feminist Criticism* 113). Charles E. Wilson interprets it as "the ritual of bathing that she performs on Ciel becomes a testament to the healing powers of sisterly love and bonding, particularly in the face of a chauvinistic, male-centered world" (48). Mattie does all this in order to negate "...the psychological destructive effects of temporality, the cycle that has led to the almost overwhelming tragedy Ciel now faces" (Montgomery, *The Apocalypse* 91). Thus, through her healing skills and ability to form a bond with Ciel, Mattie helps Ciel to survive in the face of the repressive agency of patriarchy.

It is quite exemplary in the above deliberation that Mattie has been quite successful in her life in establishing the bond with every woman who comes in close contact with her. Only she stands with the women whenever they need her, and still she does not intrude in their personal lives. Cora Lee, for example, "sincerely likes Mattie because unlike others, Mattie never found the time to do jury duty on other people's lives" (*WBP* 123). Though Mattie is the central figure, there is, in the novel, one more woman who puts in her best effort to organize and unite the women of Brewster Place. Kiswana Browne along with Mattie Michael holds the community together with a willingness to help her people. She conforms to the whole tradition of the "breed of female protagonists" who "are budding activists, product of the times" (Eko 13). She tries to bring all the women of Brewster Place under the banner of Tenants' association where they can put their problems and fight for their cause together. She goes, for instance, to Cora Lee whose life is falling apart because of her attitude towards herself and her children. Kiswana comes to her as a breath of fresh air and kindles self-confidence in her by inviting her and her children to the black performance of *A Midsummer Night's Dream,* thus providing the aesthetic satisfaction to fill the vacuum in her life. This aesthetic satisfaction is quite evident from her action after the play gets over "Cora applauded until her hands tingled, and felt a strange sense of emptiness now that it was over—Cora went down the row to Kiswana and grabbed her hands "...thanks so much—it was wonderful" (*WBP* 126). Through the play, Kiswana brings some hope in her saturated life and compels her to rethink of her responsibilities for her children. It is for the first time that Cora realizes how much ragged the clothes of her children are, and she is surprised to see so many other incidents happen in her house. She resolves to check her children's home work every night, and send them to summer school. She does also repent as to why "she had beaten him (Sammy) for writing the rhymes on her bathroom walls" (127). She would now dream about her children in "good jobs in insurance companies and the post office, even doctors or lawyers" (125-26).

Kiswana's sense of bonding is not only evident in her support to the leftover women like Cora Lee by providing something that is missing in their lives but also is willing to take a fight with the likes of C.C. Bakers who are the epitomes of masculinity and pretend to control and execute patriarchal world view in the society. One day when Lorraine and Theresa were talking, C.C. Baker appears from somewhere. He is the kind of man who knows but "only one way of doing with women other than with his mother" and "any woman who lay beyond the length of its power was a threat" (*WBP* 161). For C.C. Baker Lorraine has been a challenge due to her lesbian orientation and non-conformation of the heterosexual norms. Consequently, when C.C. Baker and his band locate Lorraine, they start insulting her. Kiswana recues Lorraine and stands with her against the band "... don't let them talk to you like that. They're nothing but a bunch of punks...C.C. Baker, why don't you just take your little dusty behind and get out of here. No one was talking to you" (162). When C.C. Baker listens that he attacks verbally on Kiswana saying "I am just gonna tell Abshu you need a good spankin' for taking up with a lesbo.... Why don't ya come over here and I'll show ya what a real man can do" (162). When the arguments went too far between Kiswana and C.C. Baker, his friends said to him "She ain't nothing but a woman" which shows their attitude towards women that is marked by humility, subjugation and suppression (162). For them a woman means only one thing and any identity beyond that is false and threatening to the male world. Kiswana not only supports the women when they are in need and helps them to stay together but she also provides them a chance to show their unmatched potential which has previously been never realized:

> This was the first time in their lives that they felt someone was taking them seriously, so all of the would-be-if-they-could-be lawyers, politicians, and Broadway actors were taking advantage of this rare opportunity to display their talents. It didn't matter if they often repeated what had been said or if their monologues held no relevance to the issues; each one fought for the space to outshine the other. (139)

Though these women live at the same place, they are quite different in their ways and perception of the society, in other words they expound the poststructuralist and modernist views on the construction of identity, consciousness and ideology. Helen Cixous in her "The Laugh of the Medusa" (1975) explains that "there is...no general woman" and no "female sexuality" that might be "uniform, homogenous, classifiable into codes" (280). This further complicates the problem of uniting them. Despite most of the women using their shared gender as the common ground for their relationship, they overlook such commonality while judging 'The Two'—Lorraine and Theresa. Mattie always sides herself with these girls because she shares the commonality of controlling the sexuality with these two girls. These women of Brewster Place have been unable to understand what Barbara Christian says in *Black Feminist Criticism* (1985) "society's attack on lesbianism is an attack on all women, not only because lesbians *are* women, but also because lesbian stereotypes expose society's fear of women's independence of man" (199) and their control of female sexuality. Without even speaking to the girls about their sexual preferences, the locals immediately begin gossiping and turning their backs to the newcomers. These women are different from the other women in Brewster Place as they love each other which has not been acceptable to the patriarchally oriented residents of the street. It is Mattie, however, who "...refuses to join in the community's condemnation of Lorraine and Theresa's lesbian relationship, preferring to mind her own business and open her mind to the kinds of love that woman can bear for other women" (Matus 52). Mattie is the only woman who respects their difference and tries to defend when Etta says that "...they love each other the way you love a man or a man would love you" (*WBP* 141). Mattie validates their love by stating "[b]ut I loved some women deeper than I ever loved any man.... May be it's not so different" (141). Mattie always aligns herself with these girls because they share this commonality. And she supports them when the other women want to take action against them. She finds nothing wrong with the two girls loving each other as she states this to Etta, "[w]ell, I've loved women, too. There was Miss Eva and Ciel, and even as ornery as you can get, I've loved you practically all my life" (141). Larry Andrews finds it as an indication of the bond that Mattie establishes with other women:

> What Mattie comes to realize, through the insight of her own experience, is that the deep bond she has felt with some women may have a wholeness and power (including the sensual) comparable to that of the lesbians and perhaps superior to any relationship that seems possible with a man in the distorted world of black gender relations. (Andrews 290)

Though these women of Brewster Place feel themselves different from Lorraine and Theresa, Lorraine constantly tries to mix with them as she is aware of the fact that "Black people were all in the same boat—she'd come to realize this even more since they had moved to Brewster—and if they didn't row together, they would sink together" (*WBP* 142) while Theresa is of the opinion that "...they weren't ever going to be accepted by these people, and there was no point in trying" (163). What Theresa emphasizes is that since they are lesbians, Lorraine must accept it and must understand that she is different from the rest of the world simply for that reason but Lorraine thinks differently, "I have accepted it.... I've accepted it all my life, and it's nothing I'm ashamed of. I have lost a father because I refused to be ashamed of it—but it doesn't make me any different from anyone else in the world" (165). Theresa further argues that she does not mean that Lorraine may not regard herself different from the others but the people of the society would not accept her not-to-be different. She puts it "[t]hey wouldn't understand—not in

Detroit, not on Brewster Place, not anywhere. And as long as *they* own the whole damn world, it's them and us, sister—them and us. And that spells different" (166 *italics mine*). Theresa's proposition that the world is controlled by the patriarch whom she addresses as *they*, emphasizes the fact that there is no space for the people who do not conform to the heterosexual norms of the patriarch, not even in a marginal space. However, they only receive hope from the likes of Mattie and Kiswana that the marginal space may provide them with a glimpse of hope in the cruel world of patriarchy.

Naylor here attempts to point out is that except Mattie and Kiswana, rest of the women act as the agents of male authority that validates only heterosexual activities, all other kind of sexual preferences are regarded as perversion. Wilson points that the story of "The Two" marks a shift in the novel by showing not the men's oppression of the women rather "...women's oppression of the women, in this case heterosexual women's prejudice against lesbians. Here Naylor examines the concept of 'the oppressed becoming the oppressor,' and what seems to be the need of all human beings to feel better than someone else" (44). These lesbian characters are created as a counter force to the Black Arts Movement which is marked by its "homophobic and chauvinistic" approach and "relegated women to an inferior status" (57).

As per the patriarchal rule of the society those women who control their sexuality or rather celebrate it are looked down upon. As Sophie puts it before Mattie "[w]hat they doin'—livin' there like that—is wrong, and you know it.... Now, you a Christian woman. The Good Book say that them things is an abomination against the Lord" (*WBP* 140). Such agents have screwed their lives since the very beginning of their relationship. They find no place comfortable and gossip free wheresoever they went as Theresa, who does not care for these people, states "[t]hey knew something in Linden Hills, so I gave up an apartment for you that I'd been in for the last four years. And then they knew in Park Heights, and you made me so miserable then we had to leave. Now these mysterious theys are on Brewster Place. Well, look out that window, kid. There's a big wall down that block, and this is the end of the line for me" (135). Thus, the major constrain to that 'the two' girls faces has been the non-assimilation in the society because of their sexual preference. Maxine Montgomery comments on the assimilation of these two lesbian girls in the Brewster community, "…they can never find complete, unconditional acceptance in a context where heterosexual relationships are considered to be the norm" ("The Fathomless Dream" 46).

Naylor makes it clear that though female bonding heals the women of insensitivity towards them and secures their survival in a marginal space; the women need to be sensitive enough to handle differences among women and a sense of commitment that constantly threatens the existence of female bonding. Lorraine's rape symbolizes that there still exist some differences among the women and that's the only reason that in the conflict between genders, women are victimized and that brings them to the level of losers. Women of the Brewster place can be held responsible for Lorraine's rape. It is the gruesome rape of Lorraine that makes the women of Brewster Place aware about their subjectivised condition and how do they work as a ploy of the oppressive power structure. The moment of Lorraine's rape proves to be spot of time or a moment of epiphany for the women of Brewster Place when they go back or discover their consciousness which further propels them to dismantle the wall, a symbol of power structure. Lorraine has been raped under the shadow of the wall which is a racial and patriarchal artifact so the women decide to uproot the wall from there. In Mattie's dream, all women contribute to bringing down the wall, smashing through the barrier that cuts them from possibilities "[w]omen flung themselves against the wall, chipping away at it with knives, plastic fork, spiked shoe heels, and even bare hands; the water pouring under their chins, plastering their blouses and dresses against their breasts and into the cracks of their hips" (*WBP* 186). Dismantling the wall is a resistance against the male-centered, authoritarian and racist society, and is an expression of their composite strength.

The discussion in the chapter concludes that the marginal space, especially the wall that stands between the Brewster Place, marginal space and the mainstream American world allows an opportunity to the inhabitants of the Brewster Place to resist what hooks says "imperialist white-supremacist capitalist patriarchy" ("Understanding Patriarchy" 2). This resistance against the Foucauldian power has been made possible by forming a bond among the women of Brewster Place on the basis of their shared common experiences of patriarchal repression and racial stranding. The chapter also adds that this marginal space is acquired or allotted to the women of Brewster Place because of the inherent rebellious tendency in them which defies the societal norms of gender, class, and racial definitions.

Chapter 3

Dialectics of the Location: Resistance through Female Bonding in Gloria Naylor's *Linden Hills*

The marginal space in the previous chapter on Naylor's *The Women of Brewster Place* (1982) is separated from the mainstream world through an unsurmounting *stoa,* the wall which not only prevents the inhabitants' access to the world of power and privilege but also confines them in the marginal spatial reality of the street. However, the women of the Brewster Place devise the technique to dismantle the embodiment of the repression by forming the bond among themselves. The remarkable illustration of the construction of Wall suggests that it comes to hold the access of the African Americans to the mainstream world, irrespective of their gender. On the contrary, the present chapter delineates on the novelist's *Linden Hills* (1985) which encapsulates Kantian antinomy and Hegelian dialectics of the progress of the history where the patriarch celebrates the freedom and material success while the women are confined and marginalized, symbolically making it a marginal space for women where the patriarchal repression perpetuates to *ad infinitum*. Further, the chapter reiterates the phenomenon of female bonding as an inevitable fact for the survival of women amidst the racial and patriarchal society which may be traced through the last Nedeed woman, Willa Nedeed who establishes correspondence and identifies herself with the previous women of Nedeed family in order to identify and to resist the patriarchal repression. Empowered and supported by her foremothers' resistance, Willa dismantles the patriarchal empire of the Nedeeds that stands for oppressive power structure in Linden Hills. However, the oppressive patriarchal structure of Linden Hills may also be exemplified by the gruesome death of Laurel who is subjugated and subjected by the power of the patriarch. The chapter also presents a critique of the capitalist hegemony by portraying the poor Anderson house which celebrates love and happiness that may further be read as a foil to the capitalist patriarchal structure of the Nedeed house which stands for subjugation, oppression, and exploitation.

In other words, Naylor's *Linden Hills* covers a complex texture of thematic interpretations which captures the role of space, Linden Hills, in the process to form the ideology, identity and the consciousness of the blacks. *Linden Hills* as a space of social reality traverses the location and celebration of Linden Hills as a geographical space as it encompasses an inevitable dialectics in its construction and function; where on the one hand Luthers (male) enjoys the content of phallogocentricism but on the other it is a site of repression and exploitation for the females of the Nedeed family which is vividly presented in the novel through the treatment, function, and the nature of the geographical space of Linden Hills, which goes under a remarkable metamorphosis as it is successively owned by different Luthers at different point in time. Linden Hills, originally a worthless space where the novel is set, has initially been construed to be an epitome of black success which may resist the hegemonic white world by the first Luther Nedeed with a "vision of what a black space should be" (Bouvier 140) or "[a] wad of spit—a beautiful, black wad of spit right in the white eye of America" (*LH* 09). However, he maintains and succeeds in adhering his vision of resistance to the white world by providing a living space to the poor blacks "who were too poor to farm and earned their living from the saw mills or tar pit" in some small wooden shacks (04). Luther's implicit desire and covert agenda to maintain the autonomy and identity of the space and the dwellers triggers him to lease the land to the poor blacks. It may further allow him to fortify the entire space of Linden Hills against the agency of the dominant and the capitalist. Moreover, his act of lending the geographical domain to the blacks provides him to play with the negative power structure. His desire of lending the space is articulated and manifested in the following words:

> Nedeed, seeing that the government and real estate developers wanted his land so badly, decided to ensure that they'd never be able to get their hands on it. So he went throughout the hill with his son beside him and, starting with First Crescent Drive all the way down through Fifth Crescent Drive, sold the land practically for air to the blacks who were shacking there. He gave them a thousand-year-and-a-day lease—provided only that they passed their property on to their children. And if they wanted to sell it, they had to sell it to another black family or the rights would revert back to the Nedeeds. (07)

The discourse exemplifies the role of Linden Hills in negating the rubric of the entire constellation of patriarchal power structure. The second Luther, a replica to his father continues with the same ideological propositions and tries to maintain the resistance to the dominant power structure. However, during the course of time, the objective of the place, which is to make Linden Hills a place for the blacks which stands for black pride, losses its original message to be replaced by a capitalist feeling turning the inhabitants symbolically white in their thought and approach shedding their blackness (in a cultural sense). Thus, Luther subjects his residents to the demands of patriarchal masculinity in the name of success and mandates that they must forget their cultural past of slavery:

> He (Luther Nedeed) started to work with the ones who would be the most eager to work with him on the future of Linden Hills. The children of the parasites and outcasts from the South, who could find a welcome only from the dead that bordered their homes, wanted nothing better than a way to forget and make the world forget their past. (*LH* 10)

The proposed desire of the capitalist patriarchal Luther that bears through the aforementioned paragraph exemplifies that the entry into Linden Hills is conditioned to only those whose minds are not preoccupied with the cultural conditioning of racial experiences so that their consciousness may easily be constructed. Eventually, the third Luther Nedeed succeeded in eliminating the unwanted residents of Linden Hills who "could do the most damage if he let them stay" because they "had rooted themselves in the beliefs that Africa could be more than a word; slavery hadn't run its course; there was salvation in Jesus and salve in the blues" (11) by "either buying or tricking them out of their leases" (12). Thus, the place is turned into a semblance of black success: "Linden Hills wasn't black; it was successful" (17). This further reiterates the fact that the experiences of repression that is embedded in African American history and is carried by the local blacks living in Linden Hills may resist or be a threat to the capitalist patriarchal project of the Luther Nedeed which is symbolically articulated through the story of Grandma Tilson, the only resistance that the second Luther Nedeed encounters while evicting the place from the unwanted residents of the place, "he (Luther) run(s) into a problem with Grandma Tilson" (12). Grandma Tilson resists Luther's project in the following words:

> I used to fish with your daddy down in that there pond, Luther, and he gave me this land and I ain't giving it up. So take your frog-eyed self and your frog-eyed son out of here. And I know your evil ways—all of you. So if you plan to try something like burning my house down while I just happen to be in it, I got this here deed *and* my will registered at the courthouse. Your daddy weren't no fool and he didn't fish with fools either. (12)

The above deliberation of the Luther family's genealogy beginning from first Luther to the fourth expounds the explicit agenda of constructing the space on its own terms. However, the gradual progression of the family exhibits a remarkable shift in their ideology with regard to the construction of the place. They initially exhibit that the purpose of forming Linden Hills is precisely to resist the oppressive and hegemonic power of the whites, however, in the later part of their journey their thoughts go under remarkable metamorphosis from the intention to provide sanctuary to the poor blacks and make Linden Hills an ideal place in the face of the whites to a patriarchal capitalist project. It is enough to propound that Linden Hills maintains its potentiality to be a site of resistance and repression along with some elements of phallogocentric carnival. The capitalist space of Linden Hills, though appears to be a place of achievement for black men, is a space of marginality for the African American women. This Hegelian dialectics embedded in the place, however, distorts the interpretation of hooks' idea of marginal space "both sites of repression and sites of resistance" for the African Americans (*Yearning* 151). The novel may be interpreted as following the dichotomy of marginal space having the potential for repression and resistance, however, conditioned by gender. The patriarchs, Luther men may only locate it as a site of repression for their women, however, the women of Luther family, especially Willa, through her identification of the repression locates it as a site of resistance.

Similarly, Okonkwo too identifies Linden Hills as space which is dominated by the hegemonic capitalist men. He adumbrates that "Linden Hills' rooted disease of male hegemony and female objectification could be seen as being only a trope to the many unjust locations of power which (Black) women dismantle not by awaiting scriptural intervention or through normative dissent but by effecting change, sometimes through stealth and through revolutionary acts" (128). Barbara Christian reiterates the similar idea when she compares Linden Hills with Brewster place, "Brewster Place and Linden Hills are geographically in the same area; both are inhabited by blacks...each of these places as proximate neighborhoods, though quite different in their orientation" ("Naylor's Geography" 106). Barbara's "differen[ce] in orientation of both the places may be traced in the conversation that Kiswana Brown and her mother have in Naylor's *The Women of Brewster Place.* She further comments from the perspective of the sense of community:

> The outside world perceives Linden Hills as a symbol of black achievement while Brewster Place is seen as a manifestation of failure. Naylor portrays Brewster Place as a black community (though flawed and vulnerable) held together primarily by women, while Linden Hills is

> characterized as a group of houses that never becomes a community, a showplace precariously kept in place by the machination of one wealthy black patriarchal family. (106)

Barbara points that Linden Hills as place is marked by the modernist and postmodernist tendencies of individualism, capital formation, human as resource and degradation of the human being to the level of commodity through the complex process of alienation, reification, and commodity fetishism. Contrary to this *The Women of Brewster Place* is marked with the gift of community or bond among the residents which seems to be missing in *Linden Hills*. Further, this is exemplified in Teresa Goddu's "Reconstructing the History in *Linden Hills*" which could be read as presenting the dichotomy of repression and resistance. The 'Mythic Model' of the history of Luther family, which is "based on repetition and replication instead of progression through difference" (216) and 'Objective History' of Daniel Braithwaite which is conditioned by "Luther's perspective" (218), present the conscious repression of a parallel running tradition of female history. On the contrary, Willie's 'Poetic History' "reads against the socialized signs of Linden Hills and recuperates a black vernacular history" and also "sees the absences in Linden Hills and recovers the female subject" (220). This resistance of Willie's "Poetic History" to Luther and Braithwaite's models is completed by Willa's "Autobiographical Herstory" (222). Teresa explains and validates Willa's version of history when he comments that Willie's "poetic story might revise Luther's and Braithwaite's logocentric histories by insisting on a subjective rendering of reality situated in the body and by signaling a move toward a female-centered story" (222), the revisioning process is completed by Willa's "discovering the names and histories of the "many mothers that Luther never talked about" (223). Gayatri Chakroberty Spivak too adds into the discourse of the repression through the erasure of female history when she says, "it is the long history of women's work which is a sustained example of zero-work: work not only outside of wage-work, but, in one way or another, 'outside' of the definitive modes of production" (501). In a similar fashion,

Moore too identifies Willa's act of resistance as a form of the subversion of the Nedeed history:

> Braithwaite's uncompleted magnum opus is designed to fabricate a patriarchy, but Willa Nedeed constructs and completes the true history of Linden Hills as she unearths the artifacts of the former Nedeed wives during her imprisonment in the morgue, her living hell at the bottom of Tupelo Drive. Her story resists the value systems of the white mythology within which Luther IV wants his story told; this resistance finally, though tragically, topples the patriarchy within which generations of Nedeed bridegrooms have imprisoned their brides. (1411)

It is evident through the preceding discourse that the whole tradition of Luther family in Naylor's *Linden Hills* explores symbolically the genealogy of male domination that further controls and defines women as a gender. It also locates and parallels the historical repression, discrimination, marginalization, humiliation, exploitation, and oppression by patriarchy of the women of Linden Hills to that of the construction of the place which has come into existence only by selling of his wife by the first Luther Nedeed. Moreover, the marginalization of the Nedeed women is performed through the silencing, effacement and baring them with property right making the novel an odyssey of "struggle against a male ideology condemning them (women) to virtual silence" (Habib 43). The established patriarchal order in the novel, *Linden Hills* confines and destroys the lives not only of the women of Nedeed house like Willa Prescott Nedeed, Luwana Packerville, Evelyn Creton, and Priscilla McGuire, but also the characters like Laurel to emphasize the eminency of the patriarchal power structure. All generations of Nedeed men, for instance, have reduced their women merely to body and shadow of men and they consequently become a non-entity. Valarie Smith states that the:

> Women have historically served only one purpose in the Nedeed household, and that is to reproduce Luther. Tolerated because their bodies are needed to reissue that same squat figure, with his "dark, immobile face" and

> his "huge, bottomless globes" for eyes, the sequent Mrs. Nedeeds have each been stripped of identity and then relegated to oblivion. (273)

They have to abide by the rules of the patriarchy else have to be condemned and marginalized. Consequently, the only choice left to the women of Linden Hills is to be submissive and silently accept the patriarchal power structure. The rebellion against the patriarchal power structure means repression and confinement in the marginal space.

The chapter explores the women's experiences of marginalization, domination, and repression in their lives that represents Linden Hills as a marginal space which results from their submission to patriarchal power structure. However, Willa's initial marginalization and isolation, which emanates from her invisible rebellion against the power structure, may not be interpreted that she lacks the potential of resistance rather the opportunity and stimulus to resist which is evident in Willa's later course of action. Initially, she is confined to the basement of her house by her husband "to teach her his lesson for her presumed infidelity, subdue her spirit, and cancel any right she thinks she might have for an independent life" because her deeds do not conform to the patriarchal tradition of the Nedeed house (Felton 89). Historically, all Nedeed men, for instance, conform to the father in physical features, "[t]he same bowlegs, the same protruding eyes and puffed lips," the color of Willa's son "a ghostly presence that mocked everything his fathers had built" is one of the monumental resistance against the established patriarchal norms of producing a son within the laid rules of Luther family (*LH* 18). This is taken as a sheer violation of the patriarchal norms that "took over a hundred and fifty years to build what he now had and it would be a cold day in hell before he saw some woman tear it down" (18). Hence, Luther Nedeed locks Willa along with her son into the basement because of her act of the said resistance:

> She became a constant irritant to Luther, who now turned her presence over in his mind several times a day. Somewhere inside of her must be a deep flaw or she wouldn't have been capable of such treachery. Everything

> she owned he had given her—even her name—and she had thanked him with this? The irritation began to fester in his mind and he knew he had to remove it or go insane. He could throw her out tomorrow; there wasn't a court in this country that would deny him that right, but no one in his family had ever gotten divorced...he had allowed a whore into his home but he would turn her into a wife. (19)

The Luther's account of irritation confirms that the women in his house are no more than the property of the men who may throw them out at any moment and the prevalent laws support his stand. Hence, Luther Nedeed's aim is to make Willa realize that she has, in fact, committed a heinous crime of the violation of the patriarchal norms by producing a pale son. However, he fails to understand that "[n]ature triumphs over [his] planning, for this son harkens back to his maternal ancestors, as the too-long submerged blood of the Nedeed women manifests itself" and "convinces himself that his wife has been unfaithful" (Christian "Naylor's Geography" 115). He further goes on to relate the act of Willa as an act of disobedience against the whole lineage of Luther family who has been very meticulous in preserving the tradition of the suppression of women and using them as a machine to produce a replica of Luthers only. Luther:

> [T]ook out the journals and charts that were locked in the ancient roll top desk in his den. Weeks were spent tracing the dates and times and dates of penetration, conceptions and births for every Nedeed in Linden Hills. He then matched all this with the positions of the stars and the earth's axis at those moments and it verified what had been passed down to him about the facts of life. "There must be five days of penetration at the appearance of the Aries, and the son is born when the sun has died."
>
> Luther slammed the journals shut. He had done that...it was followed to the word. Like every Nedeed before him his seed was only released at the vernal equinox so that the child would come during the Sign of the Goat when the winter's light was weakest. It had been infallible for generations.... (*LH* 19)

The whole process of the consultation of journals and the position of stars in making the wife pregnant to produce the identical son divulges the fact that Nedeed men consider only their side of details while the predicament of the women in process is ignored. Homans points that reducing women to produce only the identical sons in Luther family degrades women's importance and experience, "the operation of making replicas demands the elimination of a woman and of the particularity of women's bodily experience and the substitution of figures more fully under male control" (162). Homans sounds the same what Gayatri Chakravorty Spivak asserts "a non-confrontation of the idea of the womb as a workshop, except to produce a surrogate penis" (498). Consequently, Nedeed plans to punish Willa for resisting her elimination:

> Now, let her stay down here with her bastard and think about what she'd done. Think about who she was playing with. He climbed the steps and checked the iron bolt on the door. Did she really think she could pass her lie off as his son? His fathers slaved to built Linden Hills and the very home she had tried to destroy. It took over a hundred and fifty years to build what he now had and it would be a cold day in hell before he saw some woman tear it down. (*LH* 20)

Confining and degrading the women of Linden Hills to their body further conforms to their marginalization and exploitation which makes it conspicuously clear that the Nedeeds absolutely act like the imperialist white when they attempt to devalue their women only at the level of the labor who has no other utility than that in Luther house. Luke Bouvier reiterates the same fact when he explores a commercial relationship in the Nedeed family. He explains that "by adopting the producer/exploiter opposition and using it forcefully to assure the blackness of Linden Hills, the Nedeeds and the community they control are paradoxically becoming more and more white beneath an increasingly thinner façade of blackness" (145). In confining Willa to his basement, Luther experiences a strong sense of authority as he states "[b]y now she understood that he controlled her food and water and light. Whatever she had been allowed—upstairs or down—was hers not by right, but as a gift.... She wouldn't have been down there in the first place if she hadn't tried to make a fool of him" (*LH* 69). This statement indicates that in the Luther household, the women are considered to be only a maid who is supposed to do all household work and cannot claim anything to be hers despite being a housewife in the same house. And whatever she is offered, she should be thankful for the same. However, the realization of the state of marginalization compels the faceless and nameless women of Linden Hills to be resistive. Maxine Lavon Montgomery observes that *Linden Hills* is marked with "acts of rebellion arising from subaltern women" (*The Fiction of Gloria Naylor* 21) which is situated against the back drop of "women's awakening to the reality of a century-old subjugation and the power that gendered difference implies. Such an arousal occurs through a discovery of women's history and the revelation of the proactive subjectivity on the part of the subaltern" (21). Maxine presents a House/Home dichotomy presenting house as a site of entrapment which is exemplary in that Willa is "to dismantle the master's house of patriarchal privilege and thereby disrupt the aristocratic ideology governing life in Linden Hills" (22). Virginia C. Fowler necessitates the gender discrimination and marginalization in *Linden Hills*, through the reflection of Naylor's own experiences. *Linden Hills* is "Naylor's most incisive critique of male patriarchy, which provides the necessary underpinnings of economic aggression and success" which is a reflection of "Naylor's own experiences at the time she wrote the novel" (60). She further goes on to quote one of her interviews that marks her experience very different from that of a man while traveling through Europe "I (Naylor) was harassed a lot on the streets because I was a woman traveling alone. In southern Spain the women don't walk alone. So the men assumed that I was a prostitute or that I wanted them to approach me, and it was really difficult" (Naylor, "A Conversation" 570).

Nedeed men through the process of 'alienation and reification' degrade their women to the body which is to be consumed by the patriarch in every form. However, the women have to participate in the process of the production and reproduction; they have to be alienated from the product by providing the household comfort in exchange. The women very soon realize that their experience, and in a sense, their whole universe is defined by their body or gender which exemplifies Helen Cixous' concept of writing history through body. Cixous in her "The Laugh of the Medusa" (1976) establishes the fact that the body has a very complex and far-reaching role to play as it has been repressed historically by the apparatuses of male theology and philosophy, social system and even psychoanalysis. She further reinstates that "to write with the body implies facilitating a return of the repressed, a resurrection of that which has been subordinated and treated as secondary, as dirty, as weighing us down and preventing us from rising to the perception of higher truths" (290). The given apodosis explains the fact that the entire trajectory of body or the physicality of the self of the woman has been controlled and constructed by the power of the patriarch. Hence, it can be seen in the novel that the women characters are the victims of male insensitivity in their life in one way or the other except Ruth "who has anything close to a successful relationship with a man" (Andrews 293). Virginia C. Fowler is of the opinion that "Ruth Anderson does represent the purest love we encounter in the novel" (67). Unlike Luther's house where what rules is hatred for women and their marginality and subjugation, in Anderson House "Love rules in this house" (*LH* 38). The Andersons are presented to be the happiest couple in the novel simply because in their struggle against the white empire, they have managed to scrap off the pinks which are constantly associated with "obsessive materialism" (Fowler 75). Fowler further marks that "[t]he pinks thus constitute a powerful trope for the sickness underlying African Americans' embrace of white values" (75). And her further comment summarizes the whole story as "[t]he love ruling the Anderson home is glaringly absent from the houses in Linden Hills" (75). Though the house has been barred from modern day amenities, there is enough love to be called a home:

> It was difficult to notice what wasn't in the Anderson's apartment because so much care seemed to have gone into what was there. Visitors found themselves thinking, what a nice feeling to be allowed into a home. And it *was* a home with its bare wood floors, dusted and polished,

> and with the three pieces of furniture that sat in three large rooms: one sofa in the living room, one kitchenette set with plastic-bottomed chairs on uncertain chrome legs, one bed. Two towels hung in bathroom side by side with two washcloths folded neatly over them. (*LH* 33)

Maxine Montgomery finds that bourgeois capitalism that dominates marriage, family and other social relations in Linden Hills is countered by Norman and Ruth "whose filial loyalty prompts her to stay in a distressed marriage" (*The Fiction of Gloria Naylor* 24). This presents a picture of the home where "Norman assumes the role of nurturer and care giver when he tends to his ailing wife, thereby adopting a traditionally feminine role" surpassing the allocation of gender role by capitalist bourgeois (25). She further says that "[t]he code of male dominance that governs life in aristocratic Linden Hills is rendered null and void when Norman concedes, 'Love rules in this house...'" (*LH* 38) (*The Fiction of Gloria Naylor* 25). However, unlike the love governing Anderson house, the Luther house is presented as devoid of all such sensitivities. Nellie Boyd summarizes Luther's relationship with Willa as "void of emotion and genuine concern. She is regarded solely as a necessary entity for the reproduction of a son who would inherit and continue to oversee Linden Hills. This is evident in the process he uses to choose her as his wife" (78-79). Andrews goes on to state the reason for isolating and sexually ignoring his wife that Luther Nedeed has sexual inadequacy which is explored by Willa after discovering Evelyn Creton Nedeed:

> Luther had sexual inadequacy that explains his physical coldness towards her. Her sexual frustration and self-hatred were expressed in an obsession with cooking, first crazily huge amounts, then small furtive doses of aphrodisiacs designed to make her husband attracted to her, then bulimic purgative, and finally rat poison to kill herself with on Christmas Eve. (*LH* 293)

The above discussed reality of Evelyn Creton's life proposes that the patriarchal system incorporates so much evidence of injustice that women have to face the blame and reprimand of everything in the world, even the misdemeanor of the male. However, the reality of such tortuous condition never comes to the surface and the women remain absent from the historical consciousness. The female marginalization could further be traced through the confession that Luther has when he "actually had to pause for a moment in order to remember his mother's first name, because everyone—including his father—had called her nothing but Mrs. Nedeed. And that's all she had called herself" (18). The intensity of female marginalization can be imagined through this confession of Luther which suggests that the women in Luther's house remain nameless shadows who have no sense of identity and have almost been erased from any written as well as social document. Further, the condition of the women or their treatment in Nedeed family could be traced back to Luther's aside where he misses his wife in her absence or rather is irritated by the same not because he loves his wife but because there is nobody who could take care of the house in her absence where he equates her with a pair of shoes, "[n]ow her absence even lay at the base of his burning throat.... His father was right: breaking in a wife is like breaking in a good pair of slippers. Once you'd gotten used to them, you'd wear them until they fell apart, rather than go to the trouble of buying a new pair. Well, in a few weeks she would have learned her lesson" (67).

Moreover, the erasure of the women is performed by constantly isolating them from the community that further helps maintaining authority over them. Barbara Christian discovers the reasons of the erasure and marginality of women in Linden Hills when she equates the assertion of women's history as a threat to the patriarchal establishment. She writes that "Willa Prescott Nedeed relives the herstory so carefully exhumed from the Nedeeds' official records, we realize how the experiences of the women are a serious threat to the men's kingdom" ("Naylor's Geography" 115). However, the resistance against patriarchal ideology is performed through women's creative and imaginative reliance on stories, recipes, and photographs. This further formulates the collective memory and reconstructs conventional patriarchal history. This also questions and responds to the gaps present in the genealogy of written history. The written records in whatever form left by the Nedeed women are a way to construct a history which otherwise could have completely been washed out, as Charles E. Wilson observes, "[w]ith each of these characters, Naylor explores how history is recorded (what methods are used), who is recording it (and why), and most importantly, who is interpreting it (and what agenda). Clearly, the person who has the opportunity to leave a written record, enjoys a level of power unavailable to someone who is denied the chance" (81). However, the women of Linden Hills, who have ever been denied to allot a place in the written history of Linden Hills, manage to leave some sort of the documents. This is the written record of the previous Nedeed women that resists the erasure of women and further helps Willa to discover a whole tradition of repression and resistance in the basement. The basement of Luther house, Homans points "literalizes the Virgilian repression of mothers, for stacked in it, dusty and ignored, are trunks full of the memorabilia of generations of Mrs. Nedeeds, waiting to be discovered by Willa" (157). Homans associates Willa's resistance with that of Feminist critique of women's erasure when she asserts, "Willa Nedeed's story of resistance and rebirth resonates not only with classical and later Western accounts of the successful effacement of women but also with feminist critique of and resistance to such effacement" (152). The whole journey of Willa through the records of historical repression and the consequent resistance is summed up in the following words by Smith:

> These dire stories help the present Mrs. Nedeed to see how she has participated in her own erasure. Naylor's touch is nowhere more deft than in her handling of Willa's arduous process of self-recuperation—a process that requires rejecting Luther's authority, proving to herself that she exists, reclaiming her birth name and taking charge of her own history, and realizing that if she had made her own bondage by relinquishing identity and will, she could make her own freedom by forging a new self. (274-75)

However, a close observation proposes the fact that Willa's repression and confinement is prolonged in the basement in the absence of female supportiveness and cooperation which the women, for instance, in *The Women of Brewster Place* have.

There has been no Mattie Michael who could heal her like she does to Ciel in *The Women of Brewster Place.* Comparing the bond of female solidarity in Linden Hills with that of Brewster Place, Andrews comments, "Brewster Place offers close physical contact that makes the women's confrontation with each other inescapable and their mutual support compelling. In *Linden Hills,* however, the women are physically isolated in house and separated by status distinctions. The possibilities for sisterhood here are less spatial and contemporary than temporal and historical" (287). However, Willa manages to establish the bond with her ancestral foremothers and is healed by their experiences of repression that emphasizes her strength to resist the patriarchal power structure. Contrary to Luther's theory that the basement confinement will dampen Willa's spirit and she will surrender in order to save her life, her experiences and exposure to the previous Nedeed women makes Willa more confident and empowered. Consequently, Luther's authority and commandments for Willa have no meaning anymore, "[t] here was no meaning to those patterns of empty noises. The words didn't connect inside of her to any history or emotion. She was past being moved to disbelief, frustration, or anger. The power of that voice was gone.... Luther was a dead man if she left that basement alive. And so she knew she could never be allowed to leave" (*LH* 71). Her imprisonment in a marginal space provides her the strength to resist and she is nurtured by a strong sense of female relationship. Willa initially appears to be a total victim of her husband, gradually rises to the position of power to encounter him; and the power is provided by the consciousness of the existence of such mother figures in her descent who, too, have been exploited and pushed into the margin by the men in their lives. Indeed, "most of the documents Willa discovers in the basement are a record simply of effacement and silencing" (Homans 159). This interaction of Willa with the previous Nedeed women is an example of female bonding or what Andrews calls "black sisterhood" (Andrews 293). He points that Willa's "contact with previous Nedeed women through their documents is a genuine if indirect experience of black sisterhood" (293). Further, he goes on to find the roots of this sisterhood into

Naylor's *Mama Day* (1988) where Willa hails from and where there exists a whole tradition of female bonding, in fact, the whole island community of the island belongs to one maternal figure, Sapphira Wade who has been a binding force:

> The bond between women does not arise as a refuge from isolation, mistreatment by men, or loss of identity in the white and black bourgeois worlds. It predates and transcends these modern conditions. Most important is the historical connection that runs from the legendary free spirit who founded the community, Sapphira Wade, through Miranda (Mama Day) to Miranda's great-niece Ophelia. (286)

It is only when she starts reading the accounts of the experiences of her female ancestors that she becomes aware of her lineage, suffering, and a sense of belonging to the tradition of the dispossessed women. A sense of self-confidence is kindled within her by her symbolic bond with her ancestral women and she gathers the courage to climb the stairs and face the epitome of patriarchal power. While standing before Nedeed once she comes out of the confinement, she is supported by several generations of female relationship that she has discovered during her confinement in the basement. Through female bonding Willa identifies herself with Luwana Packerville, her ancestral foremother and her proposition that "[t]here can be no God" as she bears the similar experiences of erasure and marginalization (*LH* 93). She utters "[y]es, whoever you were, Luwana Packerville, you were right about that. This house couldn't still be standing if there were a God" (93). Willa tries to relate her records, she discovers, to her own life and thus forming a bond and communion with the women. She is bewildered, for instance, when she discovers Luwana Packerville's record "[h]ow strange; what must that woman have seen or lived to be moved to leave such a message buried in her wedding veil.... She was probably this child's great-grandmother or one the many mothers that Luther never talked about" (93). As she further reads Luwana's *Bible*, she explores the reason for her conclusion that "[t]here can be no God" (93). Willa discovers that Luwana's frustration has been beautifully carved in the form of the words on the Bible. Since she is not strong enough to confront Luther, she takes it to writing on her Bible. Her writing in whatever form comes out to be a resistance to her marginalization that Luther has been imposing on her. Willa reads one such incident from Luwana's Bible where she is informed that she is a non-entity in the house:

> Luther told me today that I have no right to my son. He owns the child and he owns me. He grew terribly enraged when I ventured a mild protest, and showed me the papers that were signed over to his agent in Tupelo. Foolish creature that I am, I thought my sale to him was only a formality. I thought in the name of decency my husband would have destroyed the evidence of my cursed bondage. But he keeps those documents securely locked away. (117)

Luwana's disillusionment embarks from the point that she has regarded the Luther house as her own and wants to assert her position. The tradition of the Luther house declares that she must be grateful to whatever she has and is provided with without asking for any identity and belongingness. Her further loneliness amounts when she notices that "[t]here [is]...nothing that Luwana Packerville could find to guide her in almost four hundred years of proclamation by these iron men of God" (119). Thus, lack of any lineage of maternal figures further complicates her position in the house from which this writing is the only escape. However, Luwana keeps noting every detail whenever she is being ignored, cornered and pushed to the margin of isolation in her own house "[t]his week a new house keeper came to cook for us and do the washing. I was pressed beyond endurance to voice protest" (119). It is something unimaginable and indigestible to Luwana to accept "a strange woman preparing [her] meals and handling [her] things" (119). On the one side, she is pushed out of her kitchen, the only place where she could be herself and on the other, she has already been cut off from the society and her family, for instance, "the child is constantly with his father, and with no friends around or relatives to visit me, the days drag on so" (119). Her repression in her home is inexorably aggravated by her alienation from her son, she points out that "...since my son has become stranger to me. And there are to be no more children as my bed belongs to me. The child I had hoped to be a refuse for all the love I have to give grows more like his father with each breath and the two are now inseparable in my mind. I thus live with two Luthers in truth and so I live alone" (121). The only possible logic of her being pushed from her kitchen that she could discover is the newspaper that reports "I know it is not for me, because last week the papers told me of a woman in Tennessee who was hanged for poisoning her master's soup, and Luther seemed much agitated over the account" (120). Further, the separation of the child from her mother conforms to the idea of alienation that works within the capitalist system which explains Luwana's condition very well.

Gayatri Chakravorty explains how the capitalist abandons or denigrates the labor to the commodity "the idea of externalization or alienation is of greater interest. Within the capitalist system, the labor process externalizes itself and the worker as commodities" (497). This stands quite true "in terms of the physical, emotional, legal, custodial, and sentimental situation of the woman's product, the child", however, "[i]n both matrilineal and patrilineal societies the legal possession of the child is an inalienable fact of the property right of the man who 'produces' the child" (497). Barred from her kitchen and family she looks at the community which she finds barren as she experiences the color and class differences which further stop her finding friends in Linden community as she embarks "[i]t seemed so unjust that I am barred from having friends among the white wives because of my husband's color and among the colored because of his wealth. If there were only something to do or someone to receive my thoughts so they won't fester within me" (*LH* 120). When she finds nobody around to share her domestic trials, Luwana writes the letters to herself "because I must have someone to help me bear these trials...I feel as if I could leave this world tomorrow and no one in this house would miss me" (120). Her life after that has become an empty one which has no hopes for the future. The whole dichotomy of Luwana's oppression in patriarchal Linden Hills' society can be understood in terms of Gayatri Chakravorty analysis and redefinition of Marx's idea of use-value, exchange-value, and surplus-value. Marx's idea of the same, as Gayatri explains as:

> Marx's notion of use-value is that which pertains to a thing as it is directly consumed by an agent. Its exchange value does not relate to its direct fulfillment of a specific need, but is rather assessed in terms of what it can be exchanged for in either labor-power or money.... In this process of abstracting through exchange, by making the worker longer than necessary for subsistence wages or by means of labor-saving machinery, the buyer of the laborer's work gets more (in exchange) than the worker needs for his subsistence while he makes the thing. This 'more worth' is surplus-value. (496)

The same relationship could be applied to understand the position of women in society and how the capitalist patriarchal society controls them in a domestic space, "...woman in the traditional social situation produces more than she is getting in terms of her subsistence, and therefore is a continual source of the production of surpluses, for the man who owns her, or by the man for the capitalist who owns *his* labor power" (496). Similarly, in Luther's house a woman's product, the child is controlled and owned by the patriarch. The child is the surplus value of what she receives in return—the house-hold comforts and a space called 'Home'. On the basis of her analysis, Spivak further suggests that "if the nature and history of alienation, labor, and the production of property are reexamined in terms of woman's work and childbirth, it can lead us to a reading of Marx beyond Marx" (497-98). However, Luwana Packerville attempts to overcome her marginalization without any support from anywhere and abandoned by the patriarch for her uselessness in the house. Left on her, Luwana writes to her other self in order to share her dispossessed, isolated, and marginalized position in the house. She tells and retells her other self that she has no relevance to the lives of Luther and his son, once she has produced the identical son:

> [M]y child only confirms what I have always felt in my heart. From his birth, he has been his father's son in flesh and now in spirit.... It is clear to me that I have now outlived my usefulness to them, and they are trying to push me out of this house by making me a stranger to my husband and a stranger to my son. And the true

> horror is that I am becoming, sister, a stranger to myself. (*LH* 123)

The patriarch through constant pushing Luwana into isolation in the house makes her realize her invisibility to the extent that she even cannot establish a rapport between her body and her consciousness. With no one to be called her own, she may also not associate herself with the house in which she is living that has further been pushing her to the verge of insanity. The only solution, however, she suggests to herself in her next letter is female bonding which may be the only way that could save Luwana from going mad. She writes to herself:

> Please, venture out and make friends with the other wives. I alone am not enough for you. I know you feel it is impossible because you are despised by the farmers' wives around you and distrusted by the colored women up on the hill, but for the love of God, try. Go visit and take them flowers and vegetables from your garden this spring. Do something, my dear, because I fear for your sanity. (125)

She realizes that this isolation and marginalization is driving her towards madness and if she does not find any female support she would soon become so. In absence of any female support and bonding and a constant marginalization which could not be borne by Luwana Packerville, she reaches to the conclusion that "[t]here can be no God" and finally, gets insane (93). The perpetuation of patriarchal repression on Luwana in Nedeed house reiterates the lack of female tradition and bonding to the extent of insanity.

Furthermore, the lack of a female tradition and bonding among the women of Nedeed house could be traced to the fact that Evelyn Creton, the next woman in the Nedeed house "probably never knew Luwana Packerville. As she roasted her meats and canned her apply butter year after year, she didn't know that a woman had gone insane because she was barred from the very kitchen that Evelyn Creton later filled with her damned cookbooks" (140). This suggests that though the women shared the same kitchen one after the other, they have been ignorant about each other's suffering and marginalization. Had they been aware of each other's miseries or trials, they could have reacted collectively. The strength of the collective bonding may be traced to Willa's resistance who when discovers these women in the form of their monuments, reacts against patriarchy and its epitome, the Nedeeds.

However, Evelyn Creton's story also suggests that confining and delimiting the women's space constrains women's creative potentials and establishes the authority of the patriarch. Evelyn Creton expresses a lot of anger and justifies the feminist emphasis on the space for women. Patricia Hill Collins emphasizes the relevance of a safe space where the oppressed "...can express themselves apart from hegemonic or ruling ideology" (*Black Feminist Thought* 05). She further identifies "three primary safe spaces for black women"—"black women's relationship with one another," "black women's blues tradition" and "the voices of black women authors" (05). However, Evelyn Creton is unable to occupy any of the aforementioned spaces. She even lacks the primary safe space—the relationship at her home "such as family and friends" or "black churches and black women's organizations" (05). Evelyn's only space is her kitchen where she spends most of her time. Though she has a bed room too but it is not private or her own, Luther has access to it any time while she is not allowed to enter in that of Luther:

> He needed his private space. But he would come at night. Enter and leave her body with the same quiet precision that she saw when he balanced his accounts, read his newspaper, or dissected his steak. That entrance and exit from her bedroom and her body became part of a natural flow of motion that was Luther. If spontaneity and passion didn't exist in the rooms they ate in, entertained in, and sat in, how could she expect it in the room she slept in? (*LH* 148)

The above discussion suggests that even Evelyn's very private space of her body is also controlled and consumed by the patriarch as if she is a commodity or an object of mere sexual gratifications. The description of her room as lacking in spontaneity and passion exemplifies the sexual relationship between her and her husband and that further pushes her into an acute helplessness, pain, and objectification. However, to a certain extent, these women of Linden Hills have allowed the patriarchal power structure by accepting the material success to subjectivize them. Her condition is well posited by Felton and Loris "[t]he life-records of these Nedeed women show their wasting away under the authority of their husbands, even though these particular women had all of the material possessions that myth should insure their survival" (90). Naylor adds to it when Willa feels that these Nedeed women have been beautiful, and they are very conscious of their beauty "[t]he records were so exact she could almost see her slender fingers massaging that pale face with glycerin, almond paste, and pigeon fat. She had often imagined that the cream-and-ivory women who slept in that canopied bed were incredibly beautiful" (*LH* 150). Discovery of Evelyn Creton, however, makes Willa realize that her confinement to the basement emanates from the historical conditioning of the women in the house. If something is wrong that does not lie in herself rather in the house which bears a tradition of female subjugation and marginalization. Her realization is in that sense very close to that of Luwana's thesis that "[t]here can be no God" (93). Though she is able to locate repression and consequent frustration in the women, she finds it irresistibly irritating why the previous Nedeed women have not resisted their repression. She believes that her present aggravated condition of repression is the outcome of the acceptance of injustice by her ancestral women. Had the previous women raised their voice against injustice, the situation could have not been that grave. This realization fills her with anger:

> If there was any sickness, it was in this house, in the air. It was left over from the breaths of those women who had come before her. The Luwana Packerville, Evelyn Creton, and God knows who else.... This had happened a long ago. She could taste the anger at the back of her throat as her eyes came full circle to her son...(She wanted) to destroy those beginnings. But she couldn't touch what had already escaped her long before she came to Tupelo Drive. She was left with only the ends. (204)

In her frustration of these women for not being resistive, she further discovers the photographic records of Priscilla McGuire "as one box spilled out piles of photographs and she tore at them blindly" (205). The photographs of Priscilla are a reassertion of an established private history of her own that resists the erasure of female tradition from the Nedeed house. Teresa Goddu establishes the relevance of the photographic history when he alleges that though Braithwaite, the official Nedeed historian and a history Professor, is a self-proclaimed photographer of history, he fails to understand the role of subjectivity involved in the photographic version of history as "subjectivity enters the experiment as soon as the scientist picks up the camera and looks through its lens" (218). The reason of his myopic vision as proposed by Teresa is that his eyes are conditioned by "Luther's perspective" which leads to his phallocentric vision (218). Nonetheless, if there is anybody who could be termed the photographer of history in the real sense, she is none other than Priscilla McGuire, who brilliantly marks her exclusion from Luther's family through the photographic method. A close examination of the photographs, kept safely by Priscilla McGuire, marks that she has constantly been marginalized and ultimately disappears from the photographs which further conforms to her erasure and subjugation from the historical realities of the Nedeed house. The exploration of the disappearance of the woman from the family history and realities compels Willa to reevaluate her own condition. She starts asking for the meaning of her own life when she finds the woman disappearing from the photographs and she is very disappointed that she has no history rather is lost in the oblivion. Nobody has ever talked about her as if she has never existed, "the past dissolving into the present and bringing with it the meaninglessness of whatever had gone before. Everything else, every other word or action had been only a bizarre temper tantrum against fate. Because after all that, here it finally was: a dying body, the ticking of a cracked clock and a smeared photo album marked *me*" (*LH* 267). The only statement that links Willa with Priscilla is "*I knew you would come, and I'm so pleased...*" (249) which proposes that beneath the disjunction of the historical reality pertaining to the condition of the women, they are united at least on the basis that they have been subjugated and so the coming generation of the women will be subjected to the same. Priscilla's disappearance makes Willa aware of her own presence or rather absence from the male tradition of History "[s]taring at the gaping hole that was once Priscilla McGuire, she reached her hand up and began to touch her own face, her fingers running tentatively across the cheeks and mouth, up the bridge of the nose, and spanning out over the eyes and forehead" (267). Her identification of the position of marginalization which stems from her knowledge of her previous women forces her to form a bond between them and review her own position in the contemporary reality. Once she is assured of her presence and as she has not been pushed up to that margin that she could not recover, she tries to rebuild herself "[n]ow that she had actually seen and accepted reality, and reality brought such a healing calm. For whatever it was worth, she could rebuild" (168). And that energy to rebuild generates from her fear or threat from being disappeared if she does not resist her marginalization. Another factor that goads her to act is the last words of Priscilla McGuire *I knew you would come, and I'm so pleased...*, which bestow on her a sense of responsibility to act against the force that has caused her disappearance from the family (249).

However, when Willa compares herself with the previous Nedeed women, she never finds herself even a bit resistive before producing the white son rather she has always been "...a good mother and a good wife. For six years, she could claim that identity without any reservations" (279). Once Willa registers her resistance she "sat on a cot in a basement, no longer anyone's mother or anyone's wife..." because she has revolted against Nedeeds by "...producing a white skinned child" (279). Nellie Boyd finds that "...when Willa provides him (Luther Nedeed) with a son who does not look exactly like him, he feels she has broken the terms of his marital arrangement. He no longer regards her as an appropriate wife for him or an appropriate 'first lady' of Linden Hills" (79). She loses her position immediately after she produces a son who is not identical in color to Luther Nedeed. This further indicates the truth that a Nedeed woman exists only to produce a son who must be identical to Luther Nedeed in every possible sense, else she should be ready to face the consequences like one Willa has suffered. However, it is also evident in the previous cases of Nedeed wives that even after they successfully produce an identical black son, they are pushed to the unknown world of isolation and marginalization.

After going through a symbolic journey into the history of the Nedeed household to measure the amount of exploitation, marginalization, and resistance the previous Nedeed women have been subjected to, Willa invokes in herself a divine power to confront and take revenge of the collective history of subjugation of female erasure, suppression, and marginalization. Her endeavor is further supported by Willie, a feminine poet who unlocks the door and paves her way to upstairs:

> An unconscious journey in toward the power of will that had crept alone in primordial muck eons before being clothed with fins, scales, wings, or flesh.... She breathed in and out, her body a mere shelter for the mating of unfathomable will to unfathomable possibility. And in that union, the amber germ of truth she went to sleep with conceived and reconceived itself, splitting and multiplying to take over every atom attached to her being. That nucleus of self-determination held the tyrannical blueprint for all divisions of labor assigned to its multiplying cells. Like other emerging life, her brain, heart, hands, and feet were being programmed to a purpose. (*LH* 288-89)

Naylor has beautifully imprinted how Willa's whole body and mind has been prepared by an unconscious and invisible power for the assignment that she has taken. As "Willa headed for the concrete steps", her very first destination has been "kitchen" which has served as a central metaphor in the overall discourse of feminist studies and particularly in the lives of previous Nedeed women (294). She, further, plans her daily routine, thus to assert her position and identity which has been denied ever since before. She murmurs to herself "...twelve steps to the door, then into kitchen. After cleaning that room, she would start on the den. Then up the hall toward the staircase to the bedrooms. She would begin with her, move to Luther's, and then on to the child's" (296). As the power is bestowed on her by her experiences, she is garlanded with a number of metaphors, all leading to one central meaning that is to show her confident and courageous which stems from her symbolic bond with the previous women of the same descent "[e]ach step, repeated a million times and millions of feet away on much lusher ground as the wingless queen amidst a horde of army ants trudged on, watching the deadly tarantula, the sleeping crocodile, the rifle-bearing hunter eaten away in front of her eyes. While the only thing stopping Willa was simply a bolted wooden door" (297). On the one hand, Willa is moving upwards to reestablish herself with all possible kind of historical and ontological support and confidence which she has acquired through her discourse with the maternal figures, while, on the other, Luther Nedeed has been totally unaware of Willa's tryst with the records of the previous wives, and hence he is ignorant of the secret bond that Willa has formed with these women, which in turn has provided her with determination and empowerment to make her presence felt and resist her marginalization in the family and society. This ignorance leads him to control Willa once again and restrict her entry into this world, and confine her once again to the basement. But this time the things have got changed and he faces a new Willa who is not only ready to assert her position but also to take up any challenge. Naylor beautifully carves this scene where the clash takes place which ends in the burning of the house in the following lines:

> Luther Nedeed made two mistakes that cost him his life: he thought Willa was leaving the house, and he read the determination in her eyes as madness. She was heading for the piles of boxes and loose paper in the corner by the hall door. But she kept walking when he called her, walking when he touched her, so he blocked her path with his body. That brought them face-to-face. He had never encountered the eyes of a lone army ant, marching in defiance of falling rocks and rushing water along the great Amazon, the wingless queen who cannot fly from danger, blindly dragging her bloated egg sac as long as at least one leg is left uncrushed; so the dilated pupils

> in front of him registered insanity. Her fist lashed out and caught him across the Adam's apple, making him bend and choke. As she brushed past him, he sprang up, grabbed her tightly behind the shoulders, pulling her away from the door...every cell in her body strained his hands and he found himself being pulled toward the hall. (299-300)

Their struggle makes the Christmas tree fall and the house catches fire which is articulated by Willa as "My God, we're on fire" (300). This struggle erupts because of Nedeed's inclination to push her into the kitchen and then to the basement again. However, his intention is to lock her again there threatens Willa's sense of freedom. As a result, much to chagrin of Luther Nedeed empowered Willa takes him from the front, "[n]o meaning to his struggle except that it was pushing her back into the kitchen. And now no path to the clutter by the door except through the lighted tree. They went hurling against it, the top smashed a side window, and the December wind howled in" (300). This act of Willa marks the end of the patriarchal empire of Luther Nedeed. Delineating upon the debate whether Willa's death is a matter of sacrifice or self-destruction, Christopher N. Okonkwo writes that "Willa's death should be revisioned not in the pejorative sense of suicide and self-destruction but as positive, as deliverance and self-sacrifice that open a new millennium with the possibility of multiple choices for the subdivision's residents, particularly its Black women" (130). He calls Willa "a feminist critic and historian to serving as a triumphant heroine" (117). He further deliberates that:

> Willa's revolt and victory collaborate as well as conclude the women's generational fight for face and voice. Also, one must not overlook the strength of character that informs Willa's unpopular decision to reclaim her position as a good wife and mother in a Black suburbia stratified along lines of caste, career, and class. When we analyze Willa's courage to risk her life and ultimately die, thereby indirectly delivering Linden Hills' other inhabitants from Lutheran shackles, she qualifies as a symbol of strong womanhood. (129)

As the above discussion exhibits, the basement confinement of Willa provides her the opportunity to establish the bond with her ancestral women and to resist the patriarchal order symbolized by Luther Nedeed. Using 'mirrored cave' motif, Homans points that Linden Hills like Irigaray's *Speculum of the Other Woman*, provides an equal opportunity to resist the white world, however, Nedeed men fail to do so. He reasons for the same here:

> Perhaps racial oppression puts Luther Nedeed in a position of marginality roughly equivalent to that of women in Irigaray's scheme and gives him the opportunity to perform their acts of criticism, an opportunity that he wastes. While Willa is recovering her face and her name (her will) in the cellar, Luther is upstairs in his "den," another sort of cave.... (170)

Homans' comment suggests that Luther's empire is destroyed for two visible reasons—one is that he has subjugated and marginalized his woman and the other is that he has forgotten the original motif of the construction of the place, i.e. to resist the white world. In addition, it also suggests that the marginal space of the cave is utilized by Willa to gather the strength to dismantle the authority which creates and perpetuates the marginal space for the confinement of the subaltern. In this sense, the novel repeats the same phenomenon that has been performed in *The Women of Brewster Place* where the women conceive the strength to dismantle the racial and patriarchal artifact of the Wall which has turned the street into a marginal space. Maxine Lavon Montgomery compares the ending of *The Women of Brewster Place* with that of *Linden Hills* that is marked with the emergence of 'empowered' womanhood. As at the end of the first novel women gather to dismantle the brick wall once they realize their shared subjugation in a patriarchal society, much in the same way, "Willa's discovery of the documents connecting her with the maternal predecessors who find themselves subjected to the tyrannical behavior of Luther Nedeed," leads her to "incendiary" (*The Fiction of Gloria Naylor* 28).

It is not only the women who are the object of patriarchal subjugation rather the patriarchal machine runs its course invariably crushing whosoever comes on its way as long as they do not move along with its speed, instructions, and path. There are numerous instances in the novel where not only women are the subject to the patriarchal power structure but also the men who are resistive in their act of defying the patriarchal orientation of heterosexuality and go on having homosexual relationship. Most of these characters who rebel against any such authority are to face the severe consequences as the former poses a number of challenges as well as threats to the revolutionary. Winston Alcott, for instance, is one who has been in love with David and is forced into a heterosexual marriage by his father, firm where he works, and Luther Nedeed; all of them control certain sections of his life. For instance, his familial life is controlled and defined by his father while the firm decides his career, and Luther Nedeed decides about the place he has to live in. Kimberly A. Costino in her article "'Weapons Against Women': Compulsory Heterosexuality and Capitalism in *Linden Hills*" demonstrates that how capitalism operates through heterosexuality to control and exploit the subject when she explores that Naylor's novels "...examine compulsory heterosexuality as a political institution and expose seemingly inextricable link between economic success and compulsory heterosexuality" (41). Further, what she makes clear is that Naylor finds "...heterosexuality as a strategy...not an innate or inevitable, then it is not necessarily fixed and stable" (46). Christopher N. Okonkwo comments on conforming to heterosexuality as a means of surviving in Linden Hills, "Winston Alcott comes to realize, for instance, that to reside in Linden Hills he must dump his gay lover David, renounce his homosexual lifestyle, and get married to a woman and that this woman would hopefully conceive a son to whom he would transfer his millennial lease in the subdivision" (123). Had he got married to David he could have disqualified to be a resident of Linden Hills, which is symbolically represented by Luther's offering of a flat to Winston as a gift of marriage.

Winston's case necessitates the control of patriarchy into the heterosexual system as the residents of Linden Hills are controlled by heterosexual norms. However, Willie and Lester are the two characters who reject the patriarchal masculinity's idea of heterosexual mandate. Unlike Winston, for instance, Lester rejects the idea of upward mobility and the control of economic resources as a goal of his life, thus, defying the patriarchal control. In addition, his desire to be a poet strengthens his proposition. His compatriot Willie too rejects the patriarchal control by resisting the traditional ideas of masculinity or presenting an example of what Goddu refers as "marginal sexuality" by aligning with Willa (220). It is Willie who hears the pathetic sounds of Willa for the first time in Linden Hills. This alignment with Willa and the search of her story turns him "if only for a moment, into a woman" (Goddu 222). Also, as a replica of Willa in the outside world, Willie acts as a foil to Luther Nedeed with his abilities to critically view the devastating and destructive aspects of the patriarchal system of Linden Hills. The relationship between Winston and David underlies the basic concepts of queer theory where the sexual control is guided by the rubric and texture of social formation. The constellation of experiences through economic, cultural and social path controls the relationship between Winston and David. On the contrary, the homosexual relationship between Willie and Lester survives as they do not come under the oppressive control of Linden Hills, a site of repression, and they also defy or in fact reject the socio-economic apparatuses which are important for dynamism and mobility in society. The possibility of rejecting the authoritative constellations provides them with possibilities of finding their identity and consciousness.

The possible reasons for Laurel Dumont's repression and marginalization, that the text suggests, lies in her insistence and incorporation of the values of white America which in turn demands the surrender of African values and culture, however, which have been the only way to survive in Linden Hills. Berg locates the reason of Laurel's suicide in her rootlessness when he asserts "Laurel Dumont, unable to reconnect with her family or to secure a real sense of home, commits suicide by diving into the empty pool that borders her magnificent house" (4-5). And when she tries to assert her own existence in a patriarchally established society of Linden Hills by claiming the house she is living in as her own, she is left with no option than to commit suicide because this is something unimaginable in Linden Hills.

Montgomery points "[a]s if to remind the young woman of her marginal status, Luther evicts her once he learns of the DuMonts' impending divorce" (*The Fiction of Gloria Naylor* 26). This society is designed in such a way that only a male can be heir of the property in Linden Hills else in the absence of a male member the rights of the property revert to the Nedeeds. The intensity of the favor one gains for being a male could be traced back to Dr. Braithwaite, a Professor of History, whose wife is dead and he is living in Linden Hills simply because he is a male, while for the same reason Laurel Dumont is being asked to vacate the place. Though before committing suicide, Laurel Dumont makes a last effort by calling and uniting with the other women folks of the community which could have been a way to gain support in her struggle against patriarchy but since the women she tries to call are themselves victims of the patriarchal subjectification, they could not offer any help which further pushes her to end her life. Her story suggests that had she been able to form a bond among the women of the place, she could have survived or dismantled the very orientation of Linden Hills itself at the beginning only.

Maxine proposes the reason for Laurel's position that she leads the life uprooted from "agrarian past and its sustaining traditions" (*The Fiction of Gloria Naylor* 25). She is a prototype of the people who "surrender [their]...cultural moorings in the pursuit of money, status, and power. In the purview of a Linden society, the notion of power to a woman is symbolically shattered by Luther's enforcement to leave the house once he learns about her divorce from Dumont" (25). The only home suggested by Naylor is that which Roberta offers with her "...connection with an agrarian South, evidenced by her down-home cooking stories about Br'er Fox and Br'er Rabbit, and mother wit, ground[ed]...in an insistently maternal reality that exists outside the purview of the Nedeed paternal dynasty" (26). Okonkwo further analyses that Laurel's death is not an act of resistance rather surrender before the power of patriarchy which is the result of her materialistic capitalist approach when he articulates that "[u]nlike Willa, Laurel seems unable or unwilling to locate alternative paths of self-validation besides materiality, maleness, and marriage hence the negative associations of her death" (121).

The foregone discourse and deliberation discusses the construction and location of Linden Hills which is represented as an artifact of power structure. The discussion also establishes the fact that the oppressive power structure with its agency maintains carnival as far as the place of the man is concerned. However, it is concomitantly a site of repression and exploitation for the women as it is owned and controlled by the power structure. The eminence of power is realized at all possible situation at Linden Hills, and the example of it can be seen through the control of sex and sexuality through the patriarch. It maintains the social construction of the sexuality by approving the sexual practices and heterosexuality whereas the homosexuality is disapproved and ostracized. Linden Hills subjectivizes its characters through the process of signification which is the result of a traverse between economic, social, and cultural signifier and signified. This may be testified in the example of Winston and David. On the contrary, those who may defy such signification of the signifier or signified from social, economic, and cultural realms may not be controlled by the power structure which may be appropriately identified in the case of Willie and Lester.

The chapter examines the process of marginalization of the women by all Luthers who control the subjectivity of the women, which is evident by the fact that the Linden Hills has been bought by the first Luther after selling his wife. It is a glaring example of the commodification of the women as far as the treatment of their body is concerned. The oppressive history of the process of subjectivization of the women is traced through the diachronic and synchronic remnants of the history of the women of Linden Hills. The interpellation of women is made possible through several hiatus as they lack a cohesive bonding among themselves. In Linden Hills the women are presented as highly subjective and isolated which do not allow them to interact with the larger reality of the community and brings them into a great fiasco of fracturedness. The cohesive bonding among the women of Brewster Place fortifies them with immense capacity to fight against the oppressive structure of patriarchy. The comparative picture of the Linden Hills and Brewster Place exemplifies the fact that the female bonding is inevitable in order to efface the powerful force of patriarchy.

Chapter 4

Locating Resistance in Willow Springs through Cultural Practices and Female Bonding in Gloria Naylor's *Mama Day*

The present chapter emphasizes on Naylor's strategy of constructing a marginal space of Willow Springs in her third novel *Mama Day* (1988) in order to preserve the cultural and mythical practices, which are deeply embedded into African American mythos to resist the mainstream world view. Naylor proposes with evidence that the practices of the island—conjuring, healing, hoodoo, and candle walk protest against the consciousness and ideology of the dominant mainstream. In other words, these cultural practices not only act as apparatuses to preserve the identity but they are also the potential sites of resistance to the dominant or hegemonic power structure of the mainstream world. *Mama Day* defies the notion of marginality through constantly referring to a centre to which an outsider, typically the oppressed, is always peripherally situated—a position of perpetual powerlessness that reifies the hegemonic centre. Unlike Naylor's previous two novels, namely, *The Women of Brewster Place* (1982) and *Linden Hills* (1985) that are situated in the cities of North America, *Mama Day* is situated off the mainland of America to further marginalize its location as "the only thing connects us to the mainland is a bridge—and even that gotta be rebuilt after every big storm" (*MD* 05). Further, the marginality of the place could be observed through the fact that "Willow Springs ain't in no state. Georgia and South Carolina done tried, though—been trying since right after the Civil War to prove that Willow Springs belong to one or the other of them" (04-05). Consequently, because of the liminal location of Willow Springs, the place belongs to none of the state "[a]ll forty-nine square miles curves like a bow, stretching toward Georgia on the south end and South Carolina on the north, and right smack in the middle where each foot of our bridge sits, is the dividing line between them two states" (05). The liminality of the place, however, provides it with the political autonomy, "after they passed that Sixteenth Amendment. None never went over for local elections, 'cause there was no place to go, us being neither in Georgia or South Carolina. And them local politicians couldn't do nothing for Willow Springs that it wasn't doing for itself" (80). Consequently, the island, Willow Springs celebrates the autonomy and resistance to the mainstream world as it "rejects the conventional wisdom and standards of behavior of the dominant culture and provides alternatives to the mainstream culture" (Simpson and Yinger 35) because there are no hegemonic modern agencies to control and subjectivize the people of the island. As a result, the people of the island have developed their own autonomous system which may not be identical with the mainstream world:

> And there ain't no sheriff to watch out for, and no jail to put.... The nearest courthouse is fifty miles beyond the bridge on the South Carolina side, and over a hundred on Georgia's. The folks here take care of their own, if there is a rare crime, there's a speedy judgment. And it ain't like the law beyond the bridge that's dished out according to likes and dislikes, and can change with the times. (*MD* 79)

The first half of the novel exposes and resists the modern agencies of power that work to control and to dominate the blacks in the United States which implies the fact that despite all proclamation of abolition of slavery, it still survives. The latter part of the novel, which is set on an island predominantly inhabited by the black people, offers a sanctuary for them to survive and to resist the hegemonic world with their cultural practice. Moreover, the novel offers resistance to the modern agencies of power by not letting their dreams of making Willow Springs a vacation paradise fulfilled which may be an act of colonizing the island and breaking in the autonomy and integrity of the island. The novel, thus seems to participate in what bell hooks observes "...'the politics of the location', necessarily calls those of us who would participate in the formation of counter-hegemonic cultural practice to identify the spaces where we begin the process of re-vision" (*Yearning* 203). Naylor seems to be aware and acknowledges hooks' idea of 'the politics of location' as the setting of the novel, *Mama Day* on the island of Willow Springs provides such an opportunity of counter-hegemonic discourse that is embedded in the cultural practices and the location. However, the marginal space of Willow Springs that is geographically situated at the periphery is not presented by Naylor as a site of repression but only a site of resistance with its well established culture that offers the inhabitants a sense of autonomy and authority, thus, defying, bell hooks' idea of margin as "...both sites of repression and sites of resistance..." (*Yearning* 151). Naylor also mocks hooks' idea of coming to the marginal space "...through suffering and pain, through struggle" (148) by emphasizing the essential myth of the island about the matriarch, Sapphira Wade who has tricked the island from her white master, Bascombe Wade. Sapphira Wade has been an "African-born, Bascombe Wade was from Norway, and it was the 1823 'ing that went down between them two put deeds in our hands" (*MD* 05).

People of the island are the descendents of the same matriarch and share the same historical lineage of Sapphira Wade, "[a] true conjure woman: satin black, biscuit cream, red as Georgia clay: depending upon which of us takes a mind to her. She could walk through a lightning storm without being touched" (03). However, because of its location, and a culture of its own, the island stands in opposition to the mainstream American world; points Ivey, "[i]n *Mama Day*, Naylor's matriarchal society on the tiny island of Willow Springs stand in opposition to contemporary American hierarchical society represented by New York" (98). This positioning of the island in opposition to the contemporary American society ascribes not only the marginal status to the island but also offers an opportunity to read the cultural practices of the island as a resistance to the modern hegemonic world of the mainstream America.

In a similar fashion, Maxine Lavon Montgomery adumbrates that "Naylor lends a decidedly gendered postcolonial voice to the saga of black resistance as the author relies upon subversion and disruption in the creation of an alternative reality that challenges the discourse of the larger society" (*The Fiction of Gloria Naylor* 40). She places special emphasis on the myth of Sapphira Wade as she points out that "[t]he legend of Sapphira Wade paves the way for infinite discursive possibility" (52). She also notes that the autonomy the residents of the Willow Springs enjoy hails from Sapphira Wade's conjuring practices as "[c]onjuring allows the island matriarch to maintain a spiritual connection with Africa and enjoy an expanded sphere of influence outside both the house and field. She wrests control over the land that later becomes Willow Springs, paving the way for the unprecedented self-sufficiency residents inherit" (42). Thus, Maxine attributes the potential of the inherent resistance of Sapphira Wade to her 'spiritual connections' with Africa in the form of the spiritual and cultural practices.

In addition, the myth of Sapphira Wade also emphasizes the collective bond that the island infuses, which is based on the fact that the whole island is the descendant of the same matriarch. However, Naylor also uses a collective voice of the island to articulate the possession of the island to emphasize the bond that the people of the island exhibit to resist the modern encroachers and contemporary practices of the mainland. The collective voice articulates that "[i]t (Willow Springs) belongs to us—clean and simple. And it belonged to our daddies, and our daddies before them, and them too—who at one time all belonged to Bascombe Wade (whom the matriarch tricked to get the island)" (*MD* 05). The historicity of their possession of the island suggests that the whole of the island community is the descendent of the same Wade family which also implies that the bond that the people of the island share is more filial in nature than communal. However, the collective bond of the people of the island allows the inhabitants to resist the real estate developers who have "[s]tarted coming over here in the early '90s, talking 'vacation paradise,' talking 'pic-ture-ess'" (04). The desire of the dominant class of the mainland to conquer, control, and exploit the marginal space of Willow Springs to perpetuate the exploitation of the marginal inhabitants is quite clear in their intention of establishing the real estate business on the island under the guise of "community uplift" and "better jobs" (06). The present matriarch of the island, Mama Day who is "a direct descendant of Sapphira Wade" seems to be quite aware of the power structure inherent in the lies of the real estate developers as she cautions the inhabitants lest they may get into the trap of the temptations that the modern colonizers offer (06). She also quotes the examples of the exploitation that the real estate developers have performed at other places when she articulates "...it weren't about no them now and us later—was them now and us never. Hadn't we seen it happen back in the '80s on St. Helena, Daufuskie, and St. John's? And before that in the '60s on Hilton Head" (06). Thus, Mama Day's visualization of the potential harm and exploitation that the real estate developers may cause on the island locates the locus of the resistance:

> Got them folks' land, built fences around it first thing, and then bought in all the builders and high-paid managers from mainside—ain't nobody on them island benefited. And the only dark faces you see now in them "vacation paradise" is the ones cleaning the toilets and cutting the grass. On their own land, mind you, their own land. Weren't gonna happen in Willow Springs. 'Cause if Mama Day say no, everybody say no. (06)

Such an insight into the destructive intention of power structure offers the inhabitants of the island a vision "...that anything coming from beyond the bridge gotta be viewed real, real careful" (07). This critical vision of world that they articulate and adhere echoes hooks' idea that in the marginal space "we are transformed, individually, collectively, as we make radical creative space which affirms and sustains our subjectivity, which gives us a new location from which to articulate our sense of the world" (*Yearning* 148). Thus, their insight into the nature of power structure not only provides them the opportunity to articulate their perception of the world but also provides them the sense of a community that shares the same perception and ideology. Their sense of community and bonding among themselves along with their cultural practices which they perform on the island perpetuate their retention and resistance against the hegemonic power structure of the mainland.

Furthermore, the inhabitant's lack of faith in modern sciences and their appropriateness question the whole Western academia or resist to it. This lack of faith in modern sciences may also be a shield against all kinds of relegation that the modern sciences may cause to the marginal societies by offering a misinterpretation or misrepresentation. Robin Blyn has attempted to point out the misinterpretation that the Western academia may offer to a cultural society in an article entitled "The Ethnographer's Story: 'Mama Day' and the Specter of Relativism". He resists and challenges ethnography as a genre by giving native's point of view an edge over Reema's son's ethnographic visions which posits a threat to the "cultural relativism" (240). This threat of relativism carries with it "...the veiled power structure that holds them (ethnography's "truths") in place and the consequent political impact they have on non-western populations" (240). Reema's son threatens the autonomy of the island with his [mis]interpretations of it from ethnographic perspective that he has developed during "...his training in a method of cross-cultural interpretation clearly informed by the tenets of cultural relativism and the prevailing imperative in the academic circles of his day to explicate the strategies of self-empowerment and resistance practiced by cultures threatened by colonialism" (242). Reema's son's scorn by the "community of Willow Springs", "[d]spite his efforts to 'put Willow Springs on the map' and to celebrate its culture of heroic resistance to western imperialism", emanates from "his training in the western academy" (243) where he has "...distanced himself, geographically and linguistically..." from Willow Springs (Thompson 38, quoted in Blyn). Blyn, further, quotes Susan Meisenhelder for illustrating the reason of the scorn of Reema's son as he has "[i]mbued with the values of the white world in which he has been educated..." and hence "... miss(es) the autonomous cultural identity of Willow Springs" (quoted in Blyn, 243). Autonomy for Reema's son lies in "...a strategy of resistance marked by the creative transculturation of Western identifications..." while Blyn illustrates Meisenhelder who believes that "...autonomy is assured through a contrary strategy of resistance, one defined by its refusal to admit Western ideology into the autonomous zone" (244). Misguided by his training, Reema's son though:

> [O]ffers an account of Willow Springs that celebrates resistance to colonialism, he reproduces colonial ideology, offering an account that veils his own appropriation of Willow Springs as a paradigm for "inverting hostile social and political parameters." His thesis proceeds apparently unaware that the cultural relativism it offers as a cure for stereotypes of racial inferiority has reproduced the same imperialist symptoms inherent in the original racist discourse. (247)

Willow Springs resists the Western ethnographic worldview not only by rejecting and scorning the thesis of Reema's son but also projecting an autoethnography of Willow Springs that lies in "the distinction between spatial autonomy and cultural isolation and on the dynamism of the local culture. She (Naylor) repeatedly challenges the attempts of all of its visitors to construct the island in terms of a prior, exotic, and less-sophisticated era" (249). Through the episode of Reema's son, Naylor takes an opportunity of locking the marginal space for any analysis, understanding, and encroachment of the dominant hegemonic power structure. However, the success of the autonomy of the marginal space depends upon the idea of the island's communal bonding. Reema's son attempts to unlock the central myth about "18 & 23" of the island and consequently meets with a futile attempt because of the perspective of an outsider that he carries (*MD* 07):

> When he went around asking us about 18 & 23, there weren't anything to do but take pity on him as he rattled on about "ethnography," "unique speech patterns," "cultural preservation," and whatever else he seemed to be getting so much pleasure out of while talking into his little gray machine. He was all over the place—What

> 18 & 23 mean? What 18 & 23 mean? And we all told him the God-honest truth: it was just our way of saying something. (07)

This communal bond among the people of island which holds them against the subjectivization of ethnographer's perspective depends upon the communal practices prevalent on the island. One such practice is healing which for the African Americans has been one of the ways to form a bond among themselves that further offers resistance to the conception of individualism prevalent in the white world. The knowledge of such communal practices which Naylor propagates through the text has been acquired from her household where she has listened to stories of such practices. Naylor has acquired her experiences through cultural upbringing that has imbued in her the faith for the cultural practices; it is the experiences of Naylor where the genesis of her novel, *Mama Day* may be located. She talks about the same in one of her interviews with Angela Carabi:

> It goes back to the stories I listened to when I sat in the corner of the kitchen, and to the different ideas that my parents had regarding the old women who not only worked as quasitraditional doctors, but who used roots and herbs and had supernatural kinds of powers. My mother believed that there were things that happened in life that you could not question but my father was very reluctant to accept "superstition". The structure of *Mama Day* emerged from this dual interpretation. I wanted as well to look at women in history, especially at women connected to the earth who could affect behavior. Until the Middle Ages, when the so-called "witches" were persecuted, women were the primary healers who knew how to abort or how to stop conception. They showed women how to have control of their process of creation. (121)

The aforementioned account of Naylor's experiences of the formation of her cultural unconscious and her fortitude to realize her experiences in the fictional form may have the stimulus behind the writing of the novel. However, Naylor has been quite successful in carving such an immortal figure in Mama Day. Kathleen M. Puhr has attempted to explore such characters in

Mama Day in her article "Healers in Gloria Naylor's Fiction." He discovers "the power of love as a force that heals, bringing peace and wholeness" (518). She finds Naylor's characters devising different ways of healing, "...some through literal doctoring, others through psychic healing, still other through inspirational documents that they have left behind, and finally some through providing a haven for the needy" (518). The healing and conjuring of these women offer, what Puhr quotes from Pryse "the power to reassert the self and one's heritage in the face of overwhelming injustice" (quoted in Puhr 519). Billingslea-Brown in "Yearning for the Homeland: The 'Return to the Source' in Contemporary African-American Women's Fiction and Visual Art" too explicates that "...the pivotal rituals of nurturing, healing, and renewal, recollected and enacted by women, affirm cultural and matrilineal continuity" (06). Furthermore, Puhr also places Naylor with other contemporary novelists of African American tradition who are engaged in the discourse of resistance. He explicates that Gloria Naylor resists "...a culture that has marginalized African American women, dictated where they must live, attend school, and eat, denied them economic opportunities, prevented them from voting, and psychologically abused them..." by "...depict(ing) heroic struggles and gallant role models who have helped their sisters not only to endure but to prevail" (519). Miranda Day, for instance, in Naylor's *Mama Day* "...heals many inhabitants of Willow Springs" and her "healing powers transcend the world of science and verge on the magical" (522). Mama Day appears to accept and conform to what Billingslea-Brown says "...mothering and healing as communal responsibilities" (06) rather "[h]er healing powers arise from the world of nature: from the plants she converts to medicine with the confidence of a shaman, from the chickens who surround her house, from the trees and birds of the forest" (Puhr 523). Healing, along with the resistance to the unjust world, fosters bonding among the women on island of Willow Springs. Mama Day "is the wise woman of the community, and she possesses formidable powers used in helping and healing the inhabitants of Willow Springs. Her power lies not just in herbal remedies or conjures spells; they emanate from deep recesses of the mind and perhaps more ancient sources of power" (*MD* 130). Her conjuring powers are very scientific in nature. George compares her knowledge of conjuring with that of science in the following paragraph:

> But, oh, no, there was something *strange* about this lightening. It struck twice in the same place. Theoretically, it is possible, but not probable for lightening to strike twice the same place. The first exchange of electrical charge between the ground and the clouds, which in a sense is a strike, causes the negative-charge ceneter up in the clouds to short-circuit and nullify itself. So it would take another exchange of negative electrons from higher in that same cloud to the same positive charged spot on the earth to have lightening strike twice. That's rare. Unless, of course, in a scientific experiment someone purposely electrifies the ground with materials that hold both negative and positive charges to increase the potential of having a target hit. No one was running around with that kind of knowledge in Willow Springs, and it was highly improbable that it would happen naturally. (274)

The above deliberation of George about Mama Day establishes her as the healer and conjurer whose skills stand at par with scientific preciseness; however, generally, she uses her knowledge for the welfare and wellbeing of the inmates. There are numerous examples where her knowledge is brought about for the service of the people of the island; one such instance may be visualized when she heals Bernice. The incident also reminds us of some other characters of Naylor who possess the same skills and use for the welfare of the people. When Mama Day heals Bernice, she seems to share the same phenomenon that Mattie does while healing Ciel in *The Women of Brewster Place* and Eve does while healing Jesse Bell in *Bailey's Café* or Willa feels when she discovers the documents of her ancestral Nedeed women in *Linden Hills*. Mama Day's healing power emanates from her familiarity with the herbal knowledge, rituals and an understanding of the place "the whole island was her playground: she'd walk through a dry winter without snapping a single twig, disappear into the shadow of a summer cottonwood, flatten herself so close to the ground under a moss-covered rock self, folks started believing John-Paul's little girl became a spirit in the wood" (79). Andrews is of the opinion that Mama Day's "intuitive powers and her knowledge of nature..." are on full display when she heals Bernice of her pain (296). The detailed process of healing that Mama Day performs on Bernice displays the accuracy, preciseness, and acumen of healing skills that she possesses. When she consumes fertility pills to become pregnant, Mama Day examines Bernice carefully relying upon her intuitive knowledge. She is against such unnatural ways of getting pregnant because she believes in the communion with nature and that one may achieve anything with patience and through the potentiality of nature. Since Mama Day is committed to the welfare of the inmates of the island, she goes to rescue Bernice. She examines Bernice for locating the locus of damage that the fertility pills have caused to her:

> "Now, where is the pain, Bernice?"
>
> "In my stomach."

"You sure it's your stomach?" she turns Bernice on her back and makes her fold her hands gently on her belly. "Close your eyes and try to concentrate on the pain. Is it coming from your stomach for true?"

> "No, Mama Day, it's my sides." Bernice winces.
>
> Miranda nods. "And what kind of pain is it, Bernice?"
>
> "It hurts."
>
> "I know it hurts, honey, but is it like little needles all in one spot or does it kinda radiate out and down?"
>
> "It's like it's happening in my stomach and side all at one time."
>
> "Okay, lay still now." Real gentle, she presses her fingers along the bone under Bernice's stomach, and then starts to move up along her sides. "Now, you just nod when I touch a place more tender than the rest." She ain't but a little ways up when Bernice presses her lips and eyes together and nods.
>
> "Good girl. That's what I thought."
>
> "Can we save the baby?" Ambush asks her.
>
> "She ain't pregnant." (*MD* 73)

Miranda exemplifies a real care and help for the people of the island through the example of the healing performance of Bernice. However, Naylor generalizes healing of Bernice to all the women of the island when she says "[t]hem fingers had gone that way so many times for so many different reasons. A path she knew so well that the slightest change of moisture, the amount of give along the walls, or the scent left on her hands could fix a woman's cycle within less than a day of what was happening with the moon" (75). Acting as a true African mother, Mama Day identifies the damage caused to the limbs of Bernice by the drugs she has taken. Since she has little knowledge about the mainland medicines, she prefers to invite Dr. Smithfield for further investigation; however in the meantime, she uses her herbal medicines to control Bernice's pain:

> Miranda washes off the choke-cherry bark and then cuts a piece about the size of the last joint on her little finger. She has to be careful with this stuff—awfully careful. It could kill as easy as cure.... She props Bernice up in her arms and first makes her suck on a piece of peppermint candy she had Ambush bring her. When Bernice has worked up a good spit, Miranda takes the candy from her. (82)

Mama Day succeeds in receding Bernice's pain before Dr. Smithfield reaches to investigate her:

> When Bernice has chewed for a while, Miranda makes her spit the bark out in her hand and then gives her the peppermint candy. Miranda strokes her throat to help the sweet juices go down, and then makes her chew on the bark again. They keep doing this till it's nothing but a pulp, and the muscles in Bernice's body start to relax with her breath coming in a little deeper. (82)

Mama Day not only heals Bernice but displays her witty skills in helping her getting pregnant too at a later stage by relying upon the miraculous potentiality of nature and imbibing patience in Bernice. She offers Bernice pumpkin seeds and at the same time demystifies that it's not the seeds that are the locus of the miracle that Bernice is going to experience, rather, it is Bernice's mind. She explains "[t]he mind is a funny thing, Abigail—and a powerful thing at that. Bernice is gonna believe that they are what I tell her they are—magic seeds. And the only magic is that what she believes they are, they're gonna become" (96). And she further directs Bernice:

> Every time you get your monthly, plant a gold one—let the life blood flow out of you into this seed. And come spring, she could tell Bernice, When you take the vines from them gold seeds out into the garden, you're really taking the life line between you and the baby. And the way you watch that grow—round and full—the life will sure to be growing inside of you. Yeah, she could disguise a little dose of nothing but mother-wit with a lot of hocus-pocus. But it was all leading up to the other place. Nothing would be real until the end. And in the end, Bernice would have to step over the last line all by herself. (97)

Howsoever, Bernice conceives simply because she believes in Mama Day who restores her faith in herself. She comes to Mama Day to inform her about the growth of the seeds. Bernice takes Miranda off a bit to whisper, "My seeds are doing well, Mama Day. They already are starting to make vines in the kitchen window. And I knew Miss Abigail would like my dress, 'cause when Miss Pearl said she wouldn't, I stuck a black seed right in the dirt" (115). As is exemplary through Bernice's healing and getting her pregnant by making her plant a seed, Mama Day shares a close communion and bond with nature that is the secret of her knowledge, healing power, and conjuring practices. And perhaps through her communion with nature which further helps her to hold the respect of the people of the island, she has been able to resist the oppression of hegemonic power structure on the island. She as a result enjoys a respectable place on the island and "...if Mama Day say no, everybody say no" (06). Her communion with nature is expressed in the following paragraph when she goes to find the herbal medicine for Bernice in the night:

> In the woods, Miranda follows the ground that's sloping down, stopping once in a while to place her palm against the earth to see if she is nearing the stream. If there was a

> choke cherry tree anyplace in here, it'd have to be there. A bramble scratches her on the face, and a few feet on she trips over a creeper from a sweet bay. *No point in cussing,* she hears her daddy's voice. *Little Mama, these woods been here before you and me, so why should they get out your way—learn to move around 'em.* And in her own part of the woods she could, even now in her eighties when it was pitch black. (79)

In addition, it is only through her knowledge of the herbs, nature, and graveyard (the other place) that Mama Day is able to heal her niece, Cocoa who is subjected to the jealousy of Ruby, another practitioner of black magic on the island, who applies poison to her scalp. The poison that Ruby applies to Cocoa's hair is so powerful that Mama Day's healing skills are put for real test to scrap its effect from Cocoa. However, Mama Day begins healing of Cocoa with cutting her hair and making Cocoa establish a communion with nature through a healing bath in the tub. Mama Day also applies some sort of charcoal paste in order to minimize the effects of the poison:

> There is a half tub of warm water waiting as she leads Cocoa staggering and mumbling into the bathroom. She spreads a charcoal paste on her head, leaving her slouched drowsy in the water, her head thrown back over the rim of the tub. Miranda balls up the sheets and pillowcases around the shredded hair and burns the lot in the back yard.... The warm water spraying from the shower on Cocoa's bent head brings her out of her sleep struggling. Stay still now, Miranda tells her as she massages more of the grayish paste into her scalp, this needs to be soaked in for a while. Them red welts is coming up between her shoulder blades, but Miranda's got to ignore 'em as she rinses the paste from Cocoa's hair. (265)

However, since the poison that has been applied by Ruby affects the other half of Cocoa too. Consequently, Mama Day's skills are constrained as it implies George's help too in healing Cocoa to complete health as "[h]e is a part of *her*.... And that's the part Ruby done fixed to take it out of our hands" (267). She admits, "I got rid of the nightshade Ruby put in her hair. Her vision will be clearing and she'll stop all the sleeping in a little bit. But I can't get rid of all she done to her" (267). Her agony is engraved with the realization that George has come from the city so may not believe in the act of healing that Mama Day has decided for her. Kubitschek points out the reason of George's non-cooperation with Mama Day "George has difficulty believing in the nature of the illness, much less the necessity of his participation in a cure which none of his back-ground has prepared him for" (88). However, George's non-cooperation and non-believing forces Miranda to choose to sacrifice him to save Cocoa, as Cocoa is the last descendant of the Days family and hence has to be saved to maintain the matriarchy on the island. However, Cocoa also represents the collective bonding with the previous generations:

> ["]...Baby Girl is the closest thing I have to calling a child my own. And I did say Baby Girl, 'cause she's the last of the womenfolk some into Days that I will live to see. There ain't a mama who coulda felt more pain or pride for her when she was coming up—do you understand? But it's more than my blood flows in her and more hands that can lay claim to her than [these"]. (*MD* 294)

George reiterates the existence of the aforementioned association of Cocoa with Miranda and Days family when he compares himself with her "I was always in awe of the stories you told so easily about Willow Springs. To be born in a grandmother's house, to be able to walk and see where a great-grandmother and even great-great-grandfather was born. You had more than a family, you had a history. And I didn't even have a real last name" (129). It is conspicuously clear that George realizes that he because of his upbringing has been barred from the privileges that Cocoa enjoys, however, his training into the Western academia and the hegemonic agencies that have constructed his mind have never allowed him to merge with the island. Anyhow, Miranda succeeds in rescuing Cocoa back from the effects of poison without George's support and secures the matrilineal and familial bonding. She further continues healing Cocoa to health:

> In the pantry she rolls up bundles of dried herbs into clean strips of cloth. Now that Baby Girl was going to live, she had to be nursed back to health. And Miranda

> makes sure to bottle up plenty of tonic for a sedative. She scraps the pot clean that held the balsam, rinses it, and hangs it up to dry. She closes the shutter up stairs, makes the bed, and sweeps the floor. (302)

Saving of Cocoa and sacrificing George proposes the fact that, above all, in Willow Springs the matriarchal lineage is given priority over any other consideration. Paula Gallant Eckard in "The Prismatic Past in Oral History and Mama Day" sounds the same when he says that "[w]hile race figures into the manifestation of the Other in *Mama Day*, the bonds shared within the female community and between generations of women seem to be the strongest elements" (129). Mama Day not only sacrifices George in order to save Cocoa, she also punishes Ruby who has applied the poison to her hair and has threatened the familial bond. This incident exhibits Mama Day's commitment to security and safety of the matrilineal tradition of the island. She uses her knowledge to attract the lightening to Ruby's house and destroys it along with Ruby:

> The silvery powder is thrown into the bushes. She strikes the house in the back. Powder. She strikes it on the left. Powder. She brings the cane over her head and strikes it so hard on the front door, the window panes rattle. Miranda stands there, out of breath, with little beads of sweat on her temples. There's a long thin crack in her walking cane, running down the back of one snake and cutting through the head of another. She examines it close to make sure it'll hold her weight, and then she turns around to head south on the main road. The door don't open when she leaves, and the winds don't stir the circle of silvery powder. (*MD* 270)

Mama Day punishes those who are threat to the sovereignty and autonomy of the island, as is exemplary in the case of Ruby, who is a jealous conjurer. In yet another example, Mama Day appears to be protecting the dignity and respect of the folks of the island, when a white man visits the island and addresses the folks in an insulting manner like "Nigger didn't you hear me? And nigger this and nigger that. The folks on the porch of the general store got real quiet. So he had no problem hearing Miranda. 'You'll address him proper before the night is over.' Guess he only saw an old colored lady with a bag of groceries and red straw hat cocked on her head" (80). Being an outsider, the white man has no idea about what the old lady (Mama Day) commands on the island. And when he does not abide by the rules of the island, he is punished for that:

> The rest is history. How that boy got left alone wandering down in the cypress swamp. Took him half a night to find the road again, and his patrol car sitting on three flat tires. Still could have radioed for help, except Willow Springs saw one of its worst lightening storms in a decade. Not a drop of rain or a bit of wind—just a sky lit up so with them lightning bolts that you could smell the air burning. (80)

This incident reaffirms Willow Springs' sovereignty and autonomy and that "Willow Springs was one place that's best left alone" (81). Further, it also proposes that any intrusion from outside with an air of modernity and flamboyancy which may act as a threat to the respect of the island, must be handled with collective strength which is displayed when the white hit by the storm looks for the shelter "[a] bad night to be stirring about, but it seemed nobody was home when he staggered up and down the road begging to be let in somewhere" (80).

The above-mentioned incident is one of the examples which exhibit the collective bond that the people of the island share. However, the collective bond of the communal and familial relationship or bond that exists between the generations of the African American people may also be represented through the cultural artifacts which Naylor has presented through the metaphor of quilt. It binds the several generations of the African Americans together very much like different scraps of the cloths are bonded together to make a quilt. In order to emphasize the "multifaceted lives of African American women," Floris Barnett Cash has "examine[d] the inventiveness of African American women in the decorative art of quilting" (30). He further states that the artifact of "quilts can be used as resources in reconstructing the experiences of African American women" in the contemporary oppressive power structure which tries to negate the contribution of African Americans in the American history (30). His exploration suggests that the roots of quilt making may be traced back to the period of slavery in America when, "[f]emale slaves would get together in the evenings or on Saturday afternoons to spin, weave, and sew. A former slave recalled that her mother worked in the field all day and pieced quilts all night" (32). He further establishes the efforts of the slave women in making quilting as a "culture or a way of life as a means of liberating from an oppressive environment" (32). However, he finds that such an art form has been pushed into the margin or "outside the traditional or mainstream disciplines" and that the studies of such an artifact in academia finds its place only "[i]n the late 1960s, concurrent with civil rights, the student protests" (33).

However, Naylor who is "a self avowed feminist and black cultural nationalist" seems to be well informed with the cultural relevance of quilt as an artifact as in *Mama Day* she has used the metaphor of quilt making to represent the collective bond and creative legacy that African Americans have inherited from their maternal ancestors (Fowler 01). It also refers to the traditional and cultural legacy of the African Americans where a quilt is presented to the daughter as a marital gift and thus binds her to the maternal house as she carries and bears the quilt, accommodating the scraps of the whole family and the previous generations. And this quilt has to be passed on from one generation to the next enforcing among them to have a bonding together. This is what Mama Day utters while weaving a quilt for Cocoa's marriage "[t]his'll be passed on to my great-grandnieces and nephews when it's time for them to marry. And since I won't be around to defend myself, I don't want them thinking I was a lazy old somebody who couldn't make a decent double-ring quilt" (*MD* 136). Thus, quilt is deeply embedded into the collective unconscious of the family which makes it indispensably significant for their bonding and hence, it has to be made with assiduous diligence. Mama Day articulates the same thematics in the following narrative:

> Just out-and-out aggravating, that's what she could be—demanding to have herself a double-ring quilt as a wedding present. Like all folks got to do this winter is sit around sewing together tiny bits of cloth till their fingers ache. And you couldn't send an old poor-mouth quilt with one double ring, no—from edges to center the pattern had to twine around each other. It would serve her right if it took till next year, and it probably would if they had the sense not to keep at it all day and a good part of the night. (135)

The above paragraph explains the whole texture and technique of using the quilt emphatically along with the emphasis how quilt making is a communal practice. Lamothe points that such cultural practices offer an opportunity to resist against the hegemonic power structure of the mainland. He further proposes that the resistance is not located in the place that Naylor has constructed rather the kind of the cultural practices that are being practiced over there:

> Naylor does not explicitly foreground the Gullah Island as a site of resistance to colonial domination by alluding to the myth of Africans/Ibos who reject their enslavement by flying or walking back to Africa. Rather, the locus of resistance in Naylor's text lies in the island inhabitants' retention and transmission of African-derived traditions and values, such as orally conveyed folklore, quilting, and herb and rootwork, in the face of cultural forces that would efface them. (Lamothe 156)

However, Lamothe fails to acknowledge that the cultural practices are rooted in the historicity and mythical structure of the location itself and so may not exist in isolation. Naylor seems to be quite aware of the proposition that it is only through the cultural practices that the autonomy of the place may be retained and the hegemonic structure of the world may be resisted. Therefore, Naylor discovers quilt making which is one of the cultural practices that resist the fragmented, individual reality of the contemporary mainstream world by emphasizing the communal activities. Naylor establishes quilt making as an art that has to be displayed with minute labor which is presented through the process of quilt making that Mama Day and Abigail are involved:

> Abigail bits off the knotted end of her thread. She sighs and runs her hand along her end of the quilting frame. "It may be taking forever, but it's gonna be some kind of beautiful. You were right, Miranda, using that cambric muslin instead of a regular cotton lining is gonna make this feel like velvet. But it's pain in the neck to sew—a stitch will slip away before you know it ["]. (*MD* 135)

Meisenhelder observes that the quilt offers not only the bond among the people of the island but it also provides them with an autonomy "[t]he person who is part of the quilt, stitched next to but not absorbed by others, independent but not isolated, connected to but not doomed by history, achieves peace and meaningful freedom from the white world" (416). However, this act of binding together of different pieces from different generation helps her establish an intergenerational bond with her ancestors, Mama Day adds to the quilt whatever she lays her hand on—different pieces of the scraps from several generations. Thus, making quilt is tantamount to the communal activity or a source of living with all generations:

> The overlapping circles start out as golds on the edge and melt into oranges, reds, blues, greens, and then back to golds for the middle of the quilt. A bit of her daddy's Sunday shirt is matched with Abigail's lace slip, the collar from Hope's graduation dress, the palm of Grace's baptismal gloves. Trunks and boxes from the other place gave up enough for twenty quilts: corduroy from her uncles, broadcloth from her great-uncles. Her needle fastens the satin trim of Peace's receiving blanket to Cocoa's baby jumper to a pocket from her own gardening apron. Golds into oranges into reds into blues.... She concentrates on the tiny stitches as the clock ticks away. The front of Mother's gingham shirtwaist—it would go right nice into the curve between these two little patches of apricot toweling, but Abigail would have a fit. Maybe she won't remember. And maybe the sun won't come

> up tomorrow, either. I'll just use a sliver, no longer than the joint of my thumb. Put a little piece of her in here somewhere. (*MD* 137)

Meisenhelder presents Miranda's perspective holding the whole world as nothing but a big quilt itself that brings in her proposition of the whole world as a big family, "[s]ubverting white cultural definitions, looking at the Empire State Building from her own rather than from a white perspective, she sees it not as an awesome engineering feat indicative of triumph over nature, but as an emblem of seeing the whole world as a quilt, all of its scraps connected and the human element put in perspective" (417). He further quotes from the text, *Mama Day* to support his argument "...when you stand on top of that building, you kinda see the world the way God must see it—everything's able to be cupped into the palm of your hand. Them big cities should have big buildings, with all that plenty around them—it gives folks a chance to keep things in perspective" (*MD* 306).

In a similar fashion, Sam Whitsitt in "In Spite of It All: A Reading of Alice Walker's 'Everyday Use'" explores that by stitching the pieces of the past generation, the quilt maker becomes a part of the quilt and the vice versa, thus, forming a never ending bond together. He observes "just as disparate pieces of cloth get stitched together, the quilt itself is stitched to the world that produces it. The quilt 'represents' herstory, history, and tradition, binding women, and men, to the past and the past to the present" (445). The generational bonding represented by quilt in African American community is subjected to one's being a part of the belief system it is a part. Alice Walker's Wangro, one of the sisters in her "Everyday Use" is not able to understand the meaning and share the bond with her ancestors because of her cultural upbringing. She wants to decorate the quilt in her drawing room and to make it a show piece while the quilt is meant to be used. While Maggie, the other sister would use quilts and she would continue the tradition with her own quilting when her grandmother's quilts wore out. Her quilts would not be exactly like her grandmother's, but they would warm future generations (Walker 245). Similarly, George who is an outsider to Willow Spring culture is not able to associate himself with the metaphor of quilt that stands for bonding and sharing and emphasizes to decorate the quilt which they have received as a wedding gift, while Cocoa who is aware of the real significance of the quilt wants to use it and pass it to her future generations to continue the bond among the generations:

> And then our wedding present came from home in the same summer. And I unfolded the quilt, all seven square feet of it, we stood there in awe for a moment. You wanted to clear a wall in the living room and hang it up. But it had been made to be used, and I also knew they hadn't gone through that kind of labor just for me. I ran my hands along the multicolored rings. They had sewed for *my* grandchildren to be conceived under this quilt. I looked at you standing beside me—the blue cotton shirt as always, hair cropped short and parted to the left as always. Our grandchildren? Let's see how it fits on the bed, I said. (*MD* 147)

The above-mentioned cultural understanding of Cocoa and George reiterate that George is an outsider to the island of Willow Springs and so is not able to understand the essence of it while Cocoa seems to be incorporating the ethos of the island. In such circumstances, George's death becomes inevitable on the island because of his constant resistance to form a bond with the island which has been a result of his subjectivization while trained in the Western academia. Aurelia Armstrong in her article "Beyond Resistance: A Response to Žižek's Critique of Foucault's Subject of Freedom" says that "[i]n *Discipline and Punish* he [Foucault] chronicles the emergence of a form of modern power that regulates individuals by subjecting them to disciplinary practices and norms which produce them as certain types of subject" (24). George, through his constant subjectivization has been transformed into a subject where he is unable to locate his real self and has realized his constructed self to be the real one which further constrains all his efforts of association with a non-hegemonic world. Therefore, what George could have done is what Aurelia quotes from Foucault's "The Subject and Power" as:

> [T]he task nowadays is not to discover what we are, but to refuse what we are. We have to imagine and

> to build up what we could be to get rid of this kind of political "double bind," which is the simultaneous individualization and totalization of modern power structures. The conclusion would be that the political, ethical, social, philosophical problem of our days is not to try to liberate the individual from the state, and from the state's institutions, but to liberate us both from the state and from the type of individualization which is linked to the state. We have to promote new forms of subjectivity through the refusal of this kind of individuality which has been imposed on us for several centuries. (quoted in Aurelia 24)

The process of subjectivization of George has started very early in his life even when he was a child. In the foster house where he has been brought up, George has been imbibed with the sense of individuality which has hampered his sense of community, thus his communion with the cultural practices of the island of Willow Springs. The foster house where George has been brought up has been all about "rules and facts" and they have to be maintained (*MD* 24). And perhaps because of his non-belonging and orphan state, he has to abide by the rules and thus providing the chance to the hegemonic power structure to construct his self, "[w]hen I left Wallace P. Andrews I had what I could see: my head and my two hands, and I had each day to do something with them. Each day, that's how I took it—each moment, sometimes, when the going got really rough. I may have knocked my head against the walls, figuring out how to buy food, supplies, and books" (27). Adriane L. Ivey too reiterates that "George's central flaw, one that forces him into the role of sacrificial lamb, is his inability to accept the irrational" which has resulted from his upbringing in an orphanage "[t]he proprietor of the orphanage in which George is raised reiterates for her charges the idea that all one can rely on is himself and the present; therefore, George grows up believing only in the rational and real. This belief serves him well in New York, but it causes his downfall once he enters the mystical world of Willow Springs" (103). While in Cocoa's case, power has not been able to completely construct her even after her exposure to the hegemonic world of the mainland because of her deep roots in history, community, culture and constant correspondence with her family.

> As Judith Butler (puts)...that to be constituted by power in Foucault's sense does not mean that the subject is completely determined by power. To say that power relations constitute the subject is simply to point to the fact that our possibilities for action and thought are both constrained *and* enabled by the discursive frameworks which structure these possibilities, but this is not equivalent to saying that it is the framework itself which determines our choices or how we respond to the range of options that become available within it. But while it might be possible to explain the compatibility of productive power with free agency, this explanation only makes Žižek's question about the genesis of the subject's capacities for autonomy, reflection, critique and resistance more pressing. (25)

The aforementioned proposition of autonomy of the subject that shields the complete subjectivization of the subject has been imbibed in Cocoa through history, communal bonding, and cultural practices of the island which she carries with her even to the mainland. This is exemplary in that she celebrates Candle Walk, the annual communal festival of the island in New York with George. Though Cocoa lives for a longer period of time in the mainland, the mainstream world has not been able to construct her 'self' because she has not been able to inculcate in herself the values of the mainstream world that act as apparatuses. Perhaps the strength of resistance against the mainstream code of conduct has emanated from the fact that she carries a bond with her own people of the island to the mainstream world which has consistently denied the acceptance or amalgamation with the outside world. She accepts the same in the following paragraph:

> You know, I was scared when I came to this city. Really scared. There were more people living on my one block than on the whole island where I grew up. And instead of getting better in seven years, it's gotten worse. Because just when you think you've gotten a handle on

> it, there's a new next-door neighbor or the Laundromat at the corner becomes a hole in the ground and the next year it's a high rise with even more people for you not to know. A whole kaleidoscope of people—nothing's just black or white here like in Willow Springs. Nothing stays put. So I guess the way I talk is my way of coming to terms with never knowing what to expect from anything or anybody. I'm not a bigot, but if I sound like one, I guess it's because deep down I'm as frightened of change and difference as they are. (*MD* 63)

However, Cocoa's narration of the city life which she is unable to accommodate herself with also points out the havoc that modernization has created by fragmenting the people, making them individual with no sense of harmony. In the similar way, Lamothe comments that "Naylor constructs Cocoa's and George's understanding of the island as symbolizing home in order to query the effects of modernization, historical rupture, and social fragmentation on African Americans" (156). In "Writing from Memory: The Diasporic Discourse of Abdulrazak Gurnah and Ben Okri" Maurice O'Connor echoes Cocoa's longing for the home place of Willow Springs when he points the new racism that is still prevalent in the west "[d]espite the postmodern discourses of Western multiculturalism, we are still faced with Fanon's highly perceptive psycho portrait of cultural alienation in the colonial metropolis" (02). This sense of an outsider in the mainland reduces Cocoa to the level of a marginal and the only solace she may look for is with her great-grandmother, Miranda Day. Cocoa admits that "[t]here is something hypocritical about a city that keeps half of its population underground half of the time; you can start believing that there's much more space that there really is—to live, to work.... But it took me a while to figure out that New York racism moved underground like most of the people did" (*MD* 18).

Cocoa's subjectivization may be traced through Maurice's quotation of Fanon "I had to meet the white man's eyes. An unfamiliar weight burdens me. The real world challenged my claims. In the white world the man of color encounters difficulties in the development of his bodily schema" (quoted in

Morris 04). Further modern form of racial ideology could be traced in the following account by Maurice, "...integration into a society dominated by discourses of whiteness is problematised both by the local population whose gaze discovers the underlying racist ideologies of color, and by the memories of homeland where black, as a skin color, is invisible" (08).

Naylor's *Mama Day* offers an alternative world which is safe from the depressing growth of the modernism by constructing a space with its roots in cultural practices and artifacts which is free from the subjectivities of the modern power. Candle Walk, for instance, is one such cultural practice which acts as a metaphor that is applied by Naylor to exhibit the bonding that exists among the people of the island and to mark the resistance against the mainstream celebration of the commercialized Christmas. Adriane L. Ivey explains the subversive nature of Candle Walk as "Naylor has her characters reject one of the most meaningful and symbolic Christian holidays for a more pure version of a holiday based on benevolence" (105). Wall identifies that candle walk's "ethic is communal" as it provides the residents to forge bond among themselves and to help the poor, "[g]oing from house to house, their way lit with the candles they hold, the residents of Willow Springs offer gifts to each other; many use the occasion to repay debts of kindness. The practice allows people to help those in need without making them object of charity" (1455). The practice of Candle Walk is a sort of blurring the economic boundaries too and addressing and appealing to all across the classes:

> Candle Walk was a way of getting help without feeling obliged. Since everybody said, "Come my way, Candle Walk," sort of a season's greeting and expected a little something, them that needed a little more got it quiet-like from their neighbours. And it weren't no hardship giving something back—only had to be any bit of something, as long as it came from the earth and the work of your own hands. A bushel of potatoes and a cured side of meat could be exchanged for a plate of ginger cookies, or even a cup of ginger toddy. (*MD* 110)

The people of island not only celebrate the Candle Walk with full fervor but also resist the celebration of the mainland festival of Christmas as the people like Hooper emphasize on the celebration of Christmas, the residents hardly pay attention as they go on celebrating Candle Walk on 22nd of December, "any fool knows Christmas is December twenty-fifth—that ain't never caught on too much here. And Candle Walk is always the night of the twenty-second. Been that way since before Reverend Hooper and it'll be that way after him" (*MD* 108). However, most of the people on the island are unaware of the myth of Candle Walk, they participate in it with full vigor, "[o]ver here nobody knows why every December twenty-second folks take to the road—strolling, laughing, and talking—holding some kind of light in their hands. It's been going on since before they were born, and the ones born before them" (110). This proposes the fact that people are not rational so far as the cultural practices are concerned rather they participate in the practice simply because the community believes in it. However, the people keep discussing and talking about the central myth of the island:

> Say you'd hear talk then of a slave woman who came to Willow Springs, and when she left, she left in a ball of fire to journey back home east over the ocean.... Said people kinda worshipped his grandmother, a slave woman who *took* her freedom in 1823. Left behind seven sons and a dead master as she walked down the main road, candle held high to light her way to the east bluff over the ocean. Folks in John-Paul's time would line the main road with candles, food, and slivers of ginger to help her spirit along. (111)

Mama Day knows the real myth behind the celebration of Candle Walk, "[b]y listening in a spiritual receptive way to the sounds around her during Candle Walk, however, Miranda learns that although the lights have been understood as an aid to Sapphira in her walk east toward Africa. They originated as a commemoration of Bascombe's heartbroken search for her later" (Kubitschek 79). Since then the Candle Walk is celebrated in commemoration of the same. The participation in Candle Walk is ensured by all irrespective of their age, and class. The real motif is to put all the people of the island on a common platform and strengthen their sense of bonding:

> A lot of the older heads can bring their real candles, insisting that's the way it was done in the beginning. They often take exception to the younger folks who will use kerosene lamps or sparklers, rain or no rain. They say it's a lot more pleasant than worrying about hot wax dropping on your hands. The younger ones done brought a few other changes that don't sit too well with some. (*MD* 110)

However, there are a few people who are worried about the future of Candle Walk because of the approaching intrusion of the commercialization in the form of readymade gifts that have to a larger extent replaced the handmade gifts that the people use to share among themselves in order to connect to the mythos of the culture. Further, commercialization and the utilitarian philosophy bring consumerism and which consequently infuses the sense of individualism among the people. The philosophy of commercialization and utilitarian in turn distorts the communal feeling at display during Candle Walk, and thus, distort the real purpose behind the event. It is quite noticeable in its inchoation "[t]hings took a little different turn with the young folks having more money and working beyond the bridge. They started buying each other fancy gadgets from the catalogues, and you'd hear ignorant things like, "They ain't gave me nothing last Candle Walk, so they getting the same from me this year" (111). However, Miranda, though situates the reason of the young people's inclination for modern gifts in their access to the mainland, she is not worried about the change that is taking place as her age old insight provides her the patience which is borne in her accepting changes since her childhood:

> There's a disagreement every winter about whether these young people spell the death of Candle Walk. You can't stop keep 'em from going beyond the bridge, and like them candles out on the main road, time does march on. But Miranda, who is known to be far more wise than wicked, says there's nothing to worry about. In her young days Candle Walk was different still. (111)

Miranda is well aware that the change is perennial and it must continue shaping the history of the reality. She also knows that repressing her people in the name of tradition shall very soon meet with the resistance and the whole island becomes the arena of power politics so she lets the course of time take its way. She remembers that "her daddy, John-Paul, said that in his time Candle Walk was different still" and "her daddy said *his* daddy said Candle Walk was different still" so she is confident that such changes are not powerful enough to wash out this communal event "[i]t'll take generations, she says, for Willow Springs to stop doing it at all. And more generations again to stop talking about the time "when there used to be some kinda 18 & 23 going-on near December twenty-second" (111).

In a nutshell, the entire discourse in the chapter encapsulates the politics and the history of marginal space and it further articulates the possibilities of constructing an invisible bonding among the inhabitants of Willow Springs which may bring a sense of life and community to them. The chapter initially focuses at the former point that is the location of marginal space. It is interesting to note here that the creation of marginal space is embedded into the historicity of the geography. The place from the inception itself is located at the margin. The location of marginal space through historical realities defies the principle of bell hooks' configuration about the construction of marginal space through suffering, pain, and struggle. This is indeed quite remarkable as far as the chapter is concerned as it defies the basic tenets of bell hooksian principle of creating marginal space. The gradual progress of the discourse in the chapter lights upon the possibilities of forming an invisible bond which may create meaning for the community. It explains all possible motives which become quite instrumental in forming a cohesive bond in which some that can be mentioned are—quilt making, Candle Walk, conjuring, and healing. The chapter further explicates on the process of forming a bond through the mythical practices of quilt making, healing, conjuring, and Candle Walk. It is candidly observed that these all mythical activities are archetypes and motives of African American socio-cultural and economic realities. These archetypes and motives hold the identity and the subjectivity of Cocoa who defies the processes of subjectivization, however the character who is bereft of the above-mentioned mythical practices is easily subjectivised by the dominant ideology of the dominant class.

Chapter 5

Transforming the Subject through Female Bonding in the Marginal Space: Resistance in Gloria Naylor's *Bailey's Café*

The present chapter makes an attempt to identify and to elaborate the role of Eve's boarding place, a marginal space in Naylor's *Bailey's Café*, in the process of the resistance to the mainstream world. The chapter also deliberates upon and interrogates into the basic nature of power structure that believes in confining and configuring the dispossessed, powerless, isolated, and destitute to marginal space. However, the marginal space in Naylor's *Bailey's Café* exhibits a Hegelian dialectics in the sense that on the one hand, the place perpetuates the repression of the marginals and on the other, it provides them with the potentiality of resistance. Gloria Naylor through her subaltern and marginalized characters in the novel explicates and delineates the entire process of objectification and subjectification in which her characters experience the odor of repressive, oppressive and exploitative nature of power by offering them a critical vision of an outsider in the hegemonic patriarchal world. Naylor sounds what hooks says "[w]e are transformed, individually, collectively, as we make radical creative space which affirms and sustains our subjectivity, which gives us a new location from which to articulate our sense of the world" (*Yearning* 148). The chapter also reflects upon the journey of the characters towards the marginal space which is explored through their individual narratives.

However, Naylor provides her characters with the place of Eve, only as sojourn where they may recollect enough energy so that they may fight against the power of the patriarch. The chapter explores how the marginal space fabricates the fact that the outside world stands for repression, both racial and sexual, which is elaborated and elucidated through the narratives of the socially and sexually repressed women. In addition, the process of the construction of the place also reveals that the marginal space of Eve's boarding house defies the authoritative and repressive institution of patriarchy by providing a safe sanctuary to the sexually and socially repressed women. The shared repressive history of the women, which is profoundly caused by the repressive structure of the powerful patriarchy, brings a cohesive system among the oppressed women that further creates a bonding among them, further providing unconstrained performativity to the female subjectivity at Eve's boarding house, the marginal space in the mainstream world. In other words, the chapter employs resistance through female bonding that emanates from the marginal positioning of black female subjectivity. The given proposition exemplifies the fact that the female bonding is one of the major tropes and instruments through which the female may realize the particularity with cohesiveness in the assigned marginal space.

Gloria Naylor has indeed attempted to appropriate the location of marginal space in *Bailey's Café* so as to explore the inherent potentiality of resistance embedded in the marginal space. It also exemplifies that the women have been pushed into the marginal space, Eve's boarding house, by the patriarchal hegemonic power, so that they can easily be controlled and shaped. However, the women glue together by sharing their ideological and empirical experiences which provide them with an opportunity to explore their creativity and the female potential so that they may stand against the patriarchal space. In this regard, the marginal women have discovered a central location of empowerment in the marginal space. Similarly, Margot Anne Kelley in her article "Framing the Possibilities: Collective Agency and the Novels of Gloria Naylor" demonstrates that Naylor in her *Bailey's Café* is making "the marginal become center" by using different frames for the representation of different women "that had previously been unrepresentable" (135). She puts her characters in a natural environment and empowers them without uprooting them from there, proving true to what Culler says, "the marginal becomes central by virtue of its own marginality" (quoted in Kelley 135). Bell hooks seems to propose the same ideological position when she associates the creativity and resistance with the marginal space. She calls it the "location of radical openness and possibility" (*Yearning* 148). The possibilities of radical openness and opportunity of the marginal space in the given novel have been realized by providing an ideological position and space to the women so that they may reevaluate their position in the hegemonic power structure through their narratives.

The narratives of the marginal women dwelling in the marginal space of Eve's boarding house collectively exemplify that they have been subjected to every possible kind of repression, particularly, sexism and racism that further indicates the universality of female subjugation, exploitation and confinement in the patriarchal and hegemonic society. In addition, it is the repressive experiences of the women characters in the society at large which provides them with the access into the marginal space of Eve's boarding house. Montgomery, for instance, notes that Naylor's *Bailey's Café* (1992) necessitates "the universal dimensions of oppression and the necessity of mounting a strategy of resistance that globalizes the struggle for positive sociopolitical change" ("Good House Keeping" 53) and which could be achieved through "the construction of a unifying myth" (53). She further comments:

> The liberation Naylor fictionalizes is to be global in scope and will include men and women worldwide. Naylor's texts imply that routine tasks such as cooking, cleaning, and mothering can be means of furthering the cause of freedom, and her novels chronicle an expansion of her artistic and political vision as women move—without moving—from margin to center. (55)

The aforementioned observation by Montgomery demonstrates Naylor's commitment of the assertiveness of black women's work as a means of survival and resistance in the firmament of white, patriarchal society of America which brings these women from margin to center without letting them move from their domestic space. The constitution of the self and the culture of subjectivity are controlled by more than one factor. Foucault in his *The History of Sexuality*, Vol. 1 (1990) represents that the immanent power controls the culture of subjectivity. However, the New Historicists, Marxists, and Feminists rely upon some other factors which contribute significantly in the process of subjectivization. Body, for instance, is one of the universal means by which the women write their history and it also becomes a means of controlling them socially, psychologically and historically. This has aptly been expounded by Simon de Beauvoir in her *The Second Sex* (1952). The novel, *Bailey's Café* continues with the tradition of narrative that put the body into the center of discourse. The following extract from the text explains the female subjectivity and subjectivization in the society:

> All of the care given the child, all of the teaching, and the betrayal is still coming. The girl wants to sin. She can see it in the breasts that keep pushing up over her brassieres. She buys them tighter and tighter, but the flesh keeps spilling out in defiance. The nipples so large and hard, they show through her dress. Inviting trouble. Wanting trouble. Cover yourself. People are staring. Wash yourself down. (*BC* 34)

The aforementioned excerpt is the indicator of the control exercised over women's body in the patriarchal society which at times is expressed in the form of the care and teaching in the family. It puts forward the theory that if a woman's sexual desire and behavior ever come to the notice of society, she should be sorry for this act of exposure and should feel shame which further propounds that woman's body is an object of shame in itself. This also proposes that the traditional patriarchal system views women as either virgins or whores, which further results into gender conflict, if, a woman ever tries to assert her sexual freedom and autonomy. Since men have been controlling and directing women's sexuality, they never feel comfortable accepting their sexual freedom. The patriarch always tells and retells women that they are not capable of themselves to carry out their own self alone in the society which is presented before them as a treacherous place. This perpetuates the role of visible and invisible apparatuses which not only control the psychology of the women but also their body. This is quite evident in the case of Sugar man, one of the characters in the novel, who is essentially a pimp:

> All women really need protecting. It's a rough world out there.... Most men aren't worth shit and will take advantage if they get half a chance.... Women need pretty things around them. A nice place. Nice clothes. The right man to take care of 'em. They're soft and need you to hold 'em. They need your shoulders to lean on when they have to cry. And when they get confused, they need you to be strong enough to guide 'em. (*BC* 34)

The continuous oppression and subjectivization of the marginal women compels them to imbibe the superiority of all patriarchal artifacts which may further perpetuate their oppression. In fact, they reify the entire construction of the oppressive power structure. This phenomenon establishes the fact that women have been subjected to psychological colonization to the extent where they start thinking absolutely in the same way as the ruthless patriarch wants them to think. It, further, persuades them to think that they are weak and cannot survive on their own. The snarl of women's subjectivization is accomplished and executed also through the creation of certain myths and stereotypical images of the world outside the home which is unsecured, demonic, and exploitative. The world as it is portrayed to a woman in the form of unsecured demonic and exploited sphere has been accepted by the women and as a result, they do not feel comfortable coming out. It has been conspicuously articulated by Adriane L. Ivey who explores the condition of women within the patriarchal system in *Bailey's Café*. She explores Naylor's *Bailey's Café* as rewriting the biblical tradition and recreating biblical characters. She also points out that *Bailey's Café* "offers a glimpse of the conflict between a feminine spirituality and the traditional masculine Christianity" which proposes that the women in the novel try to achieve a kind of self-actuality, dependence, and self control that goes against the doctrines of the roles assigned to the women in traditional Christian patriarchal world view (88). The novel clearly portrays the agonizing condition of women in the highly oppressive and yet protective domain of male. Further, the novel explains the dialectical condition of women with which they are constrained in, on the one hand, initially they are conditioned, controlled and subjugated by the power of the patriarch but on the other hand, when they are thrown out by the same power of patriarchy, they manage to collect themselves in the murky world of male. The novel precisely discusses the aesthetic-spiritual and socio-pragmatic condition of the women which imbue them with adequate energy not only to survive with resilience but also to reconstruct themselves and to act as savior.

Bailey's Café discusses and explains some possible construes, constituents and constitution of subjectivization in the process of epistemological construction. At first, it vividly presents the role of oppressive structure of patriarchy in the construction and conditioning of the subject, secondly, it expounds the instrumental role of racial repression in the construction of the self and subject. The oppressive structure of patriarchy is quite evident through the narratives of the marginal women. The women in the novel are constructed and controlled by the knotty and oppressive structure of the patriarch which is indeed conspicuously clear through the confabulated reality of several women characters. The novel exhibits the case of Eve who is unquestioningly controlled by her grandfather. Sadie's narrative too explicates the similar case of social and patriarchal semiology in which initially she is controlled by her mother who compels her to be a whore and further her husband continues with the same patriarchal oppressive order. Uncle Eli through the mechanism of rationalization, legitimization and aristocratic tries to control, shape and reshape the life of Jesse Bell. She experiences the suffocating and exploitative rubric of patriarchal world order. Similarly, Esther is ubiquitously controlled by the patriarchal order which is exercised by her brother and further perpetuated by her husband. The reality of oppressive patriarchal order even continues its knotty exercise of subjectivization even in the case of Peaches. She articulates her experiences of patriarchal oppression in the novel where she finally confesses that one has to succumb to the order of the patriarch which finally shapes one's world view. It is the hegemonic patriarchal order which has pushed Mariam out of her ancestral house.

Racial repression proves to be a lethal combination along with gender subjugation in the lives of the women who finally take shelter in Eve's place. The novel picturesquely presents the role of race in the construction of the self which becomes evident in the case of Sadie, for instance. It is the race that never allows Sadie to have a decent man in her life after she is pushed out of the brothel during the time of recession while all other prostitutes land up having a prosperous life ever after. She is compelled to choose a man who is old enough to become her father simply because they have one thing in common—their race which denotes the whole lot of commonality on the basis of their shared racial experiences in the society which this silent man never expresses until he is drunk. The reality of Sadie and her husband's life proposes that the dominant role of race in the construction of dominant ideology has been aptly dealt in the novel. It believes in the philosophy that the ideology of the dominant race becomes the dominant ideology; this dominant ideology and the race propel Esther's brother to sell her for the sake of upward social mobility. The oppressive nature and function of racial and ethnic discrimination has a glaring and exemplifying tale to share through Jesse Bell who marries to the person of highest and powerful racial group so that she might get her condition ameliorated and may have the sense of empowerment. But the demonic differences of race and ethnicity compel her to coming to the realm of lesbianism where she may satisfy her sexual urge which has been left unsatisfied in her relationship with her husband who hails from a powerful, dominant race. It is not only this, but the impossibility of the amicable merge between races and ethnicities brings her at a very miserable and destitute condition where the reader may have *pathopoia*. The racial discrimination becomes so penchant and poignant that the world of dominant race does not allow the repressed or the inferior to stay and to continue leading their lives meaningfully, it is quite clear in the case of Miss Maple aka

Stanley who is the best ever example of the racial oppression. Gifted with the sharp skills and wit, Stanley is a widely read man still has to struggle over 99 places but could not get a job simply because of his race.

The novel, thus, exemplifies that Gloria Naylor has shown her luminous artistic creativity by portraying the repressive lives of these women who have tried to assert their sexuality or rather resist the control and stereotyping of their self in a male dominated world. In order to present the microcosm of the women's condition, she picks her characters not from one place rather make them "step in here from all over the United States and some parts of the world" (*BC* 03). Each of these characters "...comes in here with a simple story. Every one-liner's got a life underneath it" (34). Her story is provided with a cordial atmosphere to narrate the same which is done partially with the help of Bailey, the owner of the café and the narrator. Though, he does not interrupt the stories of these women as such but rather helps in preparing the stage for the individual narratives of the women. However, the narratives of the women propose the fact that the marginal women reach to the marginal space of Eve's boarding house "through suffering and pain, through struggle to be that which pleasures, delights, and fulfils desire" (hooks, *Yearning* 148). Further, the repression of feminine sensibility and sexuality outside the marginal space through power-politics interrelation pervades throughout the narratives of the women in the novel.

Different characters in the novel experience the sexual repression by the demonic power of patriarchy and finally they are pushed into the margin. The conglomeration of characters in the novel expresses the repressive reality of power structure. It is explicit through the narration of Sadie. She is the epitome of suffering which stems from the virtue of her gender and race. Since very childhood to her landing up in Eve's boarding house, she has been subjected to every sort of subjugation, initially from her mother and later by society at large. She has been trying to make everyone around her happy, specially her mother, with her never-saying-no-spirit. However, because of her sensitivity, she starts smelling something peculiar and strange even in her childhood world "her seven-year-old, eight-year-old, nine-year-old world was when it started to get confusing, because then she could compare her bruises to the unmarked face of the blacksmith's daughter, her mother's high-pitched threats to the voice of Mrs. Johnson when she called her own boy in from play. There was a difference" (*BC* 42-43). Naylor, through the story of Sadie tries to define how the concept of being good could be contextualized and interpreted differently. What, here, she emphasizes is that one has to have a never saying no-spirit and accept all the work diligently and perform it with utmost persistence, in order to be called 'good'. However, in spite of being 'very good', Sadie is taken "into the streets" as her mother announces "I've been selling my tail all this time to feed you till I'm sick and near death..." (44).

Though superfluously, Sadie's mother appears to be an insensitive one who pushes her daughter into a dirty business for a life time, yet she points towards the society where the men appear to be such monsters who cannot see a woman other than as a sexual object. And since her mother is "sick and near death", she puts her daughter to their service or to "feed" them in order to earn her livelihood (45). This devil within the men is further unmasked when one of the customers says "yeah I like it when you scream, the very first one whispered and kissed her neck, his hands holding each side of her rigid head. I like it when you scream" (45). This is the beginning of a new life for Sadie in a world which she pretends to be liking partially because of her mother and partially because there is no other way of surviving. Her mother has a very ambiguous role in the novel as she is a victim of patriarchal exploitation herself and still she perpetuates the tyranny of the oppressive order. She not only pushes Sadie into the business but also expects her to like it and consequently because of her mother's forced expectations, Sadie "made them think that I (Sadie) liked it" (46). She "even took it in the behind" and that too without feeling "dirty with any of it, *really* I (Sadie) didn't" (46 *italics mine*). What she receives from her mother in turn are good words "I know you could do it, I'm so proud of you. You're a good girl, Sadie" (46). What her mother is unable to sense is her use of the word "really" which implies in itself that she feels dirty in doing all that but trying to suppress the same with her use of the emphasis on "really" (46). Sadie's further reluctance in the business of her body could be traced while working in a whore house, one of the blonde whores says to Sadie "It's shame you're a nigger, Sadie...or you could make out really well" (48). Though Sadie did not answer the blonde whore directly, she "wasn't dreaming of being taken on as one of the house whores; she was standing by the back gate on Saturday mornings, waiting for the wood wagon to come" (48-49) that means that Sadie is looking for some permanent love. And she eventually succeeds in getting that. Though the man was older enough to be her father, he "had given her the closest thing that she would ever have to what she'd dreamed of. And she was trying to prove that she deserved it" (52). This life of Sadie with this man is no better than her previous life because the man she has now chosen is himself victimized and has little to offer her in the name of comfort of married life. His victimization in American White world has led him to be a bitter man that by the time has become his unconscious which is expressed in his sleep when he is drunk "[m]y name ain't nigger. So he hadn't moved his wagon fast enough for a policeman that day. Pissing in my pants. Blood running down San Juan Hill. Flames. So he'd been decorated in the Spanish American War. The Ninth Cavalry charging with Teddy Roosevelt. And later his buddy got pulled off a troop train in North Carolina and lynched" (53). Sadie "sewed" his fragmented sentences which he utters while he is drunk "to form the story of a bitterman who could once ride a horse like a god and had to become a mule to keep his family from starvation" (53). He never told anything about himself to Sadie in the entire journey of their married life which lasted for around twenty-five years, simply because like other black men, he does not trust his wife. This dichotomy in the lives of black women is quite evident here as on the one side she is not accepted by the white people because she is a nigger and on the other hand, she is not trusted by her own people/ husband "if he ever found out that was the case, that she was carrying some white man's disease into his bed, he would beat her senseless" which proposes that the black women live in such a world where nobody trusts them (54).

Further, Sadie could feel the difference between the worlds of white women and that of the black women. When there is recession and the law has taken over to shun the whore houses, almost everyone has got without a job. Every woman working over there is leaving and finding a new place to survive; it is even difficult for a colored woman to stay over there as "the law at the front door, it was best to leave as quick as they could through the back. Hang around too long and the blame might be put on them for the whole idea of the place" (50). Later, she is almost stunned when she discovers one of the prostitutes she was working as hair dresser for she has got well settled within the prestigious institution of marriage while her whole life has been a struggle. This incident takes place when Sadie has been wandering here and there in order to look for a job so that she could earn enough money to retain the house of her husband from his daughters who have claimed her house after the death of Sadie's husband:

> She was concentrating so hard, she almost collided with the two women leaving through one of the wrought-iron gates...but it was the laughter of the women that made her stop. *Damn fools,* the echo hit her, *there's no way for them to nail a vacate sign on...*the blonde was streaked with silver and swept up with pearl-studded and topped with a black cloche. The pearls were real and so was the mink stole. The wedding ring was platinum. And the green eyes were still beautiful, the makeup expert enough to mask the spreading crow's feet. (58-59)

The above incident makes Sadie review her condition in a patriarchal and racial society as while she is turning every stone to save a ghetto house, she discovers that the woman who is once a whore now living a respectable life. However, she makes every possible effort to save the house as this is the only thing in the world left for her after the death of her husband. She even sells herself here and there and works at several places to earn money "[s]ome evenings she would only need to sell herself for 23 cents, some evenings 15. And on the rare times she'd find a silver dollars, it meant four whole evenings could pass without her picking up a man" (67). However, despite her continuous efforts "[d]reams had been dying around Sadie all of her life. And the last star for her was dimming quickly inside. The last thing holding her back from falling to her destruction, an endless plunge through the endless space of the black hole waiting to open in her heart" (64). Consequently, she could not retain the house and hence have been forced to embrace the life of the street. Hence her journey to the marginal space of Eve's boarding house starts amidst "suffering and pain" (hooks, *Yearning* 148).

A close insight into the narrative of Sadie suggests that she has been subjected to the tyranny of her mother and whole range of power structure, however, subjectivization has offered her a critical insight into the rubric of power structure on the one hand and provides entry into the boarding house on the other. Similarly, Eve's life experiences the similar condition of oppression. Initially, she is controlled by her patriarchal grandfather. Prima facie, Eve's grandfather appears to be loving and caring as he provides everything she needs. However, the care and love seems to be the ideological methods to control Eve which is quite evident in that the moment grandfather discovers the fact that it is not he who controls Eve's sexuality but she herself owns her body and enjoys her sexuality, the grandfather turns indifferent and in fact becomes demonic and oppressive in his attitude towards Eve. Consequently in a fit of moment, he throws her out of his house and commands, "I (Eve) was going to leave him the same way he'd found me, naked and hungry" and he even "burned every one of those brown sack dresses he'd sewn for me. And then he made me strip off the one I was wearing—and he burned that, too, along with the cotton underpants and cotton wraps I used to bind down my breasts" (*BC* 88). In addition, Maxine Lavon Montgomery also points out the influence of her grandfather which is exercised through the institution of church "Godfather, a figure for male authority, is ubiquitous in his influence within the delta community. Perhaps the most definitive change in Eve's evolving consciousness occurs when she comes to recognize his church as a social construct..." ("Authority, Multivocality and New World Order" 188). This reflects that Eve's subjectivity and sexuality is controlled by all forms of institutions namely family, educational, and religious. It reverberates the philosophical position of Althusser with regard to the formation of subject which he clearly expels in his famous article "The Ideology and the Ideological State Apparatuses" (1970). In addition, her initial consciousness of patriarchal subjectivization comes in the form of the male gaze which makes her aware of her female sexuality at every point of time. She discovers that "[t]he men had only one question in their eyes when they looked at..." her that is they want to have sex with her (83). It gives a reflection of Beauvoir's famous proposition that "one is not born woman but becomes a woman" (301). Not only the male gaze which acts as threat to her existence in her spatio-temporal reality but she finds that the women who are the agents of patriarchy also control her subjectivity. In fact, Naylor here refers to the Foucauldian critique of power oppression which is evident when she says "the women's eyes held other questions, unnatural questions, as their heads followed us (grandfather and Eve) when we rode in the wagon" (*BC* 83).

Further, the chapter attempts to untie the inextricate relationship between power, knowledge, and sexuality which is perpetual and pervasive that maintains dialectics of subjectivity and the formation of the self. The entire process of subject formation through self disclosure to the power structure, and governmentality controls every individual; however, it exhibits some aporic nature. When the power of the dominant ideology operates all other forms of ideology move to the margin and hence, the whole world automatically supports patriarchy. A decision taken by the ruling ideology and dominant ideology is not questioned as it holds the power which is aptly explicable in the case of Eve's grandfather, as he throws Eve out, "...there was nobody who would dare to take me (her) in" (85). It forces her to start her journey in utter despair and despondency "from east of the delta to follow the riverbed north...a long walk in a dry winter through the manes part of Louisiana" (89). The extrication from the power politics or from the power itself may make one feel stranded and helpless like orphan. Eve when she is extricated or chopped off from the power machinery almost feels and experiences the similar situation. She is sans clothes, shelter, and food and faces the challenges of life moving through the delta that has been very harsh which is exemplary in that she has inhaled and exhaled the delta dust through every pore of her body. The oppression and the sense of destitution as she goes under can easily be explained through the following paragraph:

> And since that was the driest winters in living memory, the dirt sought out what wetness it could and clung to the tiny drops of perspiration in my pores. It used that thin film of moisture to creep its way up toward the saliva in my mouth, the mucus in my nose. Mud forming and caking around the tear ducts in my eyes, gluing my lashes together. There was even enough moisture deep within my earwax to draw it; my head becoming stuffed up and all sounds a deep hum. It found the hidden dampness under my fingernails, between my toes. The moist space between my hips was easy, but then even into the crevices around the anus, drawing itself up into the slicks walls of my intestines. Up my thighs and deep into my vagina, so much mud that it finally stilled my menstrual blood. ...Godfather always said that he made me, but I was born of the delta. (90)

And "...it's no more possible than washing away my fingerprints or my color. I guess because it's only dirt, and there is something that makes you believe you can wash away dirt. But it's not a part of me—it is me" (82). Delta dust is the metaphor that symbolizes the repression in her story and through the delta passage "I'd already clearly seen enough of the world to know there was little I needed to laugh about. And the only road that lay open to me was the one ahead, and the only way I could walk it was the way I was" (91). Her thousand years walk through delta symbolizes the period of women's collective historical exploitation. This is what Maxine Montgomery points "[t]hat Eve walks, she tells us, a thousand years before reaching Bailey's, is an important allusion linking her role among a community of women to the millennial reign of Christ" ("Authority, Multivocality and New World Order" 189). Once she reaches the other part of the world after crossing the delta, she constructs her boarding house "which is full of nothing but sluts and whores and tramps" (*BC* 80). Like Mattie Michael in *The Women of Brewster Place*,

Eve "passes no judgment on the behavior of those women once she lets them live there, and she passes no judgment on their visitors" (92). One of the many characteristics of this boarding house is that it lets the women to be themselves and live their life on their own terms. The place also offers a kind of solace to the women torn apart by the concurrent treachery of men in their lives. The new location of Eve is essentially marginal as it is far-away from the power of dominant class and ideology but it is also a place which can house the marginal, the dispossessed, the oppressed and subaltern who share the similar experience of pain, agony, destitution and deprivation. It is evident when Eve says "I'm tempted to let a woman stay here because of the pain in her story: daddy beat up on her. Mama beat up on her" (81).

Often the perpetuators of the violence, in the lives of the marginal women, are their own people. It is quite evident in the case of Esther who is subjected to sexual exploitation by her husband and is pushed into this confinement and perennial sexual slavery by nobody but her own brother who tells her that "[t]his is your husband.... Do whatever he tells you, and you won't be sent away like the others.... I believe in my older brother. He is kind to me and calls me only little sister. And there is much more food here than at home" (95). The force of power is felt more forceful in the state of economic, political, and social deprivation and the condition of deprivation does not allow one to negotiate with the power structure but to accept the stock reality as it is offered. Esther who is the subject of demonic power structure and deprivation cannot negotiate with the given economic, political, and social power but is left with no choice but to accept the words of her husband. And "[s]o I (she) come down when he calls. And rejoice that it is dark" as she functions not more than the concubine of a powerful dominant patriarchal master (96). Esther takes refuge in this slavery from escaping herself being a whore, however, she becomes one unconsciously the moment she accepts the sexual and physical slavery of the master. However, she has lived for around twelve years consoling herself that she has escaped being a whore. Moreover, she does not accept the slavery but suspends her rejection for twelve years because her family gets benefitted out of her slavery. She confesses that "I stay with this man for twelve years because I am a good sister. My older brother gets higher wages with each passing years.... And each time I am called into the cellar to kneel among the sacks of potatoes and flour, I count the days to repay my debt. I count the many ways in which you can hate a man" (99). Initially, she seems to surrender before the demands of her husband, as she always goes down the cellar whenever she is called and allows him to do whatever he likes, in her deeper consciousness she has some feelings like "I thought of killing this man when I was within hours of becoming the next lying bitch to leave. I thought about sparing the other young girls waiting in line to sleep alone in his pin-and-lace bed. The other twelve-year-olds with brothers. But my guess turned out to be right. There are too many of them to kill. And there are just many twelve-year-olds" (99). Maxine Lavon Montgomery traces Esther's hatred towards her master that the:

> ...pervasive hatred for men stems from the commodification of black women within the context of a rural economic system. Esther suffers exploitation as her elder brother barters her to an older, propertied farmer in exchange for higher sharecropping wages. Passively, Esther surrenders to the farmer's whims while he chooses to be intimate with her only in the cellar of his home. The pink and lace-trimmed bed where she must sleep alone reveals her confinement to a socially prescribed gender role. ("Authority, Multivocality and the New World Order" 191)

Naylor has universalized the experience of women's subjugation through the experiences of Esther. Her experience denotes that she is only one of those girls who are forced to live such a miserable life. Maxine Montgomery finds sweet Esther full of hatred which "stems from the commodification of Black Women within the context of a rural economic system" ("Authority, Multivocality, and the New World Order" 191). Naylor's construction of the places like Eve's is a counter establishment of patriarchal institution where the socially, racially, and sexually exploited women find solace and at themselves. Esther, for instance, is doing the same here at Eve's place what she was doing with her husband in the dark, the only difference is that here she has control over the men who visit her. At Eve's place she has certain conditions, "men must only visit in the dark. And they must bring me the white roses. And they must call me *little sister*. Or I no longer come" (*BC* 99).

The process of objectification and subjectification fosters a rebellious tendency among the characters because the process of objectification is based upon the process of the deadly weight of sexual exploitation and control too. The graphic example of Esther and Peaches makes an attempt to divulge the role of oppressive power structure in controlling the sexuality. It exemplifies the relationship between power, knowledge and sexuality. The power structure modifies the entire domain of discourse on sex and desire through displacement, intensification, and reorientation. Foucault in his *The History of Sexuality* Volume 1 (1978) explains the entire process of sexual exploitation and repression through his "the repressive hypothesis" (12). Naylor, through the vivid depiction of Esther's portrayal who is cheated by her greedy brother and his demanding wife which triggers her to realize that her sexuality is being controlled by the power structure and which finally turns her into a rebel. Further, Peaches also shares the similar experience of sexual control through power which in turn makes her rebellious. Foucault explains the same phenomenon by delineating the inextricate relationship between power and sex which is conspicuously clear when he says "power is essentially what dictates its law to sex which mean first of all that sex is placed by power in a binary system; licit and illicit, permitted and forbidden. Secondly, power prescribes an 'order' for sex that operates at the same time as a form of intelligibility; sex is to be deciphered on the basis of its relation to law" (83). Hence, Foucault further says that "there is no escaping from power that it is always—already present, constituting that very thing which one attempts to counter it with" (82). The form of power structure of patriarchy, "father" controls the sexual urge of the daughter which is clear in the case of Peaches, her father tries to protect or rather control her sexuality from the other young boys of the street as she was such a beautiful girl that "you see and don't believe"; someone who "live(s) just outside the limits of your imagination" (*BC* 100).

No boy dares to enter into "the wall he started building around the house when I (she) was nine years old" (103). If anybody does, they are given proper treatment as they "...choke up the breath to whisper that they wanted to see Peaches" and then they never show their face (103). It is not simply out of affection for her that he is protecting his daughter rather what Peaches' mom says "[o]ne dog knows another" (103). And he appears to admit that "I already know why you want to see my daughter, and you know I know why" (103). Though her daddy has been able to control the boys to visit her, but what he has not been able to control is the inner instinct of Peaches which sometimes reflect in the form of her other self and which she constantly tries to deny. Though she puts her best efforts to suppress her sexual desires, she succumbs before them which brings a sense of freedom to her "[i]n horror I watched her grow up (whore in her), and I learned to hate her for breaking my father's heart" (105). Peaches' consciousness of her sexuality is reflected through the metaphor of the mirror in the novel:

> Every mirror outside had told me what she was.... I saw her standing there unclothed with the whispered talk among my brothers.... But there was a difference when it came to women: the young and unmarried reflected her with an envy so intense it bordered on hate; those older and married, with a helpless fear. Yes, they all looked at me and knew just, what she was. (104)

The history of Peaches' sexual oppression and control is not only confined within the walls of her father but her father's friends through their male gaze control her sexuality and shape her body. This act of sexual control and repression by the patriarchy in the form of male gaze turns Peaches into an object of sexuality. This reflects upon a sexual dialectics as on the one hand father, a form of power structure controls her sexuality but on the other hand her father's friend, another form of power structure objectifies her body as she discovers herself as a sexual object in the eyes of the friends of her father. They use to say "the gal has promise, Jim" and she was always wandering as what do they mean by that and tried to discover "...upstairs in my mirrors I would try to see what she had promised that would cause the heat to seep up through the rough denim of their pant legs and melt the corners of their mouths" (104). The incident shows clearly that the woman is commodified and looked at only as a sexual object of their sexual gratification and nothing beyond that and that too since her childhood. However, she does everything to suppress her sexuality and being a sexual object but it is always reflected in the male gaze outside "[s]he was always there, reflected in the wetness of men's eyes. Tormenting me. I wore high-necked shirtwaists and loose skirts, thick woolen tights, even in the summertime that scratched and left welts on my legs. But I could feel their eyes stripping my clothes away: they knew her promise was there" (105). The continual oppression of Peaches sexuality impels her to develop two different selves; on the one hand she has the oppressed self which is the part of symbolic order and on the other the real self of her which is rebellious in her nature. The real self in the course of time becomes dominant upon her oppressed symbolic order and makes her 'self' indulged into a sexual act, however, she knows that it may be an act of sin but there is no option to rebel against the patriarchal order or to get rid of the oppressed self. Peaches sexual encounter makes her father furious and it instigates him to revenge against the men who have exploited her. She is aware of the fact that her father always wants to control her and this desire of her father makes her desirous to get rid of him or the oppressive power structure. She requests her father when he makes an attempt to control her "[d]on't lock me in my room, not there, I pleaded; I'll have to find a way to get out again. I tried to stop him from wasting his money on doctors. I tried to stop him from hurting himself by beating me with razor straps, leather shoes, his fists. I tried to stop him crying. I didn't want to leave home, but I had little choice" (106).

The exasperating and ignominious power structure with all its apparatuses has been trying and has in fact made the individual as subject. Any attempt of getting rid from the power structure may bring one into the vortex of inescapable power structure. It proves to be an absolute dialectics where a self tries to be conscious of itself away from the absolute (power) but every movement away from it is a perennial and imperative and indispensable turn towards it. Gloria Naylor through the example of Peaches movement away from her father's home, a place of patriarch (power structure) into another anonymous world sphere or spatio-temporal reality tries to establish the fact that every escape from the power structure leads into another. Naylor, here, echoes the Hegelian dialectics with regard to power structure. The movement of Peaches from her home space, however, gives her a sense of availing an opportunity of raising unhearable sounds against the power structure and at least to be able to control her own body, however, she later identifies that the entire world is in reality a big trap or snarl of the power structure itself. Every open space becomes a replica of home space for her, particularly about her oppression of her sexuality by her father or patriarch which she also experiences at all places wherever she moves on. And she keeps on moving from one place to another and "the men who only took care of me (her) to the men whom I (she) stayed with long enough until they made the same mistake of caring about me" (107). Once she gets a husband who was very caring and nice but he "made the same mistake Daddy Jim had" (109). Soon she discovers that the care was nothing but a fine way to exercise control over somebody. And when she starts visiting other men, he discovers it and he turns violent "[h]e didn't curse. He didn't plead. He just took out his straight razor one morning at breakfast, pressed it against my throat, and told me very quietly that the next man I was with, I would have to watch die" (110). She knew very well that he was a man of words so she takes the beer opener and rips her face apart as a mark of protest against his patriarchal practices. Her act of defiance against this man marks the protest against the commodification of women who must look good in order to be appreciated well in the manmade society and the moment they wither they become burden and tough to be accommodated:

> First, I took the tip of the beer opener, smiled into the mirror, and traced the path I was going to take; under the right cheekbone—yes, it must be the right—then a straight diagonal across the Dimple, all the way over to the left side of the chin. A thin red line was left on my skin for me to follow, so I didn't need to smile again as

> I grasped the opener in both hands and dug down. But I wasn't prepared for the first bolt of blinding pain; it took precious seconds to catch my breath. And now the opener hanging in my ripped cheek was too slippery to hold firmly because of the gushing blood. (111)

The above-mentioned form of rebellion against patriarchal institution once again compels her to move and she is on her own as she starts her journey towards the east. She meets a number of people who are sympathetic towards her after discovering her ripped face and one of them even suggests the names of the doctors too, not knowing the fact that she "didn't want to fix" her face (112). This incident once again brings her to the streets to survive on her own and now she could identify the promises that her father's friends have been discussing, are there in this girl. It is only after becoming a whore; she could identify her conscious self with her unconscious one:

> ...I was forced to admit that I actually enjoyed being held and touched by some of the men I lived with. I was even starting to look forward to their coming to bed. There are no words to describe how ugly that realization was. I knew she was a whore. Had always been a whore. Was probably born a whore. For as long as I could remember, I could see her in their eyes. But now as I looked in the mirror—thinking of how my own body had betrayed me with him—I could see her in my eyes. (107)

This realization leads her to hate herself as she could introspect that it is only the other self of her that "was probably always enjoying those back rooms and back stairs.... I was probably always making men in the streets look at me that way, my father's friends look at me that way" (107). What is important to look at this stage is that she directs the whole guilt on herself and consequently punishes herself for something that she is not responsible. This complies with a general phenomenon in the patriarchal society where women are held responsible for something they are actually not responsible for. She finds her search ending at Eve's place where she is not exploited as a commodity rather she is allowed to lead her life with all possible dignity and self respect and it is precisely accomplished for the women who live at Eve's place share the similar oppression and exploitation. The common experiences of objectification and subjectification develop a female bonding among them. It allows them to lead a peaceful and cohesive life, however, it is the marginal space which provides them a temporary recluse from the oppressive world and prepares them to fight against the oddities of their lives that they may face in the forth coming odyssey in their lives.

The reality of women's sexual oppression continues through different forms of power structure, Jesse Bell is a special case in this regard as she is not exploited by her husband rather by her husband's uncle, Eli, "the horrible old man, may he rot in hell.... He was a murderer—a cold blooded murderer" and always directing how to act and dress (118). This is the man who never accepts her as Mrs. King and he has been responsible for detaching her own son from her, "he took my husband and son. And they were all I lived for" (118) and "...killed me (her) in my (her) home" (130). Her isolation and marginalization at her husband's home pushes her to the space where she drinks heavily and seeks the company of lesbian relationship. Her husband has been authoritatively impotent that she has "no point in going to" him (128). She, thus, finds an alternative to express her grief "[s]o, yes, I went to...her. And I cried in her arms, never talking much sense and drunk lots of the time. She'd really become, as my husband called her, that special friend" (128). And she goes even beyond to find the solace in the arms of her special friend and finds so much relaxed in her arms that she asserts "I couldn't stand to have my husband touch me after that. I looked for the answer in her arms, but now even she wasn't enough. But there were hidden places, smoky back rooms, with others like her" (130). Through her experiences, Jesse discovers that men only want to control and enjoy sexual activities with a woman and never take her seriously which is not a case with a woman as a lover. Consequently, she decides to control and practice her own sexuality. But she has to pay for controlling her sexuality because her husband and Uncle Eli belong to such a patriarchal society where, "a woman can be only one kind of wife and mother.

Any deviation in terms of sexuality is ostracized" (Ivey 92). And when she is discovered practicing her sexuality in different clubs:

> Uncle Eli used every bit of influence he had to make sure my name hit the newspapers and stayed in the papers, throwing dirt on everything about my life, just digging, digging, until they dug up my special friend and my husband *had* to say he didn't know, cause, after all, he was a man and a king and there was his son to consider, so I'm out there by myself, on display like a painted dummy in a window as the name Jesse Bell came to mean that no-good slut from the docks and the nineteen years I'd put into my marriage didn't amount to dog shit; the care I'd given to my son—dog shit. (*BC* 131-32)

Like Eve who is abandoned by everybody when her grandfather pushes her out, Jesse finds nobody who could support her not even her husband, "...nobody was interested in my side of story, not the reporters, not the neighbors, not the divorce court, nobody, cause everybody was standing like vulture looking at me fall fall fall, waiting for me to smash my brains on the pavement, yeah, waiting for me to lose my mind" (131-32). The whole system of the society for a woman on her own is treacherous simply because the world is largely controlled by men who can never see a woman empowered rather she should be dependent on her men and act accordingly.

Another reason which could be traced behind the behavior of Uncle Eli is that he is a man who takes the white as his standard and wants Jesse to act accordingly who in turn is proud to belong to the docks, her ethnic tribe and "didn't see a damn thing wrong with being colored. And where did Uncle Eli want us to be lifted up to? Why, white folks" (125). What is applicable here is best stated by Bailey, one of the leading characters in Gloria Naylor's *Bailey's Café*, "[w]ealthy negroes held the same kind of attitudes as wealthy white people but more so, feeling that they had more to prove" (07). Uncle Eli always acts as a prototype who looks at the whites as his role models and is always conscious to act accordingly but Jesse is not willing to follow either to what Uncle Eli says or what white standard is "[w]hite folks are looking at us. White folks are judging us. They were Uncle Eli's gods. And it was a god I wasn't buying. But he was always up in my face, thinking he could tell me how to act and dress.... I let it go in one ear and out the other and did just what I wanted to do" (125-26). The disobedience of Jesse leads her to become an object of contempt by Uncle Eli. Resistance against the white ways and white gods of Uncle Eli has led Jesse to the condition she has ultimately reached. The reason of not complying to the rules of Uncle Eli like any other woman of that place is that the women coming from the downhill have more respect for themselves that the women from the sugar hills, but the women of downhill are looked down upon because of their ethnicity "[w]omen up there (Sugar Hill) look at other women as nothing unless they're attached to some man's name. And attached they stay, no matter what he does. And I personally knew a few of them who actually got their butts beaten by stone sober men behind stained-glass doors. And with all their money, they couldn't afford to cry" (121-22).

Naylor's novel has critiqued the male centered discourse through the story of Jesse Bell "giving voices to those individuals whose experiences are often excluded from written history" (Fowler 190). In continuation, Esther who is commoditized within the rural economic center "adds her solitary voice to those of the other women whose stories are included in 'The Jam'" (192). All the women in the novel are elevated "in the text to a position of honor with what is a womanist reconceptualization of the once-burdensome domestic sphere" (192). Fowler further appreciates Naylor's effort as she "dares to engage important issues affecting women of color world-wide and thus rescues the stories of women from silence and oblivion. At a time when women across the globe are experiencing unprecedented oppression, Naylor's voice is a clarion that demands to be heard" (193).

In addition, the narrative of Mariam exemplifies the similar phenomenon of repression by the oppressive machinery of patriarchy. Mariam's story blurs the national boundaries sketching the female exploitation across the world. Her story is the strangest of all as she is a fourteen year old girl and gets pregnant even when "no man has ever touched [her]"

(*BC* 143). She belongs to a society which is highly patriarchal in its thought and approach which reflects in that the women, there, are regarded impure for longer period of time for giving birth to a girl child in comparison to that of a boy. And punishment of a rape of a virgin is that "he must marry her and pay her father just restitution" (154). This indicates that the violation of a woman's body is measured in the form of just money as there would be nothing more insulting to a woman than to get married to the violator. The men are very powerful there and have full command over female sexuality which is exercised in the form of female circumcision which in turn prevents and denies any sexual pleasure to women. In such a society, when Mariam gets pregnant even when no man ever touches her, everyone is shocked. Her mother tries to know the name of the person who has done that "[s]he lifts the girl's skirt and, taking two fingers between her legs. Here, she says, who has been here? And here? Here?...and when the girl repeats her innocence once again, the woman raises her fist and strikes her" (154). This incident in a strict sense reminds of Mattie Michael, one of the characters from Naylor's first novel, *The Women of Brewster Place*. Mariam is beaten by her mother in the process of finding the name of the person who has violated her sanctity while Mattie Michael is beaten by her father who in turn faces the resistance of Mattie's mother. Consequently, Mariam is exiled from the village after much drama and left to her own which could be looked as one of the ideologies of the society that if any woman commits adultery she has to bear the same consequences.

When she is thrown out of the village, there is none than only two women who come to her rescue; they are Mariam's mother and priest's wife. Mariam's mother goes to the extent that she is sacrificed by the priests and becomes martyr in the history of gender conflict and female bonding. Her only fault is that she considers the men's gods to be her own too "I am also His servant...I am also His servant and He is my God too" and she goes inside the god's abode no woman is allowed, expecting to have God's grace on her, not "to bargain with God, to plead her goodness. She was going to demand pure and simple justice" (156) which is outrightly rejected to her in the men's world as she is wrong in her perception; God favors those who are in power and in her case men hold that privilege. As she enters the holy place, she is soon discovered and "[c]haos breaks out. The woman begins to run in circles. She knows that the Holy of Holies must be somewhere toward the center, but there are so many people shouting now, hands reaching out to strike her as she's shoved against walls and spat upon" (157). She gets herself sacrificed and does not fight back because she must keep forgiving them as she has to ask god to spare Mariam. Another woman who dares to support is High priest's wife who hides herself at the end of the village to help Mariam with an address of an old friend of hers who could help Mariam there at Addis Ababa.

Further, the journey of Stanley from his agrarian reality to the marginal space of Eve's boarding house explicates that racial identity of a person constitutes and constructs his or her life. Further, Naylor shows that society controls the gender of a person by attributing certain kind of dresses, language, and behavior. Stanley's aka Miss Maple's taking of female dresses could be interpreted as a resistance against gender stereotyping. He sends a message to the world that though he is wearing female dresses, he is still a man and wearing a particular dress does no good than wearing a woman's clothes at least for a black man in American society. The conflict arises between how he perceives himself and how the world perceives him. Most of the people around take him to be a homosexual simply because of his dress which he is not and at times he has to defend himself for the same perception of the world for instance, "it does no good to tell him (Sugar man and the likes of him) for the thousandth time that Miss Maple isn't a homosexual" (163).

In addition, he comes from a very cultured background as when "he opens his mouth, you can tell he's not from the rough side of town. If anything, it's a cultured voice and it's clear he's had a lot of schooling" (164). Initially, he is not sent to the schools, as his father "didn't trust what I'd be taught in any of their schools so he hired a special tutor" (172). His father's lack of trust in American school system echoes Bailey when he says "school isn't where real learning happens" (03) and Kiswana Browne in Naylor's *The Women of Brewster Place* when she leaves her college and joins Brewster place to serve her own people. Stanley, before landing to Eve's place after much of the experiences of racial discrimination while attempting to find a job, has lived with his father a very luxurious life with a lot of property. It is difficult to retain the property for a very long time in a racist society by a black man and at time to time, they have been victims of the maltreatment in the hands of the racists for whom it has been almost impossible to digest to see a black so rich and owing so much property:

> We were pretty much ignored by the Americans until they found out we actually owned all of the land we were farming, and the barns and the reapers and the trucks and the gin mills. They'd stand speechless at the edge of our fields, which stretched farther that they could see over any horizon; progress had given them no vocabulary to reconcile the land and us.... And having no words for what was in front of them, they believed it had no right to exist...he'd come back out of the bank to find all of his whitewalls flat ad that six-letter word scrawled in mud over his windshield. Hoodlum pranks, the Sheriff would tell him. And yes, he'd tried to find witness from even the last time, but it was funny how nobody claimed to see things. (172)

What Stanley feels strange about this is that his father never fights back. He goes even to the extent that he starts hating his father for the same. And there have been numerous such incidents where they have felt embarrassed, "[h]e had to know it wasn't accidental that a wad of tobacco spit would splatter right in front of us, staining the cuffs of his slacks. No storekeeper was so nearsighted that he waited on everyone else at the counter before he finally saw us" (173). Though he respects his father for his scholarship and prudence but "Philosophy hasn't saved my father the contempt we met in town. Philosophy didn't give him guts. I hated being ashamed of my father and when I finally told him so, there were tears in his eyes. And I was ashamed of him for that" (174).

A peculiar incident happens when Stanley is going for his higher education and his father has come to post office to parcel some plays of Shakespeare for him. This incident is remarkable for compelling Stanley to review and revise his conception of his father. Gatlins, a group of white ruffians arrives, "[t]hey entered one at a time, the bell clanging, the door slamming behind each one, until all four stood blocking...Papa ignored them" (178). They become even more irritated on being ignored, so they "...jabbed Papa in the middle of the chest: we came in here to ask you a question" (178). And the question that they ask has nothing but to express insult to his father for daring to wear proper clothes "how it is that a low-down, scum bag, filthy piece of shit like you—ya know, something that looks like it swung in from a jungle—how it is that he thinks he can parade all up and down town wearing them clothes?" (179) and when his father answered that he "wear(s) these clothes because I (he) can" (179), he is punished for that:

> No, you can't wear those clothes. Hear me? You can't—and knocked the straw hat off Papa's head. As Papa bent over to retrieve it; the fat Gatlin grabbed him by the back of the belt, pulled out a Bowie, and slit his trousers straight down the rear seam before shoving him over on his knees. The blade also ripped through his boxer shorts and at the sight of one of his testicles hanging beneath the torn clothes, I felt something and sick lodge in my throat.... (179)

After that both of them were stripped off their clothes and locked in a room. And "[a]fter being flung naked into the storeroom, I felt on my elbows and the pain made my eyes sting. I sat on the dirt floor rocking and holding the bruised arm. I won't cry, I kept thinking over and over; I'll kill myself before I cry" (180). Initially, Stanley hates his father for being so much submissive as he reacts in hatred when his father tries to reach to him in the dark room in order to pacify him "[d]on't you touch me. My teeth were clenched. Just don't touch me. My eyes were adjusting to the dark and I could make out the shadowy silhouettes of packing crates and of his bare feet as he stood beside me. The air was close and stale; a trickle of sweat run down the side of my nose and pooled in the crevice on my upper lip" (180). He goes even further in accusing his father "[t]here is no God, or he would have struck you dead a long time ago. You're worthless.... You don't even amount to the ape they called you—you're nothing. And you've always been *nothing*. Nothing...nothing...noth..." (181-82). The Gatlins do not get satisfied by stripping them and locking them into the room rather go on to books "[t]he silk cover was gouged with holes, the spine busted and bent over double. They'd torn out handfuls of pages, crushed what was left between their fists, and then urinated on the whole thing. The stench of *The Tempest* was quickly filling that close room" (183). His father being educated does not mean that he is not brave. His bravery comes on full display when he fights with Gatlins. When Stanley along with his father comes out of the room, wearing the women's clothes, Gatlins laugh "so hard their knees got weak" (184), thinking that they are surrendering before them as for them women's clothes are the mark of surrender and then his father "headed straight for the big one and spoke to him first. Grabbing him by the collar, he slammed his face down on the counter and dragged his unconscious body along the whole length of it, the fat Gatlin picking up splinters in his broken nose and leaving behind a trail of blood and chipped teeth" (184).

And his anger stems from what they did with the books as he states "[t]here is no greater strength than what is found within. There is no greater love than reaching beyond boundaries to other men. There is no greater wealth than possessing true peace of mind. When my son left me to go out on his own, I wanted to give him the vision of such a brave new world. You pissed on that" (186). Stanley was unable to understand that his father accepts this submission before Gatlins because of him as he expresses after being insulted by Stanley "I kept hoping you'd understand. I should have just come out and explained why. I've lived the way I have. It hasn't been easy, Stanley, but I did it for you" (*BC* 182). The fault of his father has been that he always wants to make Stanley learn the language of his masters and in turn expects to be accepted by them as he puts "[f]rom the day you were born I've been speaking to you in a language that I wanted you to master, knowing that once you did, there was nothing that could be done to make you feel less than what you are, and I know that they would stop at nothing to break you—

because you are mine" (182). It poses a remarkable question about the role of language in the construction of consciousness, ideology and subjectivity. The language is the phenomenological tool through which even the epistemology and the ontology of knowledge come into the fore. The language does not only construct the consciousness but even the unconscious is structured like language echoes the sounds of Jacques Lacan. The process of enslavement and the perpetuation of master/slave dialectics may continue with the power and politics of language. Stanley's father tries to motivate him to learn the language of the masters so that Stanley may share his master's experience and world view. Further his father motivates him to learn the language of his master and says "I am a man of peace. I am a sensitive man. I can spend hours with Proust and have been known to weep at a sunset. Those are the qualities I wanted to pass on to my son. I believe he has the capacity to be a great leader. And I've tried to teach him that a man rules best when he rules with compassion" (185).

This encounter with the Gatlins and his experiences of racial discrimination along with his father at the market are not first of its kinds that Stanley faces; he has been facing the same from the day when he joined school. Almost at every step he finds racism blocking his way one way or the other. Once "[t]here was a massive blood drive going on at school and, like the rest, I went down at the Red Cross to contribute. I found out that they weren't taking Negro blood at the banks" (188). This blood drive has been organized against the backdrop of the Second World War. That was quite a frustrating experience for him and his only argument that is not answerable was "[i]f my blood wasn't good enough for the Red Cross, why was it good enough to be spilled on the battlefield?" (189). This incident supports the theory that the blacks are Americans as long as they are ready to sacrifice themselves for the country and the moment some benefits are to be conferred to them, they become blacks with no self-respect and almost non-human.

Another encounter which is even brutal in its nature, he undergoes in the Jail where he is forced to have a homosexual relation with a man whom he does not know despite the fact that he is not a homosexual as he states "I am not homosexual, but I'm not stupid either" (193) which implies that he is not raped in that homosexual encounter rather he surrenders before that man who "was six-feet-two, as broad as he was tall, as ugly as he was mean, a repeat offender serving for three counts of murder with nothing left to lose. And he wasn't a homosexual either.... They assigned me to his cell as a reprisal for helping to organize the hunger strike.... I had to hear each night after the lights were out, I'm gonna fuck you...nothing more than that" (193). After that begins his journey for searching a job. For a black man in America, getting a suitable job is next to impossible thing. He applied everywhere from Los Angeles to Philadelphia but could not get a job despite his high credentials "...the people who kept turning me down, and I was even able to feel pity for them as they avoided my eyes and wilted a little with each page of my impeccable sales charts. I could feel desperation in the way they kept reading and rereading my college transcripts, flipping through the charts..." (197) and this "scenario repeated itself (with slight variation) in six major cities a total of thirty-five times and still counting, when a massive heat wave hit the northern section of the country" (197).

Later he "divides the number of times I (he) had been rejected for a job by the number of places where I had applied, which brought me towards a probability estimate of total failure" (197). But he does not lose hope and keeps applying thinking "[m]y past experiences should not have any bearing on the next experience to come; someone, somewhere, is advertising for a qualified man as a marketing analyst and they actually want just what they print in the newspapers and tell me over the telephone, a qualified man. If it turns out to be false, the next time it might be true" (199). He also tries different kinds of clothes "[a] gray flannel suit made no more measurable difference than a brown tweed, a brown tweed than a pinstriped" (200). Such clothes even offered certain skin diseases in the summer, "[t]he only business clothes that could keep me going through that summer were ones designed for American females" (201). And people comment on his wearing of a woman's dress as "[t]his man isn't really serious. What chance does he have of being hired for such a high-level position wearing a woman's dress?", they are not aware that wearing man's or rather gentleman's dress too does not either have a chance for being hired (203). Ultimately, he gets a job at Eve's place who "after taking one look at me in that gray flannel suit with my open shirt, she offered me a job as a housekeeper with terms that I couldn't refuse" (213). And what draws Stanley at Eve's place is the "Eve has allowed Miss Maple to be one of the freest men I know" (216).

This gender and racial repression that every character encounters in American society or elsewhere in the world tear these women apart and pushes them to the edge of the world where they have to survive on their own. In such an isolated, dislocated and displaced condition, the least support and care that they receive comes not from everywhere but only from the world of women. It helps them to have a bond among themselves and, hence, strengthens a sense of community and cooperation. Montgomery comments that "[u]ltimately, Naylor's goal as creator and sovereign...is to affect some sort of unity among the widely disparate voices of women" ("Authority, Multivocality, and the New World Order" 188). Eve, for instance, represents the collective bond between all these women. Her boarding house acts as a place of solace and comfort for them. They get healing from Eve who acts "as a matriarch and guide for most of the characters" on the one side and feel free from patriarchal jaws that has crippled their lives, on the other (Ivey 89). Though, these women are involved in sexual activities here, but the only difference between the life at Eve's and the life before arriving at Eve's is that they here control their own sexuality. Here, they are not supposed to reach to the cellar when the husband calls, as in the case of Esther, rather they decide whom to see and whom not to and in what circumstances. Eve provides them full autonomy in this regard. She is sensitive enough to admit a woman with a painful story "I'm tempted to let a woman stay here because of the pain in her story. Daddy beat up on her. Mama beat up on her" (*BC* 81). In turn, the women believe in her as Esther shares what happened with her in the dark only with Eve. Her healing of Jesse Bell reminds us of Mattie Michael in *The Women of Brewster Place* and Miranda Day in *Mama Day* (1988), both of them are the epitome of female bonding and solidarity; her way of healing is a bit different from the earlier healers of Gloria Naylor. While Mattie gives Ciel a healing bath to save her and Miranda uses herbal medicines to save Cocoa, Eve takes Jesse to hell as Jesse describes:

> Imagine, she said, that you're speeding along at, say like, seventy miles an hour. No car, no nothing, just your body, seventy miles an hour. And suddenly your whole body slams right into this brick wall. But you don't go unconscious, so you can feel crushed pieces of your skull stabbing back into your brain, your lungs collapsing in, each snapping and crumbling, your inside busting open as your guts rip apart. That's how much it hurts. Now, imagine, she said, that your body gets slammed into that same wall again and again. Red-hot bricks one time. Block of ice the next. Imagine it going on for four straight days. And imagine, when it was over, that bitch put me through it all again. (139)

Yet another evidence of Eve's care and supportiveness is manifested when she helps Mariam deliver the child while "[n]one of Us had the answer for what was to happen when Mariam's baby came due. Her situation was a first for everybody" (221). Eve transforms herself into a real African mother. When it were almost the last days of Mariam to deliver the child she was "crying for days, asking for her mother. And Eve had told her she was going to her village again, and in a way she was" (224).

Bailey's Café and Eve's boarding house are places which provide characters with a short time break from the journey of life where the passerby stops and regains his/her energy to go back to his normal life with renewed energy or "you head to the back of the café and end it (life)" (221). This beginning of life proposed by Mariam who herself is "born black and Jew" poses a serious question as what would happen to this street (221). But this brings other women of the boarding house to unite for this cause. And Mariam's delivery could be looked as a perfect example of female solidarity and bonding as "...everyone who lived on the street was gathered inside. And I mean everyone, even strange little Esther. She'd squeezed herself into the darkest corner of the room, sitting on the floor with arms wrapped around her bent knees.... It went on for four hours.... Then we heard the baby's first thin cry—and the place went wild" (225). And Bailey explains the event in the following paragraph:

> Nadine hugged me so tightly she almost lifted me onto my toes. Then Gabe grabbed me around, and we started to dance.... Miss Maple took his other hand and the three of us were out in the middle of the floor, hands raised and feet stomping.... Jesse had her skirt raised in the throes of a mean flamenco. And wonder of wonders, Esther smiled. But I think it was Peaches who started to sing. I know she has the best voice and the spiritual off high and sweet. (225)

This birth of the baby by the virgin mother has been made special by the inhabitants of the place and "nothing important can happen unless they're all in it together as a community" (227). Montgomery explains the role of Mariam in *Bailey's Café*, "Mariam, a curiously virginal unwed mother whose touching account of anti-Semitism and sexism recreates a vital sisterhood among women of color across the Diaspora who often find themselves at odd with notion of female sexuality prescribed by patriarchy" ("Authority, Multivocality, and the New World Order" 188).

Virginia C. Fowler locates the bond shared by the women of Eve's boarding house in the subjection of their physical repression. She comments "[b]eing defined by the world exclusively in terms of their bodies is the bond shared by all the women in (both) the novel(s)" (*Gloria Naylor: In Search of Sanctuary* 132). And this consciousness of only physical definition of their self by the world leads these women to define themselves or control their sexuality which in turn puts them in conflict with their male counterparts or more precisely the previously controller of their sexuality.

The chapter has made an attempt to explore the uncanny world of power which is inescapable as it is inextricable embedded into the rubric of knowledge and the process of subjectivization. The chapter begins with the basic philosophy of nature, form and function of power. It also explains the oppressive tendency of power which expels the dispossessed, isolated, and destitute to the brink of margin and thus creates a marginal space for those who are powerless. The marginal space contains a Hegelian dialectics in itself as it becomes a recluse or sojourn for the dispossessed but it also becomes a site of resistance. The antinomy of power does not only allow the character to explore its space in the world but it allows the character to be trapped into the eminence of power which is imminent. The entrapment of characters into the vortex of power at the marginal place inculcates a rebellious tendency in them. Gloria Naylor through her characters in the novel *Bailey's Café* explicates and delineates the entire process of objectification and subjectification in which her characters experience the odor of repressive, oppressive, and exploitative nature of power. This allows the characters of the novel to play with the aporatic nature of marginal space. Further, the novel expounds the fact that female subjectivity can enjoy its reality only at Eve's place as it is the place of female bonding where the female share common experiences and the world view. Naylor provides her characters with the place of Eve, only as sojourn where they may recollect enough energy so that they may fight against the power of patriarch and may continue their search into the dismal and eliminating space where they may find their subjectivity or the world view.

Chapter 6

Dialectical Opposition and Continuum: Resistance in Gloria Naylor's *The Men of Brewster Place*

The present chapter attempts to explore how the mechanism of repression subjectivizes both African American men and women, irrespective of their gender. The chapter exemplifies the shared phenomenon of repression in the lives of the characters in Gloria Naylor's *The Men of Brewster Place* (1998), which emanates from their shared experiences of the process of subjectivization by the hegemonic power structure. The men in the novel share the same marginal space, 'Brewster Place' along with the women in Naylor's *The Women of Brewster Place* (1982). However, *The Women of Brewster Place* is largely dominated by the female characters where men are mostly absent or they are presented as the perpetuators of the oppression on female autonomy. Moreover, *The Men of Brewster Place* provides the men with an opportunity to justify their deeds and to prove their instance to be the compatriot in the saga of resistance against the power structure. Further, the chapter also explores how the experiences of men extrapolate the process of an implicit continuum between the condition of the oppressor and the oppressed in the novel which conspicuously reveals post structuralist concepts of dialectical opposition and continuum. In other words, 'men' are oppressors as far as their relationships with the women are concerned; however, the same men become oppressed when they come under the aegis of the oppressive system of subjectivization through the power structure of a hegemonic society. The synchronic phenomenon of black men to be oppressor and the oppressed at the same time may be traced through Gloria Wade-Gayles *No Crystal Stair: Visions of Race and Sex in Black Women's Fiction* (1984). She expresses the omnipresent phenomenon of racism in the lives of the black people, irrespective of their gender, through the imagery of circles in the following paragraph in order to specifically sketch the condition of black women in American society who by virtue of their race and gender are the most oppressed category, however, it equally expresses the liminal condition of the black men:

> There are three major circles of reality in American society, which reflect degrees of power and powerlessness. There is a large circle in which white people, most of them men, experience influence and power. Far away from it there is a smaller circle, a narrow space, in which black people, regardless of sex, experience uncertainty, exploitation, and powerlessness. Hidden in this second circle is a third, a small, dark enclosure in which black women experience pain, isolation, and vulnerability. These are the distinguishing marks of black womanhood in white America. (34)

The aforementioned paragraph proposes the nature of duality as far as power, function, and place of black men are concerned. They confront the phenomenon of discreet oppositions and continuum between the oppressor and the oppressed in their everyday life on American soil with regard to the condition of women. They are the victims of racial discrimination but perpetuators of sexism against their own women. Confronted with the reality that the patriarchal order around which society is structured does not allow black men an equal access at par with their white counterparts, the exploration reveals that the black men act both as the oppressor and the oppressed. Gloria Naylor's novel *The Men of Brewster Place* is a running discourse on black male sexuality and stereotyping which adheres to the fact that they are both the oppressors and the oppressed. These males are the product of socio-economic and political situations with which they are constantly at conflict. Moreover, the men of

Brewster Place like the women of Brewster Place are constantly being controlled by the power structure of the imperialist, capitalist society. The phenomenon in context avers for the fact what Raymond Williams and some other Marxist thinkers call the nexus between the base and superstructure/infrastructure "which can be discovered by analysis" (5). The control of the base, "the means of production or capital" allows the white imperialist and capitalist to incisively control the superstructure of the socio-political order (05).

However, a close examination into the contemporary African American women's literature establishes that black men have not been portrayed positively. Edward M. Jackson in his book, *Images of Black Men in Black Women Writers 1950-1990* (1992) mentions the negativity of the descriptions of black males, citing an example of Alice Walker, Ntozake Shange, and Maya Angelou. He writes "[p]ositive images of black males are the exceptions, rather than the rule" (22). Black masculinity is, as suggested by Delgado and Stefancic, "the social construction of men of color is even more troublesome and confining than that of men in general" (211). For instance, their research into black manhood in contemporary America, lead White and Cones to assert, "the racial stereotypes [related to black masculinity] have been confirmed, validated, and deepened until they have taken on a life of their own" (47). Black males are viewed as "... uncivilized and subhuman...[and] sex obsessed..." (Johnson and McCluskey xiii). Such and some other stereotypes negatively affect black men's quests for normative manhood. The possible reason for the negative stereotyping of black males is that the women feel that black men do not acknowledge the gender struggle within their own race. If black women feel completely neglected and are misunderstood by their own men, how can they define themselves in fiction as supportive partners? In addition, black women have been trying to find their niche in the feminist movement. Feminist literature has often represented males as oppressors, and such an act of scripting men as oppressor in black women's literature may present a negative impression of the black male. Naylor has participated in the discourse of the hegemonic control of African American men with the publication of her first novel *The Women of Brewster Place*, itself through "the superstructural process" of representing "the reality of the base" (Williams 5). Naylor makes an attempt in the following paragraph to justify her negative portrayal of African American men in her first novel *The Women of Brewster Place*:

> [T]here was something that I was very self-conscious about with my first novel; I bent over backwards not to have a negative message come through about the men. My emotional energy was spent creating a woman's world, telling her side of it because I knew it hadn't been done enough in literature. But I worried about whether or not the problems that were being caused by the men in the women's lives would be interpreted as some bitter statement I had to make about black man. (Naylor and Morrison 23)

Naylor makes it clear that her negative portrayal of the men is the consequence of the underlying sexist and patriarchal behavior that they exhibit in their relationship when they negotiate with their women which is vividly delineated in her first novel *The Women of Brewster Place*. Hence, she does not depict and voice the male world view in her novel rather she constructs a sanctuary for the dispossessed women, and for which she is criticized. Further, Naylor discovers that she has not been criticized for the non-portrayal of men in her first novel, *The Women of Brewster Place,* rather how she has been militant or radical enough to portray only women. This attitude underlines the sexist color of the critics; she deliberates the same in one of her interviews:

> But I've always thought that was not what they were really asking. I always thought what was under that was not, "Why haven't you written about men here?" but, "How dare you write about women? How dare you highlight or celebrate this which we have despised to the point that we weren't even taught that they existed or that they did such wonderful things for this country and the arts? How dare you be so militant about this happening?" But I never apologize, never ever. I will say, "I was not telling your story; I was telling your mother's

> story. Now please tell me what is wrong with that?" and then they'll say, "Well, but the men are all so negative." (Perry 85)

Naylor recognizes that the black male and female cannot be separated as both of them spell two vital issues of race and gender. She proposes that though the men may be patriarchal and oppressive as far as the gender relations or familial issues are concerned, they act as the compatriot of their women in their struggle against the hegemony of racial power structure. Men and women, Naylor explains to Felton and Loris, are:

> [I]nterwoven. Like how do you separate being a black woman? I think that when I am in a certain situations that it is not my gender that will govern the interactions, it is definitely my race. I think that my race has a more powerful effect upon influencing an environment or shaping a perception of me than my gender. I think the gender is the subtext to text for me as a black woman. ("The Human Spirit is a Kick-Ass Thing" 146)

Further, Naylor, in another interview with Virginia Fowler expresses her feeling about the African American men what she presents in *The Men of Brewster Place*, "I think if you want to know how I feel about that subject; the last work is probably more telling of my feelings on the whole subject. There the men, if they do fail, they are well meaning in their failures" ("A Conversation with Gloria Naylor" 135-36). Naylor tells Charles Rowell, before the arrival of the novel, *The Men of Brewster Place* that the novel primarily focuses upon the men and their positionality in relation with their family and the power structure that constructs them:

> Now what's going to be interesting for me is to see how *The Men of Brewster Place* finally comes to being. I'm pretty sure it's going to be looking at relationships between men and their families. When you do get writing about black men, normally it's directed at men struggling with the white world for something—for dignity, for self-respect, for some gains, financial or psychological. Their opponent is always the white world. I would love to

> look at black men in relationship to their families. Don't take them anywhere out there to meet what's going on past Brewster Place, but right there—right there where they're standing. (159)

In the very beginning of the novel, *The Men of Brewster Place* itself, Naylor makes the aforementioned proposition of the existence of African American men together with their women through Ben, a leading character who reiterates the fact that the men and women at Brewster Place share the same helplessness and hardship as both of them are the integral part of the marginal space and both of them have been subjected to the racial repression in American society:

> I'm not about to argue was it harder for some than for others: Who's got it worse, the Him with nothing in his pockets, scared to turn the knob on the door; or the Her waiting on the other side to stretch that nothing—once again—for supper? When your shoes is worn down ragged and loose, what hits the ground hardest—the heel or the toe? Them are questions that ain't got no easy answer and I'm the first to admit I ain't got no fancy words. (*MBP* 03)

Ben further supports the proposition of the mutual existence of men and women in the society when he reiterates that "I don't know a man who would be anywhere without a woman. And don't know a woman who'd be anywhere without a man. It's how God did it; and we sure can't undo it" (07). Naylor attempts to exhibit further that the men are not only patriarchal and oppressive as has been portrayed in the first novel rather have love and respect for their women too, however, their affection meets with sheer helplessness because of their socio-economic conditions and their marginal reality "...their men loved them too.... There's a lot of sad things in the world; but a poor man having to keep looking into the eyes of a poor woman with no earthly reason why is one of the saddest things I know. And I saw it over and over here on the Brewster Place" (04). However, despite their socio-economic constraints, the men always put their all hard work to make their women happy because they are integral parts of their lives:

> But if there was a woman anywhere around him, he had to hope for better 'cause she was the other half; the other arm, the other eye—stepping right up on his shoulders to reach for a dream. And that's about as much poetry you'll ever get from the likes of me. I do not know fancy words, but I do know men. And the ones here, proud most of 'em, pitiful some—but hard working, all of 'em. If they was working at a job or just working at despair. And with each of 'em—no matter who he was—there was always a Her in his story. (08)

As the above paragraph suggests, there has always been a woman in the life of every man here on Brewster Place which also reinstates the fact that these men like the women of the marginal space have gone "through suffering and pain" to reach to this marginal space (hooks, *Yearning* 148). This proposition reasserts the fact that the African Americans are subjectivised to the power structure irrespective of their gender. The realization of the commonality of their shared experiences of repression in hegemonic world may goad them to form a bond among themselves to resist their subjectivization in the capitalist hegemonic world order. However, the only hope of forming the bond among the men of Brewster Place emanates from the fact that they all share the same marginal space or the state of marginality which the Brewster Place alone represents. Jackie Thomas avers the same in his review of Naylor's *The Men of Brewster Place*, when he says, "[a]ll of these men have unique situation that tie them to Brewster Place. The gifted piano player, Brother Jerome, captures the plight of all black men of Brewster Place through his playing of the blues. Although he is labelled a "retarded child," he is the silent, brilliant force that is able to put things together through his music" (NP). The discursiveness of the text exemplifies that the sound of Jerome's music is the only comfort that the men of Brewster Place may receive after the work of a hard day; the only hope which gives solace in the mundane world of oppressive structure. Also he acts as a binding force in the neglected, repressed and oppressive arena of the marginal space of Brewster Place because almost every man in Brewster Place identifies himself with his music as if "[h]is music is telling us [them] about our [their] lives" (*MBP* 37). What appeals to everybody in his music is the plight of the black man in oppressive world that he sings and which invariably affects everyone who lives in Brewster Place and "he could make that piano tell any story that he wanted. And it was *your* story if you listened real hard" (32). However, those who are not able to identify themselves with his narrative may "just hear what he was playing and be amazed" but those who "really listened... [may] began to cry. Because it was the blues, nothing but the blues coming from that boy's heart through that piano reading your life—and sometimes his" (32). It also reiterates the fact that only the repressed may appreciate Jerome's narratives through his playing of blues. It is the wish in the form of the 'Amens' coming from almost every apartment in Brewster Place which unites the oppressed and the exploited through Jerome' blues:

> Maybe he heard the Amens coming from a tired man dragging his body up the cracked and dirty stoop of 314 from a job where he was overworked and underpaid. The Amens from an apartment in 312 where a man is fighting back tears as he smashes his fist into a wall to keep from hitting the bitter woman who's thrown his life back into his face telling him that whatever he's doing is not enough. The Amens from 316 as a man turns over in bed having lost the strength to get up and keep looking for another low-paying job. The Amen brothers coming from every brick; every piece of concrete and iron railing on Brewster Place as Jerome played, filling the sweet with the sound of a black man's blues.... (*MBP* 37)

It is rightly divulged from the foregone discussion that the implicit or explicit bonding among the men at Brewster Place is programmatically made possible precisely as they share almost the same aesthetic experience of the music which coevally incepts from the *Melopoeia* of Jerome which further creates a *phanopoeic* and *pathopoeic* situations. There is yet another element which creates an inextricable bonding among the men at Brewster Place. It is the motif of Barber shop. Naylor has used the metaphor of the barbershop to carve a space for black male and to exhibit the bond that they may share "[t]his is the only place for us men to get together, to look into each other's eyes and see what we need to see—that we do more than just exist—we thrive and we are alive" (167). Jackie Thomas has also found the barbershop as a creative and potential site for black man. He explains that "the barbershop is the central metaphor that serves as a house of refuge, a place where debate and understanding take place. The barbershop is the place where all the Black men come to be themselves and to discuss their lives and society...they discuss their present conditions, vent their frustrations, and dream about more promising future" (NP). Similarly, Terry Sinclair Bozeman too points out in his thesis that:

> The barbershop is a space that finds a home in virtually every community in which you find Black males. To some degree, virtually all genres and periods of African American literary expression have situated the barbershop as a mediating space in the formulation of a Black masculine identity. The barbershop as mediating space allows Black males the opportunity to view themselves and also critique the ways in which they are gazed upon by the literary imagination. (02)

His finding "that we cannot fully understand the literary formation of Black masculine identity unless we attend to the barbershop as a formative mediating space" (02) may appropriately be applied to understand the condition of the black males in the Brewster Place which provides the aesthetic, political and creative space for the men. He further argues that:

> [T]he intrinsic nature of the relationship Black men have with the barbershop as mediating space and their embracing of "cool aesthetic" in their quest for an American masculine identity proves to validate the need for such spaces. This need primarily rests in Black men needing to shape their own sense of masculinity against and/or as refutation of a negated masculinity in a hostile society. (03)

The black men get a chance to discuss so many issues at Brewster Place that they hardly find any chance to speak about anywhere else, "[t]he issues they solve boil down to three subjects: white men, black men, and women. The white man carries all the guilts for messing up the world; the black man gets all the blame; and women are just a downright confusing issue that a hundred barbershop politician wouldn't be able to solve. Why are women so difficult to get along with?" (*MBP* 158). Sometimes people do scan the problem of the white people which comes out to be something serious among the general gossip of these men. Generally the blame for everything is laid down on the shoulders of white men but a couple of them are those who see the things in different light "[t]he white man. The white man. I'm so sick of hearing about the white man. When are we gonna face up to our own lives and the stuff we do. The white man ain't in that bed helping these girls get pregnant just to then run off and leave 'em" (159).

Naylor presents the barbershop to trace the evolution of black masculine identity and the creation of the black subjectivity by providing some kind of space or platform for their ideas. The barbershop on the one hand is a location of the marginal space where the characters from different locations of the marginal space and from the state of marginality throng to discuss several issues which are inextricably intertwined with their lives. It depicts the fact that the motif of the barbershop is a site where marginal can locate his identity by discussing the self and the others. The entire ambit of discussion among several characters who themselves and with their datum represent a kind of bricolage and space for attaining their subjectivity of black masculinity. Characters who generally approach to the place in search of their subjectivity of course, with a given trace, is first identified in the form of Greasy who looks within himself and tries to relate himself with other men when he says "I'm a man" (161). Greasy responds with all candidness to all men who assemble at the site of the barbershop, however, nobody knows as what exactly has happened to him but it could be guessed that he has been on conflict with something either with himself or with the white culture around him that he loses his job and is driven mad:

> To look at him the way he is now it's hard to imagine that this man once had a job, a home, and a future. But

> when crack started eating away at his brains, he lost it all in just that order: first his job as an airline ticket agent, then his brick home complete with a wife and two kids, to finally be left with a future in which his head was an empty shell, allowing only space for the winds of his nightmares to keep howling and howling. (159-60)

Initially, Greasy represents an aporatic condition because on the one hand he recognizes himself as a part of the complex world of black masculinity but on the other he behaves irresolutely towards his association with the entire group of the black male at Brewster Place. Similarly, the male world at barbershop also treats him contingently without any firm belief in his subjectivity. Thus, the discussion may explain the fact that the black people are unable to associate themselves with him and they feel that they are different from him, ignoring the fact that the society where they live, the same may happen with anybody. This realization comes to these people quite late when Greasy ends his life. Greasy has been "bleeding inside. But we were so busy being thankful that we weren't him; so busy judging and feeling superior, pitting our half a minds against his none, that we forgot he was our 'brother' and where he goes we go—if we like it or not. Yeah, if we had remembered that things might have turned out real different that muggy day at the end of October" (163). The sudden and uneventful suicide of Greasy, however, reminds the men of the Brewster Place of their historical, political, and social realities. Maxine Lavon Montgomery in her review of Naylor's *The Men of Brewster Place* explains that the purpose of the construction of the barbershop remains unfulfilled as the men could not rescue Greasy from succumbing to his death. She explicates "the barbershop, a well-defined space, with its emphasis on male bonding and brotherliness, is limited in its role in bringing about solidarity. The brothers, however, well-meaning, fail to rescue the suicidal Greasy, whose crack addiction leads to and is the consequence of despair. Greasy's final unraveling plea 'I'm a man. I'm a man' falls on deaf ears" (NP). After his death, men definitely feel sad and they know that they have been responsible to a certain extent for his death but are not able to take the blame, "[w]e all remembered what it was like to go home and wash his blood from our clothes, our faces, and above all, our hands. To have a look into our mirrors and lie to ourselves it wasn't our fault" (*MBP* 166). However, Jackie points that through Greasy's character, Naylor has tried to universalize the subjectivization of all blacks, "[i]t is through Greasy's death that the black men notice that, they are all the same, that their problems are also the same ones that Greasy once fought on a daily basis. They are all men who are hurting, struggling, coping and trying to make the best of what is left of their lives" (NP). It is not only the story of Greasy which narrates several untold narrations which are teamed with miserable plights and predicament and articulates a repressed story of subjectivization; in fact, there have been hundreds of such stories—they have been some "rejoicing" as well as of "grief" because grief is not something that is experienced by a woman only rather men too feel it but their way is different (*MBP* 163).

A man cannot cry out because a man hardly shows his grief to the outside world but remains choked within himself, "[a]lthough a man grieves different from a woman, a whole lot more is kept inside to bite him a little here, a little there, until the blood begins to flow. And when the blood begins to flow, it'll have to fill up every space in his body before you finally see it in his eyes. Men cry as much as women—but most just cry inside" (163). Naylor's emphasis again on marginal space of Brewster Place to portray the men is an attempt to represent the other side of the gender dynamics which narrates the fact that the men too may have a feeling of love and hatred. They also carry the same experience of repression which is laid upon them by the power structure in the society and at times, it really becomes difficult to express the unspeakable. Gloria Naylor presents several characters who experience severe pain and agony which is indeed an outcome of the repressive white capitalist world order. Characters identify themselves with one another as they share the same experience. However, the shared identification of their experiences of with one another may reiterate the phenomenon of the perpetuation of the repressive ideology in the lives of all men. In other words, the experiences of the trials and tribulation of the men of Brewster Place bind them together. The saga of their marginal experience and bonding now can be viewed and examined through initially with Ben, a marginal character in Naylor's first novel *The Women of Brewster Place* acts as an archetype of the repression in *The Men of Brewster Place*. Maxine points that "his (Ben's) history of injustice, anger, powerlessness, and despair offers a historical frame for the contextualization of the stories the other men relate" (Montgomery, "Review" NP). Ben's story also allows an insight into the deep seated anger in the black men that emanates from their condition of helplessness, partially because of his wife's inclination towards mainstream white culture and partially because of his socio-economic conditions. Ben's retreat into the alcoholism is an example of his frustration and helplessness that he encountered in his life because he could not save his daughter from being sexually exploited by his landlord, Mr. Clyde. In order to further universalize Ben's experiences in the racial hegemonic world order, Naylor has illustrated his grandfather's story which exemplifies the experiences of the same helplessness in his life. Maxine explains the shared helplessness of Ben and his grandfather when she articulates that "Ben, like his grandfather, an ex-slave turned sharecropper who is unable to protect a sister from the sexual abuse black women often experiences, fails to rescue his daughter from Mr. Clyde's sexual exploitation" (NP). Grandpa Jones initially appears to be a very calm and quiet man; he has been holding a silence within him "because there was no words he could use to talk about silence" (*MBP* 15). Grandpa's silence stems from his helplessness in a white world to protect his sister, a ten year old girl from being raped by the white master on the one side and the acceptance the brutality by his own people on the other:

> The slaves all go back to work. A new day begins. But Grandpa listens for someone to say, It was wrong. He listens in the field, in the slave quarters beside the door of the house servants—all in vain.... And that is when he understands that—freedom or no freedom—his people are doomed. It doesn't matter what's in their hearts; what's in your heart only God hears. But they—each of them—need to hear, among themselves somewhere, somehow, that this was wrong. (15)

As a result, Grandpa has lost his faith in God and religion because he finds it all favoring the dominant white. Grandpa Jones questions the power structure that unjustly favors the whites, the locus of power; he always asks "I'm opening this Bible when someone shows me the place that says white people is going to hell" (12). Grandpa here extrapolates the fact that the power structure functions through its close association with religious institutions and the civil society. Religion functions *in tandem* with power in the entire process of subjectivization. He therefore "shunned the church, holding a closed Bible, while he searched for another kind of God in another kind of world than the one who told black men that the only way to be a man was to suffer and be still" (15-16). Contrary to his Grandpa, Ben's Grandma is a religious lady who has faith in the almighty and hence says "be grateful for what the Lord gives you, she said over and over throughout my childhood. Be grateful" which used to make Ben bewildering as "which Lord she meant—her God or the one my grandfather waited on to wreak vengeance" (16). When Ben comes out of the farms, he is able to realize the theory of his Grandpa which has always tried to establish the fact that white men are privileged in this society while blacks are not. Ben discovers "coming out of those back fields, I kinda understood. There wasn't a whole lot of work for black men like us outside of picking cotton; and some would do anything to keep from having to go back to the fields" (18). Ben further in his life experiences everything what his Grandpa has never shared in his life time. His first exposure introduces him with a clear demarcation of black and white territories when he is working as a shoeshine boy:

> The shoeshine chairs were set up in a row of twelve—ten for the white customers and two spaced a bit apart for the Negro customers. Somehow all the passengers knew this arrangement without the railroad needing to put any sign up...I didn't mind working the Negro chairs. There was usually a line of Negro men waiting their turn for those two seats and they tipped as well as any other customer—sometimes more. (19-20)

Maxine finds Ben's experiences addressing the concerns of all black men in the community. She explains that "Ben's touching story links the past, present, and future in such a way as to direct attention to the timelessness of the black male situation" ("Review" NP). Ben's silence and alcoholism, like his Grandpa, have a story of helplessness and socio-economic exploitation. Since once Ben reaches to the Brewster Place, he becomes silent, his story remains untold:

> Nobody knows my true story—and never will—as it is my turn to be the silent old man as I inherit more than my share of the pain riding on the question, What does it mean to be a man? Even now at sixty-eight I'm still wondering. If I had killed Clyde Haggard, the law kills me. If I had killed Elvira, the law puts me in jail for life. If I killed myself, there was no one but an understanding God to face. So I settled on killing myself—slowly with booze—and on God understanding that I'm fighting for my manhood. There is no way to face my daughter's eyes, even in memory, as she said, He laughed, Daddy. He laughed. And laughed. (*MBP* 28)

The aforementioned account of Ben's helplessness and subjectivity as a poor black man narrates the uncovered story that impels him to take refuge in alcoholism. A close examination of Ben's story exemplifies that his whole journey of life in itself has been a struggle since the very beginning, "...I ain't never been in a situation where anybody called me sir" and the place that he hails from is Richmond, "a place where you worked until you were bone-tired and then had a choice to pray—or party—the misery way" (12). His miserable life is entrenched by a white-masked black wife, Elvira whose entry in his life gets him back to farming where they hardly meet with their livelihood "you ended up farming for the sake of a place to eat and sleep. A little more than slavery but a lot less than doing well" (21). It marks the beginning of Ben's sufferings caused by his wife who unjustly favors his white masters simply for being white. A close observation into the life of Elvira negotiates with the fact that this abhorrence by Elvira for her family stems from her belief "everything white that God put in this world was good. And everything black was to be despised. Elvira didn't even take her coffee black; "It'll just make me darker," she said" (22). Ms. Elvira continues with her project of subjectivizing her daughter and for that she brings Mr. Clyde into the entire matrix of her family discourse. In relation to this the position of Ben reiterates the silencing of blacks for economic reasons as it is Mr. Clyde's farm where Ben works as sharecropper which in turn is the only way of their survival. Mr. Clyde takes benefit of the situation by asking Ben and Elvira to let their daughter help him in his house where he takes the advantage of seducing her. It is exposed when after two months their daughter explodes:

> Things went well for about two months, and then I noticed that when she came home there were tears in her eyes.... And she began to cry. That's when she told us everything: how Mr. Clyde had been trying to mess with her almost from the beginning, how it was hard 'cause he'd follow her around the house, whispering nasty things in her ears. (22)

The very realization of his daughter being subjected to sexual abuse by Mr. Clyde makes Ben restless which is expressed in his aside and which presents a picture of collective helplessness of all black males in a racial society:

> I watch my daughter come through the gate with her eyes on the ground, and she slowly climbs up on the porch. She takes each step at a time, and her shoes grate against the rough boards. She finally turns her beaten eyes into my face and what is left of my soul to crush is taken care of by the bell-like voice that greets us. Mornin' Daddy Ben. Mornin', Mama. (23)

The perpetual effort of the oppressor to engrave the pain of Ben who is now helpless as he finds himself entrapped into the suffocating and murky world of dominant power structure. This helpless man is further disheartened by his black-masked white wife, who is white in her taste and temperament though black in color. She supports whatever is white and despises the black. She stands as a replica of the dominant ideology and power structure and hence, functions as an apparatus to perpetuate the oppressive machinery of the white. Her hegemonic and colonized attitude does not allow her to support Ben, and for that reason, the helpless Ben is unable to save his daughter from the tyrannical hands of the imperialist-capitalist white. In addition, Elvira takes Mr. Clyde's favor and despite knowing everything, asks Ben to thank Mr. Clyde for everything, in a sense she forces him to accept everything unquestioningly of whatever Mr. Clyde does. Ben is aware of Clyde's cobwebs that exist in his psychological realities as far as the dominance of the marginal through the power structure is concerned and hence, whenever Ben sees Mr. Clyde, blood runs through his ear pits and he loses his senses. However, he is rebuked by his wife "Man, what is wrong with you? Ain't you heard Mr. Clyde talkin' to you, and you just standin' there like a hunk of stone. You better get some sense in your head 'fore I knock some in you" (24). Ignoring his wife, he "stand[s] there with my hands in my pockets, staring at the tracks in the dirt where the truck had been. I keep balling my fists in my overalls until my nails dig into my palms" (24).

The preceding examination of Ben's condition in his family reveals that Elvira, who is psychologically, economically and socially interpellated by the powerful structure of capitalist society, ignores almost all beseechments made by her husband and she in fact rebukes him and propels him to accept the dominance and the bounty of the white master, Mr. Clyde. In addition, she accuses Ben of his lazy and unlivable conditions. She with her all whims and fancies supports the behavior and the function of Mr. Clyde. Naylor has indeed represented through Elvira's character a person who is the perpetuator of the capitalist machinery as she is deeply conditioned by the sense of power. It is exemplary in that Ben's request to his wife to look seriously into the matter of their daughter's exploitation by Mr. Clyde meets with all suspicion and complaints because Mr. Clyde spells power and superiority. Consequently, Ben meets nothing but contempt for complaining against Mr. Clyde who holds a godly figure for Elvira as she answers Ben's complaints with all possible bitterness in her mouth "She came to us with a bundle of lies 'bout Mr. Clyde 'cause she's too damn lazy to work. Why would a decent widow man want to mess with a little nothin' like her? No, anything to get out of work—just like you" (25). Whenever he tries to communicate Elvira about the miserable condition of his daughter and of her exploitation by the white oppressor, her "voice gets shrill[ed]. So it's a big house. It ain't like this shit you got us livin' in. It takes her longer to do things than most of folks. You know that, so why stand there carryin' on like it mean more than that?" (25). Once after he mutely resisted Mr. Clyde by not greeting him, he is rebuked for doing so by Elvira:

> Elvira comes across the porch and sneers into my face. If you was half a man, you coulda given me more babies and we woulda had some help workin' this land instead of a half-grown woman we gotta carry the load for. And if you was even a quarter of a man, we wouldn't be a bunch of miserable sharecroppers on someone else's land—but we is, Ben. And I'll be damned if I'll see the little bit we got taken away 'cause you believe that gal's low-down lies. So when Mister Clyde come by here, you speak—hear me? And you act as grateful as your pitiful ass should be for the favors he done us. (26)

Elvira's constant abhorrence of Ben and his inaction makes the girl leave them one day "leaving behind a note saying that she loves us very much, but she knows that she has been a burden and she understands why we made her keep working at Mr. Clyde's house. But she feels that if she has to earn her keep that way, she might as well go to Memphis where the money is better" (27). After their daughter disappears, Elvira too leaves Ben "for another man who worked on the next plantation over. And I left Tennessee and moved up north, taking one job after another, until I stumbled upon Brewster Place; I've been ever since" (27). And thus his expedition to Brewster Place begins and ends. Ben's narrative is an example of the socio-economic challenges to keep a family intact and immune from the oppressive power structure of the capitalist whites in America.

The forlorn and untold story of the subaltern, marginal speaks with all volume of the role and the function of the oppressive power structure in the process of subject formation. The novel exemplifies the process of subjectivization in which all characters are conditioned and constructed. In other words, characters in the novel are subjectivised and oppressed by the hegemonic power structure simple because they are black and poor. It is not only Ben who narrates the story of oppression and subjectivization but even Basil also narrates the similar narratives. Basil is described as a "no-good" son who is said to have been the reason behind Mattie's marginalization in Brewster Place "[r]umor had it that it had given her a no-good son who caused her to be on Brewster Place" (41). This impression is taken from Naylor's first novel, *The Women of Brewster Place* which narrates a story till Basil jumps the bail and Mattie has to leave the house which has been taken for bond. He leaves Mattie with no choice but to move to Brewster Place as Ben points "[t]he only thing I did know—for a fact—is that she ended up on Brewster Place, just like the rest, 'cause she had no choice. And she stayed for the same reason" (42). Naylor shifts the narrative perspective towards Basil and a sincere effort is initiated to understand why he runs away leaving a loving mother who has been everything to him. A close examination of Basil's narrative reveals the fact that Basil jumps out the bail because of his distrust in American system of power structure and its orientation towards the black males which explains the situation of every black man and his subjectivization. His impression of the judicial system which is one of the institutions that perpetuates the ideology of the dominant class is expressed in the following paragraph:

> The state nails me for involuntary manslaughter. Some high-priced lawyer my mother hired said, Don't worry, a clean record, no prior arrests, they'll dismiss the charges. Sure, for white men like him—no charges. But the court already had my butt in jail with bail set at an outrageous five hundred thousand. Ten percent down, said the bail bondsman. The only thing she had was her home—free and clear—after thirty years. So her hundred percent went into their ten percent. And if I could have believed in the system the way she did, I wouldn't have run. (45)

Naylor explicates the process of subject formation through the case of Basil. It is evident that the experiences of the African Americans and their socio-economic conditions allot a back seat to them. Basil experiences the mechanics of rationalization, institutionalization and bureaucratization, which are important instruments of subject formation. Basil along with his mother also experiences the clumsy and oppressive system of bureaucratic machinery which operates in such a way that rationalizes the category of possessed and oppressed. The process of rationalization sets the dominant free from the mechanics of institutionalization and bureaucratization, whereas the oppressed and exploited as in the case of Basil, is forced to go under such processes. Basil's act of running away from the unfathomable and intricate process of bureaucratization may be regarded as an escape of temporal victimhood; his resistance may be observed to surface when he plans to save two children—Jason and Eddie from being victimized by the power structure and repressive socio-economic conditions. They are the poor kids of Keisha, a mother who lives on welfare and always mistreats her kids which is evident in when outside the church "...little Eddie looked up at me with large brown eyes and asked, 'Are you my daddy?'", he is threatened by Keisha "[w]hen I get you home you're really gonna get it...I am sick of you doing this and embarrassing me" (53). Basil believes she needs a sensitive man who may come as a savior in her life and everything comes on the track, "unless someone breaks the cycle for her. And here's a chance" (57). Basil on the one hand is conditioned by the apparatuses of subjectivization but on the other he also defies the process of bureaucratization and rationalization. His ability to defy the social institutions allows him to shun his girlfriend and to share the experience of the oppressed or dispossessed Keisha. It is evident when he goes on to leave his beautiful girlfriend, "nut-brown skin, short natural hair, and a really nice body—small at the waist and full in the hips" (51) and marries Keisha. He ignores her girlfriend's concerns and reiterates his motif of helping the young boys "[y]ou know, Helen, we keep talking and talking about the situation with young black men. They're endangered species; they're a lost generation; on and on.... I can't solve the problem of a whole generation; but there are two little kids right here who I can help. So who not? Why couldn't I stay in their lives forever—why couldn't we both?" (56-57). For a girl like

Helen, all these points are irrelevant as she is concerned with her own benefits only. Helen is unable to understand that it's less of Keisha's fault than of the system that they have been living in such a situation. Basil who is aware of the power structure through his experiences believes that he "can make a difference in the lives of those boys" (57). Basil wants to fill the gap which has been created by the absence of a father in the lives of the boys. He "took the boys to the circus the following Saturday... I would've given anything if life was going to allow them to keep the look on their faces that day: the wonder and the magic of watching the impossible done again and again. Jason drank it all up like a sponge, but little Eddie needed convincing that the tigers weren't going to eat him" (55). He has several other plans for the boys too "I wanted to build a college fund for the boys.... They could be *anything* they wanted. I kept telling them. And Daddy's gonna be right there to cheer you on" (60). He marries Keisha for the sake of boys so that he may officially own the boys and may stop the maternal violence that Keisha uses to inflict on them. He eventually succeeds in "stop[ing] her from hitting my boys—for any reason. You don't always have to discipline a child with your hands. And I stopped her from telling them they were nothing when she was angry with them" (60). However, Basil's attempt to save the children from the subjectivization of the power structure meets with hopelessness as he is detected by the detectives when Keisha informed them and when he returns, he finds that the boys have been subjectivised by the hegemonic white world "Jason had already done time himself in juvenile detention for car theft and aggravated assault. And little Eddie had built a shell around himself, hard and permanent: he said he didn't know men. And that he didn't want to" (64). This underlies the fact that black masculinity is a construction of the power structure which is controlled as well as defined by the white world. Naylor with great astuteness and appropriateness portrays the patronizing and condescending attitude of the white, imperialist-capitalist power machinery. She reveals the fact that the process of subjectivization and acculturation continues by the white and it subjects almost all blacks who dwell in that domain. Basil's attempt to stop the subjectivization of the boys by the power structure may be said to have been a stand against the hegemonic world order which through socio-economic conditions may criminalize the black kids. However, his stand may also be read as an act of repentance for what he has done to his mother, Mattie Michael. He has broken his mother's trust in him and that's what has been ailing him ever since. However, he has been constantly planning to "honor her trust in...[him]. To take her away from that dead-end street where her love had placed her" (43-44). And he has also been grateful to his mother for the trust and care that she has imparted to him "[y]es, I thank my mother. I thank her for putting up her house for bail. For believing in me.... There she was, forced to leave her beautiful home to live on a street like Brewster Place. And you know what the funny thing is? I used those three years, when I didn't have the courage to call or write, doing exactly what I promised myself: I'm gonna pay her back" (43). However, when he goes to Brewster Place and discovers that Mattie is dead, all his dreams to see his mama and pay her back are shattered. He admits that "I can't undo my past, but I would find some woman, somewhere, and make her life happy. I would be the father I never had; I would act like the man I'd finally grown up to be" (44). Furthermore, when he goes to search for Mattie's place in Knoxville reiterates his proposition. When he reaches to knock at the door a woman comes out "I know instantly that she was alone. One baby holding onto the frayed hem of her housedress and another balanced on her hip. This is what happens without a man in the house, I thought" (49-50). This incident further reiterates his proposition to be a responsible man as he says "[a]nd I swore, once again, that I would not be that kind of man. I was going to be there for my children, that is, if I could have any.... I was here on earth for a reason. And I decided that reason was to be a solid family man..." (50). As discussed before, Basil makes a sincere effort to keep his promise, however, he is not able to confront the eminence of the power structure and is caught for his past misdeeds. Basil's case is a narrative of an individual who has himself been subjected to the repressive ideology of the hegemonic order, attempts to save his community from the oppressive structure which is exemplary in the case of the boys.

Like Basil, Eugene, Ciel's husband, carries a negative image in the community that he has deceptively cheated his wife. He is subjected to the power structure and compulsory heterosexuality. The capitalist patriarchal society does not recognize any other sexual orientation other than heterosexual, even any other orientation may be regarded as a potential threat to the existing social order and thus, to be abhorred. Homosexuality which may in one civilization and culture be treated as one of the supreme forms of relationship is treated as deviant relationship precisely because the character believes in the process of perfecting the self through the process of rationalization and bureaucratization. The social constructionism constrains his attempts to disclose his gay identity to his wife that keep on soaring the gap between them. Eugene's condition also invites the patriarchal order to revise the sexual norms of the society which often treats homosexuality as an abnormal activity. He is perfectly a normal man who loves his wife and his daughter, may experience the condition of human normalcy. He expresses his love for Ciel, his wife and Serena, his daughter and he expresses his happiness when he becomes father:

> But before I begin, you must believe that I did love you and Serena. I was so proud the day she was born; it was like a miracle watching you give birth. Can you remember that about me, with all the other crap that went on between us, can you at least remember that I was in the delivery room that day? Yeah, I know, crying and laughing at the same time. Acting like a stone fool, but proud, sweetheart, so proud of the daughter you gave me. It made me believe that we could really make it together after all. (69)

The aforementioned paragraph clearly explains that he loves his wife and daughter but there is some unrest deep within him which causes "crying and laughing at the same time" (69). His indecisiveness is explained by him as "[f]or the longest time I never picked up a man there or allowed myself to be picked up.... I would go home, kiss you hello, and then go into the bathroom to put my head down and cry. I turned the water on full force in the sink to cover the sounds of my crying. Proof again that there was something wrong with me" (83). Here, Eugene reflects upon the Nietzscheian philosophy of the subject as multiplicity which is deeply related to the condition of epistemological and ontological performativity. Eugene maintains multiple identities within himself, which tears him apart and he wants to tell everything to Ciel about himself but his sense of the manhood and his love for Ciel comes in between "[w]oman, I loved you so much, it hurt. But there was no way to tell you about myself. Do you understand? There was no way. And since I wasn't with you any longer, I could go to the Bull & Roses and ask myself, 'How does all of this feel now that I'm a single man?'" (84). Whenever he tries to go out with a man to satisfy his sexual urge with a man he feels contended but the very reminder of Ciel makes him feel guilty "[t]he first time I went home with another man from that bar, it felt so complete. At least, for a short while until the guilt of what I was doing to you came back to wrap itself around my chest and tighten into an iron knot" (84). Naylor suggests that Eugene is indeed in search of an ontological autonomous self rather than the one which oscillates between dialectics and ambivalence. She lights upon the fact that Eugene tries to make an attempt to debunk social constructionism but could not do so because of his love for Ciel and his desire for perfecting the self:

> ...I *was* afraid of what you would think of me if I walked into our apartment that very night to tell where I'd been and—more importantly—to tell you why. I decided, right there, for both of us, that you would hate me. I couldn't bear to think of the contempt that would be in your eyes. I was a man; and you would no longer see me as a man—your man—but as some sort of freak. Yes, Ceil, I decided right then and there that you would hate me as much as I hated myself. And so the lies began.... (82)

The viable apparatuses of social constructionism in the form of social acceptability and respect of oneself do not allow Eugene to unveil his identity as gay that keeps worsening the situation and ultimately, Eugene has to lose Ciel as well as Serena. Ben explains Eugene's grief when he comes to Brewster Place when people have been taking his daughter Serena for funeral. There has been pain in his eyes and he has been on the verge of committing suicide:

> He was grieving too hard to accept that child was dead. And I knew that his was the kind of grief that could swallow the whole world—himself included—if you let it get out of hand. I saw suicide in that boy's eyes and I prayed for him to get a grip on things. Just let the pain and the regrets wash over you; you won't drown although you'll feel like you will. No, the one fact about regrets is that they do ebb in time and you're faced with the hard decision to let your life go on or not. (162)

The death of Serena aggravates the pain of both Eugene and Ciel. They take different course of actions to heal the exacerbated situation. Ciel is healed by Mattie, the matriarch, whereas Eugene goes to Chino, his gay friend for redemption as he is getting restless and feels choked in the hotel room where he is staying in after Serena's death "the pain was circling and moving around me; making the air so thick I moved from place to place in that hotel room as if I were underwater.... Could there be greater pain than this? I didn't know but I was going to try and find out" (92). Chino directs him to a space where he lets his grief down:

> ...he said. "Assume the position." And so I pulled off my shirt and went to my knees. He whipped me until his arms grew tired, specks of my blood covering everything but the tiled ceiling.
>
> "Enough Sweet Water?"
>
> "No."
>
> "Please...."
>
> "No."
>
> So he kept on trying to stomach the work that was replacing my pain. Little by little replacing it.
>
> "Chino...."
>
> "Surely, it's enough, Sweet Water."
>
> "No," I said through a throat that was like sandpaper. "I'll tell you when to stop.... I'll tell you when to stop...." (93-94)

As it is evident through the above deliberation on Eugene's position in his family, his love and his oscillation between his urge of homosexuality and the compulsory heterosexual mask that he bears, have ruined his life. The hegemony of the power structure that necessitates heterosexuality, for instance, is an apparatus to control and to define the marginal people. However, the power politics subjectivizes the subjects not only from outside but also from inside. The process of subjectivization and the cruel game of power politics continue with Moreland T. Woods who cheats his own community and uses the conscience of the community for his selfish gains. It is interesting to note that Moreland is born and brought up in Brewster Place itself in dire economic circumstances. His grandmother works hard for providing him with whatever she can with "her fingers stiff with arthritis, sewing into the wee hours of the day to keep him in good schools, had been both mother and father to him for as long as he could remember" (100). However, his deceit emanates from his position where he may not identify and associate himself with his own people. Ben explains his position in Brewster Place:

> It's like his soul's been greased with Vaseline and nothing much really sticks there, nothing much is real. Is the man making a game of religion?... I do think that if your soul's so smooth it can just glide you right on through life, there's no way to understand that, how do you help him to heal the little wounds inside? The little wounds that can grow into big wounds, that can grow so fast they take over a life? I'll bet my bottom dollar that the Reverend Woods ain't never felt a wound like that. (98)

As expressed in the above paragraph, Moreland T. Woods makes religion a game and a stepping stone for his goals as he "...just have to take his ego and his plans for using Sinai Baptist as a political launching pad..." (107). Charles E. Wilson identifies Moreland T. Woods "as a colonized egomaniac whose only goal is to exalt himself" (159). However, his insensitivity towards his people brings him into conflict with Deacon Bennett who puts church over anything in his life and he "free from colonizing impulses, has different goals" (Wilson 159). This man has worked a lot to get more and more people into the church and has encouraged black men to recognize that the church "could be a place—and sometimes the only place—for a black man to exercise leadership and responsibility" (*MBP* 106). Moreland wants to satisfy his ego by constructing a new church as this may support his cause of political gain. Moreland exemplifies the Marxist position where it is established that religion is an institution which is exercised and employed by the forms of power structure to interpret realities for their personal benefits. However, Deacons' case is entirely different because he plans the funds of the church to be spent for community welfare:

> Not a larger church to fit the ego of this present minister, but larger contributions to a scholarship fund for some deserving college students; a community center with tutors for the younger children, a gym for the older ones—a refuge after school until evening when it was time for the parents—or parent—to come home from work. Deacon Bennett even visualized the church building or subsidizing low income housing for some of its members or the community at large. (107)

Moreland's will to power blinds him so conspicuously that he is ready to sacrifice the welfare of the people for his own selfish gains and "...had never understood the people who argued that building such an elaborate church was a waste of money that could be going out into the community to help fight poverty or drugs or a host of other concerns..." (105). Woods is "a heartless son of a bitch who wanted to get to the top without thinking about the people he had to step on?" (143-44). While the efforts of Deacon Bennett, Wilson finds, as way of rejecting the white society's definition of success "Bennett wants to help the community. His manhood is tied to his ability to improve the lives of others rather than paddling his own personal coffers. Bennett has rejected mainstream (white) society's definition of successful man (given the circumstances, an unattainable definition) and has embraced a notion of manhood that helps not only him (because it is attainable) but also others in his community" (160). Moreland is determined to have a new church to serve his own purpose and he has been so powerful on dice that losing him would affect the membership of the church badly. The boards, thus appears dwarf before Moreland and that is what Moreland takes advantage of. There is one flaw in

Moreland which everyone in the board knows that he is a great womanizer but proving this seems almost impossible, "[h]e is discreet with his womanizing, that was for sure. And when the women were called before the Deacons' board they all denied the rumors that had been circulating" (108). For Moreland, a woman is a non-entity because he knows how to handle them. Moreland thinks whatever the Deacons do to drag him out of the church, "[a]s long as he stayed single there was no chance of that: the married ones wouldn't talk, of course, and neither would the unmarried, hoping that they might be the next Mrs. Woods" (109). Much to the chagrin of Deacons' board and their continuous effort at opposing the construction of new church, Moreland gets a chance to attack the board when Sister Louise appears pregnant, allegedly by one of the members of the board. He takes the congregation into confidence and provokes the crowd to vote in favor of the construction of new church and Deacons' board is forced to allow the construction of the new church. Though the crowd could not understand his real motif, Bennett utters while the cornerstone of a new Sinai Baptist church is laid "I guess we'll be calling you Councilman Woods soon" (118); this is what Moreland is looking forward. The precedent discourse expounds the fact that the social fabric of Brewster Place is deeply woven into cruel, hegemonic and repressive power structure. Each character of Brewster Place covertly or overtly is entangled into the complex rubric of oppressor and oppressed. It represents a dialectics of the condition in which one is subjectivised and is oppressed and how the same character takes an important part into his movement from the oppressed to become an oppressor.

Similarly, in continuation of the narrative of Moreland T. Woods, the narrative of C.C. Baker explicates the same movement in which how an oppressed makes a willing attempt to become an oppressor. It exemplifies the reality of socio-economic condition which is woven into the complex knots of power structure and politics. Baker, once an oppressed kills his brother to get hold of power structure so that he may become an oppressor. The following narrative may sketch Baker's journey from an oppressed to the oppressor. However, it is his location into the marginal space which symbolizes the neglect and confinement of the subalterns into the periphery that motivates him to become the oppressor of his own people which he discovers as a step towards the economic dependence:

> He moves in a world where he doesn't need more than a fifty-word vocabulary. And half of that is some variation of the word, fuck.... And in his nineteen years he's never taken a trip out of the city. But he knows the streets around Brewster Place like the back of his hand. And in those thirty square blocks he has a place to sleep; finds food to eat; beer to drink; and a movie theatre to handle his dreams. He makes his money from pretty bustling; snatching a bag or two; running messages between a lady and her pimp; dropping off dime bags for mid-level drug dealers. But he dreams of so much more; he dreams of escape. He doesn't want to be a punk all his life. And the way out of the ghetto is to be taken on by Beetle Royal—a top-level dealer who keeps his business tight and his lieutenants in good cars and good clothes. (121-22)

The above deliberation on C.C. Baker exemplifies the fact that poverty, lack of education, and unemployment are a few constructs that subjectivize and construct an individual's conditions in a capitalist hegemonic world order. When he looks around himself in Brewster Place, he always discovers the synonyms of the same poverty and unemployment. His family too acts as an agency in motivating him to become the oppressor because of the economic condition "[h]is mother works full-time to keep them off welfare. But there are six children in this home—two his father brought from another marriage—and only so much energy to go around. ...C.C. Baker...sees missing in his father's life: money, power, and respect" (123). The intensity of the economic deprivation and hardship in Baker's family may be guessed by the fact that Baker "lies about the money he's bringing into the house—and they pretend to believe the lies because they need the help" which further encourages Baker to reveal his deeds in his family "No make-believe, no damn fairy tales: He is dealing and proud of it. And wants his old man to be proud of it too" (124-25).

His journey from the state of being economically and socially oppressed to be an oppressor is also motivated by his imposed sense of manhood. Naylor makes it quite clear how the black manhood is the construction of the society in one of her interviews with Virginia Fowler when she is asked about the rape scene in her first novel *The Women of Brewster Place*:

> I remember deliberately taking the narrative risk with that rape to stop the action...and to explain why that young man is raping her and to point the finger toward society and their definition of manhood. I wanted them to see that what's raping this woman, among other things, is society's conception of manhood, and their low evaluation of women. And no, I don't connect that at all to mothering, to how C.C. Baker was mothered. It was how he was taught he could be a man by society. (134-35)

The aforementioned paragraph explicates the fact that the societal power structure dictates the black man that in order to be a true 'man', one needs to be cruel, courageous, and fearless. He should also know and learn to control, to define and to subjugate women whose liberty may act as a threat to his possessed manhood. Complying with the definition of black manhood, he rapes Lorraine and kills his own brother, "[h]e does as instructed: he throws the gun by the body and runs off. The punk-ass deserved it. C.C. runs and he runs...C.C. runs and runs until he's crying from the cold wind whipping his face as he thanks God for giving him the courage to do it. The courage to be a man" (129). C.C. Baker appears to be a victim of social constructionism and state apparatuses which not only have subjectivised his self but also have pushed him into the game of power structure where his fate is waiting the same end as his brother has met.

However, the only character who may identify marginal space as a "site of resistance" is Kiswana's boyfriend Abshu (hooks, *Yearning* 148). He too has been born and brought up in the same poverty-stricken Brewster Street "...his father was a brutal man; a man who brought every insult, every failed job application, back to their home at night. And what he couldn't say—or wouldn't say—to the outside world, he said to Abshu's mother with his fists" (*MBP* 136). It is because of his socio-economic conditions, he is brought up in a foster house. The people he has been living with in foster "weren't mean people, but they were stingy—stingy with their food and with their affection. Existing that way all the time, on the edge of hunger, on the edge of kindness, gave Abshu an appreciation for a life fully lived" (140). Anyhow he has promises to himself not to let any black child suffer like he did and committed himself for the cause of them. He is also a playwright which he uses "to broaden the horizons for the young, gifted, and black—which was how he saw every child milling around that dark street" (135). His motto of life is "Lose no child to the street. And on occasion when that happened, he went home to cry" (140). Unlike, Moreland T. Woods who has "consciously betrayed the trust of the community," partially because of his will to power and partially because of his economic circumstances, Abshu makes an attempt to uplift his community and foster awareness among the residents of Brewster Place (144). Moreland T. Woods, with his will to power and deceit incarnates the hegemonic repression of the power structure and denies the community upliftment to his people by constructing a new church for his sole aim of achieving power. Abshu determines to resist and to bring down Moreland from the state of power. In his proposition, he is assisted by his friend B.B. Rey. Moreland has beguiled the congregation against Deacons to serve his purpose of the construction of new Sinai Baptist church which further paves his ways to become the councilman. B.B. Rey says "[e]verybody's got a vice, Abshu; some little secret thing lying around in the closet at home. From what I've heard about Woods it's probably women. As a matter of fact, I can almost bet it's women" (148). Abshu applies the same method of bringing Moreland down which he has applied to climb the ladder of success:

> About fifty women, half of them with baby carriages and the others seeming to be in various stages of pregnancy, holding placards, formed a small army as they marched, double time, toward City Hall. They were a living United

> Nations: some brown, some black, some red—and even some white. Soon their chants could be heard even in the auditorium where the council was seated.
>
> *Moreland, Moreland*
>
> *Where's your shame?*
>
> *You left and didn't give*
>
> *My baby a name.* (150)
>
> Their placards read: DADDY, GIVE ME A HOME; and MORELAND IS THE ONE.... So when they finally marched into the council meeting, there were about a hundred people, ninety percent of them women. (151)

Despite Moreland's repeated plea to the council that these women want to destroy him, he is not heard as women keep impelling that they want blood test to further prove their claim. He gets down as he could not afford to have enough blood for so many tests, "And besides he didn't believe that he had enough blood to take that many paternity tests. So he was history by the end of spring; and the summer brought another clone to stand in his place. Still another conservative, except that this one was white" (153).

In conclusion, the chapter responds to the process of subject formation and acculturation through the unavoidable, complex net of power structure. In the synchronic study of power structure, the place of the black men is exemplified as people who are oppressed on the one hand and are oppressor on the other. The chapter expounds the concept of Hegelian dialectics in which each anti-thesis tries to reach to synthesis because each order resists the order itself. Further, it also explains the fact that the men at Brewster Place share the same marginal space as the women of Brewster have shared at the same place. The odyssey of the men towards Brewster Place has been full of suffering and pain as they have in some cases tried to debunk the order of the power structure which is evident in the case of revealing homosexuality by Eugene. Finally, it is made clear through the entire discourse of the chapter that all characters explicitly or implicitly experience the process of subjectivization but they also perpetuate the same process of social constructionism.

Chapter 7

Writing from the Margin: Reading Gloria Naylor's *1996*

Previous chapters in the book have extensively reflected upon the process, function, nature and construction of the marginal space in the fiction of Gloria Naylor which she has created over a period of twenty years since she published her first novel *The Women of Brewster Place* (1981). In an attempt to carve her fictional space, she has presented the marginal space in varying capacities which not only is shaped by the inhabitants of the space but it also shapes decisively the lives of the dwellers. Perhaps, this reciprocal relationship has been at the locus of Naylor's strategy in bringing about a differing account of the marginal space which has been not only the 'site of repression but also resistance'.

With her recent novel, *1996*, Naylor once again enters in a socio-political discourse of marginality and marginal space. She tends to expose the dominant hegemonic power structure which has relegated her life to the brink or margin and continually reminds her that "my life no longer was mine; it belonged to the strangers in dark glasses. It was invasion in its crudest form and it robbed me of my sense of peace. It also robbed me of my privacy for reasons that were still hidden to me" (Naylor 49-50). In particular her home space has been under surveillance snatching away the only space she had where she could gather herself against the hegemonic forces outside. In addition, Naylor's consciousness has also been targeted making her crippled to the extent where she gets almost insane. The exercise of control and construction of her mind by implanting the idea of suicide have been achieved by the powerful through the incessant assistance of modern technology reinstating the fact that technology is not democratic tool rather a deadly weapon of the state, indeed an apparatus. The novel in the context typifies the fact that the subjectivization of the women is the consequence of their ideological interpellation which is installed through technology. Adorno and Horkheimer in their *Dialectic of Enlightenment* (1944) explain the fact that enlightenment with its technological and scientific instruments exhibits some inevitable dialectics because if scientism and techne aims at liberating the human from the world of darkness of ignorance, it also perpetuates the pre-conditions of technological dogmatism. Technology, as Adorno and some other Frankfurt School of philosophers believe, is one of the dominant agencies of human objectification and interpellation. Further, the world of technology with its capacity to turn the world into culture industry transforms the existential reality of human life into simulation. The process of simulation also engraves upon the unconscious of the human mind which further controls the human consciousness. The novel elucidates the situation in which it is vividly exemplified that technology is not the means of human liberation rather it is one of the powerful tools of subjectivization, objectification and interpellation. Naylor's condition may refute the basic argument of Walter Benjamin's *The Work of Art in the Age of Mechanical Reproduction* (1935).

However, Naylor survives through the trap of the power structure only when she discovers the community with similar experiences being pushed to an unidentified space of utter alienation where nobody can even guess the intensity of marginalization and subjectivization. Her attempt to share her experiences through writing is not only a method to communicate to the marginalized community but also an aesthetico-spiritual resistance to the subjectivization by the hegemonic power structure.

A close examination of the entire trajectory of Gloria Naylor's fiction since the publication of *The Women of Brewster Place* to *1996* may reveal that there is a constant growth and development of her lexis and forms. Unlike her rebellious characters like Etta Mae Johnson and Kiswana Browne in *The Women of Brewster Place,* Naylor's central character i.e. Gloria Naylor in *1996* appears to be more cool and unruffled. In addition, she also adopts an aesthetico-spiritual method to combat the hegemonic world order. Writing to Naylor appears to be a libratory exercise as she feels "[w]henever I walked up those vast steps to the main branch of the Brooklyn Library, I felt like I was getting out of slavery and moving towards my freedom. And to leave was to go back into bondage again. So I stayed from the time the building opened until it closed" (*1996* 127-28). So the library came to Naylor's rescue and provided her a space where she could be herself, a space where she was in control of subjectivity "knowing that in there, my thoughts were my own" (128). As a result she picks up pen to fight the "BATTLE FOR MY MIND" (129). However, Naylor discovers the stimulation and inspiration of writing in various kinds of writing by black people who have written their "dreams" and "nightmares too" amidst "[t]he death of children, fires, hunger, years of no recognition, but they wrote through it all. If so many could find a way to soar, couldn't I?" (128).

Naylor's *1996* also brings about the politics of representation which always aims at not only constructing the black consciousness but also controlling their image by associating them with some 'anti' images. Like other black people, Naylor is dragged into such circumstances where she is represented as "a threat" simply by denying entry to the cats of a white lady into her compound (39). It further suggests that if you claim your space to be yours, any space where you try to be yourself or speak for your people, you become a threat to the white power structure and consequently you are given different names to control you. This is what Barry means when he associates Naylor with "Louis Farrakhan and the Nation of Islam" (39). However, the moment Barry alleges Naylor to be a "supporter of...the Nation of Islam", Yuri hurriedly utters "[s]o she's black?" (39).

Thus, Gloria Naylor is subjectivized owing much to her race and being different: "She's a writer. She's black. And she wears dreadlocks. Some kind of radical, that was for sure..." (21). Being a writer with a nationality other than the US has been a threat and as a result "[e]very black, Latino, and Asian writer who has had any press coverage is on the NSA's watch list" (33). *They* also assume Naylor that "she is a sympathiser of Louis Farrakan..." which enables them to put her under surveillance (33). Soon:

> All of her books are assigned to readers for a detailed synopsis of each one. Every newspaper article, every book review, is to be read and analyzed.... She is to be followed wherever she goes in Beaufort, with a report to be filled about her destination and whatever groups she speaks to. Files from the FBI and CIA are ordered. And just to be thorough, a background check going to her college days. (33)

The surveillance has been put on Naylor because she is a potential threat to the white community; she is a black and tries to assert her blackness. The surveillance initially robbed off her sleep as she "had stopped sleeping soundly during the night. I would wake up in fits and starts. It wasn't because of the increasing heat; I liked warm nights and didn't even own an air-conditioner. It was just general unrest. The surveillance was never off my mind" (61). The surveillance by the state agencies has been a process of subjectivization, robbing Naylor's subjectivity, identity, self, and consciousness. In addition, *They* have also made a point to label Naylor as "anti-Semitic" which "meant a slow death to my career in New York publishing circle" (43). Though, "[i]t was infuriating to think that any people for any reason felt that they has the right to harass and torment me when I had done nothing to them," Naylor has simply been helpless and clueless how to overcome the problem (44).

The process of subjectivization exposes the complex socio-cultural reality of the blacks in the contemporary world. It may also explicate the intricacies of territorialisation which has indeed been at the locus of subjectivization of Naylor. However, Naylor's isolated state through her stay at St. Helena and beyond has intensified or aggravated her sufferings which symbolically come to an end when she discovers a community of the people with same kind of oppressive history and subjectivization. Her discovery of this community of the oppressed reminds of Willa

Nedeed who discovers the community of oppressed women in the process of an attempt to locate the rationale of her suffering in Naylor's *Linden Hills*. The similarity between the two subjects lies in the fact that both of them, apparently, discover a tradition of oppression by the hegemonic power structure:

> I typed in "electronic surveillance" and immediately hit a gem. A man named John St. Clair Akwei, a former employee of the National Security Agency, was bringing a civil suit against the agency for electronic harassment from October of 1990 to May of 1991. Akwei claimed that through use of the most advanced computers in the world, the NSA has the ability to read the EEGs of a person wirelessly to determine what they're thinking. He also claimed that there is a domestic surveillance in operation that tracks tens of thousands of Americans through covert agents and phoney business fronts. It all began to fall into place and make sense to me. I didn't know how or why, but I had gotten tangled in a net that involved this agency. I didn't have a chemical imbalance, and that's why the medication wasn't working.... Typing in "mind control" on a search engine eventually brought me to the Mind Control Forum on the internet. It's an impressive site with, among other things, links to similar sites, a research archive, and a section for victims' stories. (*1996* 117)

The aforementioned account of her discovery states that Naylor in an urge to resolve her suffering discovers an authentic source which informs her that she is being watched and controlled by state based agencies, however the logic of the surveillance remains mysteriously hidden. In addition, her discovery brings her closer to the reality of her victimization. Further, the "section for victims' stories presents before her a community of victims who have similar experiences. Naylor may be searching for a bond with the people who have similar experiences. The similarity of experiences may bring them close and Naylor may be supported and her invisible victimization is believed in. It further compelled her to look "for experiences that might mirror mine, or for stories that seemed to ring true" (117). However,

Naylor's attempt to look for a community to establish a bond on the basis of shared experiences of victimization does not go unattended; she identifies three women who have been resisting the repression in their own ways:

> The first was Barbara Hartwell, who had worked for CIA and was now blowing the whistle on them for the abuses she experienced under the MK Ultra program. MK Ultra ran from 1950s to the 1960s officially, and was a research program that tested the effects of LCD and other biological agents on unwitting victims to see if the drugs could be used for mind control and behavior modification. The second story that intrigued me was Eleanor Whites. She had done extensive documentation on the unclassified technology that could be used to produce microwave hearing as well as synthetic telepathy. The third woman was Cheryl Welsh, who formed a group called Citizens Against Human Rights Abuses. Welsh had done exhaustive research on the background and history of mind control in government experimentation. Eleanor white and Cheryl Welsh designed their websites for people who simply will not believe that this technology has existed or that the U.S. Government would have a hand in tormenting unwilling subjects with it. (117-18)

The invisible bond that Naylor establishes with the above-mentioned women on the basis of the shared victimization relieved her as "[t]heir problem was the same as mine and other victims of mind control technology", however, the challenge has still been there; to prove your victimization as the information of mind control technology has not been much circulated one (118). The very realization of being in a helpless position further aggravates her as she not only wants to rescue herself but also to the "people out there crying for help" (118). The only salvation that she discovers lies in the words. As a result she attempts to write down her experiences, "although I resisted the idea for moths, that the only real way for me to fight back was by writing it all down. I had no other defence except my gift with words. I remembered what my agent had told me earlier in the year: "Your Work is your only salvation" and he was right. "If I let this ordeal keep me from writing, it was the same as keeping me from living" (122). She thus decides traversing through her inhibition to resist the wrong done to her and being done to "hundreds—if not thousands—of others" (123). She wants to write for an unprovoked invasion as she recounts:

> Mine had been a quiet life—a large extended family, a few friends, and my work. I hadn't asked for this invasion into my very being, but it had come. They had slowly eaten away at the edge of everything that was important to me. Now they wanted my mind. I had no choice but to fight. I had only one simple thing to say in what would be a complex book—this is wrong. It's wrong that it happened to me, and it's wrong that it's happening to hundreds—if not thousands—of others. (122-23)

The preceding deliberation of Naylor reiterates that writing is the only form of resistance available to her. And her writing would be a candid attempt to unravel the state apparatus and "to shed light where there'd been only darkness, so people could finally see what has been happening all around" (123). Her intention would be to inspire the victims to action which is indeed impossible unless people understand that they are being subjectivized and perhaps then "may be those who have hidden themselves behind a veil of silence will feel that it's okay to come out. That there are now more than a few who would believe them. I wanted this book for this, but above all, I wanted it for me. If I could finally manage to write it, then I have won the battle for my mind" (123).

An insight into the biographical details of Naylor may lead us to establish the proposition that writing which she eventually discovers as a method to overcome her present unhappy condition connects not only to the other victims but also to her own mother who also finds salve in the books. Naylor writes about it in the following paragraph:

> I inherited my love of books from my mother, who was never able to completely satisfy her hunger for reading. The public library was off-limits for black people in those days, and as tenant farmers, her family did not have the

> luxury of buying books. So, after working with her own family in their fields, she took her spare time on Saturdays to hire herself out in someone else's fields for the day. She made fifty cents for a day of labour, and at the end of the month, she had two dollars, which she used to write to book clubs and obtain her reading material. (03)

Naylor has been condition by her mother in a way that she always values books more than mere books and finds in them a salvation, a "passport to a world that held endless possibilities" and the library for her is "a sacred place" that she "used like a shrine, to read, to think, and to dream" (04).

A close scrutiny of the entire process of subjectivization through surveillance may establish that there has been a gradual movement of surveillance from public to private world of Gloria Naylor. The chapter attempts to examine this gradual intrusion of Naylor's space; form outside to Naylor's house to her laptop resulting in the violation of her mental space. Also the chapter aims at locating the use of technology by the state to subjectivize the people, enthusing in them a sense of marginalization.

The entire process of Naylor starts with alienating Naylor from her neighbours and consequently delimiting her access to her communal space which has indeed affected Naylor's consciousness. One day while communicating to her neighbour Betty, Naylor eventually comes to know that something unusual is happening to her. Betty told Naylor that:

> "There's been talk.... A sheriff's deputy was calling around not too long ago, asking questions about you."
>
> "What kind of questions?"
>
> "Just who you are. How long you been here. That kind of thing."
>
> She was having trouble meeting my eyes. The evasiveness disturbed me. Betty was one of the most straight forward people I knew. (24)

The aforementioned piece of conversation between Naylor and the neighbour may endorse that *they* have succeeded in insinuating the process of Naylor's alienation from her neighbours. This has indeed disturbed Naylor, "I felt a flush of shame that my neighbours would believe that someone like me would be dealing with drugs" (25). However, Naylor does not notice that she is being followed, until she notices something strange:

> It wasn't until February that I noticed I was being followed I was on Ribault Road near the government complex, on my way to have a nicked front windshield checked at the dealership. While stopping for a red light on the intersection of Highway 21, a man with brunette hair and a woman with shoulder-length, fluffy brown hair, looked away attempting to hide their faces, the instant I peered into my rearview mirror. This alerted me that something was amiss. Then several artificial moves were performed by the couple. The woman applied lipstick, kissed the man, applied lipstick again. They did not have the body language of people so taken with each other that they kiss publicly. I faked a left turn into the government complex on highway 21, and they sped off. My intuition was confirmed half an hour later when I left the dealership. There was the same gold Honda, pulling out from a side-road and staying three cars lengths away from me. When I turned, they turned. When I sped up, they sped up. I thought the tail originated with the Sheriff's office, and that it was about that drug business again. The Honda left me when I turned into Coffin Point Road and headed for my home. (34)

The recognition of the fact that she is followed forces her to believe that her public space is shrinking because of such an intrusion. However, she could not locate the reason why that was happening to her: "I had the very same question with no clear answer—why?" (42). However, with her close scrutinized wit, Naylor reaches to the conclusion in the letter that she writes to Peter that there are three levels behind this situation:

(1) Private citizens

(2) A private security agency

(3) Government participation. (44)

She further narrates her being followed everywhere:

> I am always in the middle of a formation when I leave home, with cars coming very fast toward me and turning on either side. Why? God knows. Whoever thought this up must have some sort of military training.... It's a pattern that plays itself out if I's at home, in my car, or at a restaurant. (45)

The very identification of the entire process of her surveillance by Naylor further infuriated the state agencies. And *they* decide to use modern technology to further subjectivize the victim which is indeed evident in Dick's words:

> Who are you Gloria Naylor? He thinks. Nobody. Living in a nowhere town on a nowhere island. And you're about to dip heavily into my budget because I's putting a Code 3 on your file. You're going to be watched my dear, like you've never been watched before. (48)

And as a result, Naylor is put on a surveillance 24/7 which has further started intruding in Naylor's even personal space, her laptop:

> In the day I had my garden and my books; at night I was on the internet talking to friends. And then I realised that they had even broken into that bit of my life. I was on my laptop making notations for my journal when a "spoof box" popped up on my screen. The window read: "Paging Idle." I couldn't get it to disappear and when I clicked on the button for "Answer," nothing happened. I had to shut down the computer to get rid of it. I booted up again, went back into my WordPerfect program, and after a short while there was another spoof box that was labelled, "Trouble." And the text in this window read "Big Trouble. We're Gonna Die." I tried to use the "print screen" key on my laptop to have a proof of this window, but it didn't work. And the only way to get rid of this window was to turn off the laptop and reboot the system. I am not a computer whiz; I knew the rudiments of how to use the system from owing computers over the years. But you didn't need to be an

> expert to understand that someone had hacked into my system. This fact distressed me more than the message, which I put down to childish prank. But it also made me have second thoughts about whether or not the government was part of my surveillance. (50)

The above-mentioned account of Naylor's victimization by *them* is indeed unbearable and throws Naylor into a state of total disruption. She thought "...someone, for some reason, was monitoring what I did on my laptop. Another invasion into my life. And if they were able to do this—and they were—what about my phone line? My fax machine? Were there even cameras in my home? A lot of questions for which I had no answers. Possible scenarios kept playing around in my head" (50). Not only this, the intensity of surveillance on Naylor can be imagined by the fact that "[t]here were people from the Drug Enforcement Agency, the Anti-defamation League, and the National Security Agency all involved with following this woman" (51).

Naylor is forced to have trouble sleeping as she spends sleepless nights because she could never put the surveillance thing off her mind. The sleepless nights also make her further find the subjectivization:

> As I lay in the darkness wide awake, I heard them for the first time. The birds. The sound carried well in the still of the night. Tweet. Tweet. Tweet. There were no birds in that part of the island that sang at night. So I knew it had to be them, the people who were watching me. They had come onto my property and were circling the house. I got out of bed and went to the window, but I saw nothing in the pitch black. (61)

Naylor's movement to the public space was curtailed by such an intrusion confining her first to house and then the domestic space was also violated reaching out to her laptop, monitoring even what she was doing on internet and beyond. She admits how she was being surrounded by *them*. "Going out for a peaceful drive was out of the question, because I had to deal with the cars zinging by in my ears and the blinking brake lights in front of me. I only went out when I absolutely had to. I was surrounded. Whenever I turned they were there to manipulate my environment. Slowly, each day, they were closing in" (62). *They* have also targeted everything related to her or the things that she loves the most. It is her garden that becomes a soft target of *them*. Naylor once notices "...that one of tomato plants had drooped and the leaves were starting to curl up. I checked for bugs, but there were none on it..." and the next day when she goes to check on it "the plant had gone totally black as if someone had scorched it with fire. I also saw that my Brussels sprouts were beginning to wither. I dug up the tomato plant and all the Brussels sprouts. It was like losing a part of myself. I had worked so hard on that garden" (64-65). She reaches to the conclusion that *they* "poison[ed] the garden" (65).

The intensity of Naylor's subjectivization may be observed by the fact that "[m]ost of her waking moments were spent thinking about the surveillance: the drive-bys and the noise" (83). In addition, Naylor's subjectivization has tremendously affected her consciousness. She confesses it like "you are changed by an experience like mine. I would no longer look at this country with the same innocence as before. I would no longer trust bonds of friendship to be unshakable" (84). The worst part of the experience that Naylor was undergoing was that "...things happened around me that I couldn't control. I had been outmanned and outgunned, with *them* bringing in friends to betray me" (90). The hardest part of the entire story that has been pinching Naylor a lot was she was not in control of her space. She confesses "what would I be guarding? Nothing except my space and the right to have my space without violation. The most bitter pill of all to swallow was that I couldn't guard my space effectively" (91). It is further exemplified by her subjectivization that she has been completely drifted away from her normal life and the surveillance thing is always up in her mind:

> Always back to the surveillance. I don't know what bothered me the most: the surveillance or the fact that *they* had the ability to hack into my computer. I had to accept that every thought I wrote down was possibly monitored. It was like living my life in a glass cage at

> a zoo. People I hadn't invited into my life had entered anyway and were watching my every move. (99)

Soon, Naylor realises that it is not only that she is being watched by the strangers rather they have also started controlling her mind and implanting thoughts. The idea behind this move has been to drive Naylor crazy where she is completely broken. Some strange things suddenly start coming up in her mind like "*I am a bitch*" and "*I am the worst bitch in the world. I want to kill myself*" (99). Naylor is taken aback as there has been no correlation between the context and the words or idea in her mind. Soon enough the accusation and abuse take momentum and it becomes a daily practice:

> *We rule the world....*
>
> I was watching television when a strange hissing sound came into my head.
>
> *You hate Jews....*
>
> I don't hate anyone. I thought.
>
> *Yes you do. You hate Jews....*
>
> I'll be glad when the medicine kicks in, I thought, so all of this can stop.
>
> *Medicine can't help you. Nothing can help you. You need to die....*
>
> Why I would want to die?
>
> *Because you hate Jews...and Eskimos. You hate Eskimos. The Eskimo people are unhappy with you now.*
>
> This is stupid.
>
> *This is not stupid. These are facts being brought to you by the Eskimo people.* (114)

Naylor is being subjected to so much violation of her personal mental space and she may not even guess about that she is being controlled because "...it was too horrible to think that someone had actually entered my mind. To believe that would be the first step on the road to madness" (115).

Naylor discovers that her mind is being controlled one day when she "decided to sleep on the couch in my study. My head was clear as a bell. When I decided to do it again on the second night, I heard bumping and thumping on the other side of my study wall. Then there was a strange sound at the base of my nose. The voices returned" (115):

> *You can run but you can't hide....*
>
> *Did you hear us, bitch? You can run but you....*
>
> *Face it, bitch. You need to kill yourself.*

This has given Naylor a realisation that "Whatever was going on, they were doing it to me. These voices were not originating in my own mind" (115). This has furthered pushed Naylor to reflect upon the issue as to how can somebody read your mind. The next moment a thought pops up in her mind, "*nobody's reading your mind, bitch. You're crazy*" (116). It went till she falls asleep, however, as she woke *they* were there "*Good morning, bitch. Did you sleep well?*" (116). A deep speculation on that matter led her to search internet to locate the problem and assumably the solution. Much to her surprise, there she located entire community of people who have been subjected to the surveillance or mind control. This is assured Naylor that she is indeed been monitored by an external agency. In an urge to save her mental space from being violated, she apparently decided to write down her experience and for that reason she located library as the safest point.

The novel, *1996* has been an odyssey that Naylor has taken while preparing to write a book. The novel offers an insight into the complexities of being black and woman in the capitalist, patriarchal society of the United States. In addition, Naylor has also attempted to make a point that the people who are marginally located have a different point of view which is always different from that of the people who live in the mainstream.

Chapter 8

Conclusion

The thesis has made a candid attempt to locate the marginal space in the first five novels of Gloria Naylor—*The Women of Brewster Place* (1982), *Linden Hills* (1985), *Mama Day* (1988), *Bailey's Café* (1992), and *The Men of Brewster Place* (1998). The marginal space in the aforementioned novels has been represented through its dialectics as it is a spatial reality which on the one hand exercises and perpetuates repression and resistance, on the other, it is a desired space of a few who acquire it through labor so that they may be able to resist against the oppressive, exploitative and demonic exercise of power structure. The study has also explored the spatial and temporal reality of marginal characters who dwell in a marginal space with a history of repression that they carry. Further, the shared experience of marginal characters of their repression culminates into a shared bonding among them which enables them to resist collectively against the hegemonic power structure. The thesis in context also expounds the fact that gender responds differently to the marginal space. The marginal space on the one hand elaborates the fact that it is constructed by gender which may function as a site of celebration for one gender (male) and marginal for another (female). It covertly signifies another significant shift that the marginal space may present an alternative world order with its well established cultural practices, language, community and cooperation that may be parallel to the mainstream world and so it offers a resistance to the hegemonic power structure of the contemporary world. Finally, the study has identified that men are proved to be the compatriot of the marginal women, despite their patriarchal attitude; they share the same marginal space and are subjected to the same repression of the power structure and experience the process of subjectivization. The study has extensively elicited, and has quoted some remarkable theorists and critical thinkers like Foucault, hooks, Fanon, Cixous, Beauvoir, Lacan, Spivak, Zizek, Collins and others to support and prove its proposition of marginality, repression and resistance along with the phenomenon of bonding to analyze the first five novels of Gloria Naylor.

The discourse and the discussion accomplished in the introduction of the thesis have underlined the fact that the African American resistance inevitably necessitates the process of subjectivization, through ideological apparatuses, among African Americans in American society. Formation of different viable strategies and sites for accounting the socio-economic, political and ideological phenomenon of resistance has been devised and discussed by some erudite theorists and thinkers along with some mentionable critics. There are many theorists and thinkers who have located the strategies of resistance at different sites, for example, critics and theorists like bell hooks, Surya Nath Pandey, Barbara Christian, and Margot Anne Kelley have emphasized on the fact that the marginal space is a site of repression and opportunity for resistance as it provides the marginal to obtain an outsider's view of the hegemonic power structure. Again authors like hooks, Collins, and Marshall along with Lavon present 'Home' as a site of resistance against the imperialist and capitalist world view that controls and defines women outside the home space. Some other critics and thinkers reiterate that the female bonding is quite instrumental in resisting the patriarchal and racial repression, for instance, Andrews, Brantley, Matus, and Awkward, etc. have supported the female bonding. In addition, there are some other methods of resistance which can be seen through the lances of revision and representation. Both revision and representation provide an opportunity to review the state of black people in classical and contemporary literature, media and consequently resist and reconstruct the repressive images of the African Americans. The introduction is concluded with the proposition of a gap for further resistance as has been proposed by Tapan Kumar Basu and Pickett.

Chapter two of the thesis has illustrated the apodosis that the marginal space of Brewster Place with its wall that separates it from the mainstream American world, provides an opportunity to the inhabitants of the Brewster Place to resist against, what bell hooks calls, "imperialist white-supremacist capitalist patriarchy" (hooks, *Understanding Patriarchy* 02). The wall exhibits an antinomy or pharmakon in its nature and function, as it, on the one hand, has been constructed by the power structure to exercise different apparatuses of power machinery which control the consciousness, ideology and identity of the marginal, but on the other, it also provides the marginal with an opportunity to resist against such oppressive power structure which always aims at 'will to power'. It has also traced the odyssey of the women of Brewster Place which is replete with racial and gender repression in hegemonic patriarchal world. The repressive condition of the women is located into the process of subjectivization, in which the socio-economic, political and linguistic realities play vital roles, has also been aptly discussed in the chapter. Further, it has also elaborated upon the condition in which the women of Brewster Place come forward to resist against the power of patriarch. The resistance that emanates from their positionality in the marginal space against the Foucauldian power has been made possible by forming a bond among the women of Brewster Place on the basis of their shared common experiences of patriarchal repression and racial stranding. The chapter also adds that this marginal space is acquired or allotted to the women of Brewster Place because of the inherent rebellious tendency in them which defies the societal norms of gender, class, and racial definitions. Again, it exemplifies that though marginal space stands against the mainstream world in so far as its construction is concerned; there are some characters who defy this definition by making a labored choice to live in the marginal space.

Linden Hills, the place which acts simultaneously both as marginal and mainstream in Naylor's *Linden Hills*, has been examined, discussed and debated in the third chapter of the thesis which divulges an inherent dialectics in its construction and location; however, the dialectics may depend upon the role of gender in context. It is represented as an artefact of oppressive power structure with its agency that maintains carnival as far as the place of the man is concerned. However, it is concomitantly a site of repression and exploitation for the women as Linden Hills is owned and controlled by the patriarchal power structure. Primarily, the power structure at Linden Hills functions through necessitating the condition of heterosexuality which conforms to the dominance of the patriarch in its all forms whereas the homosexuality, which defies the principles of social constructionism, is disapproved and ostracized.

Linden Hills subjectivizes its characters through the economic, social, and cultural signifier and signified which may be identified to have been the controlling tools of the power structure which may be verified in the example of Winston and David. On the contrary, those who may defy the social, economic and culture privileges may not be controlled by the power structure which may be appropriately identified in the case of Willie and Lester. Further, the chapter also explores the process of marginalization that the women experience in the Nedeed house. The process of marginalization is entailed upon the women by all Luthers who control their subjectivity which is rooted in the fact that the very foundation of Linden Hills lies on the auction of his wife by the first Luther. This represents a glaring example of the commodification of the women and their controlled subjectivity in a patriarchal capitalist society. The oppressive history of the process of subjectivization of the women is traced through the diachronic and synchronic remnants of the documents that the previous women of Luther family have left in the basement. However, the interpellation of women is made possible through several hiatus as they lack a cohesive bonding among themselves. In Linden Hills the women are presented, conditioned, subjectivised, and isolated which does not allow them to interact with the larger reality of the community which brings them into a great fiasco of fracturedness. The cohesive bonding, for instance, among the women of Brewster Place fortifies them with immense capacity to fight against the oppressive structure of patriarchy.

The comparative picture of the Linden Hills and Brewster Place exemplifies the fact that the female bonding is inevitable in order to efface the powerful force of patriarchy.

The arguments in chapter four encapsulate the underlying propositions with regard to the role, nature and function of politics and history in the construction of the marginal space, Willow Springs, in Gloria Naylor's *Mama Day*. The chapter further articulates the possibilities of constructing an invisible bonding among the inhabitants of Willow Springs which may bring a sense of security, carnival and community to them with an insight into the web of the power structure. The location of marginal space through historical realities since its very inception defies the principle of bell hooks' configuration about the construction of marginal space through suffering, pain, and struggle and the notion of segregation of the subalterns by the power structure which is indeed quite remarkable as far as the chapter is concerned. The gradual progress of the discourse in the chapter lights upon the possibilities of forming an invisible bond which may inculcate a sense of autonomy, self-respect and resistance against the power structure. It explains all possible motives which become quite instrumental in forming a cohesive bond in which some remarkable motives are—quilt making, Candle Walk, conjuring, and healing. It is candidly observed that all mythical activities are archetypes and motives of African American socio-cultural and economic realities. These archetypes and motives hold the identity and subjectivity of Cocoa, the protagonist who defies the processes of subjectivization through her roots in the community and practices of the island, however, the character who is bereft of the above-mentioned mythical practices are easily subjectivised by the dominant ideology of the dominant class. In its all capacities, the marginal space of Willow Springs also offers an alternate world which resists the mainstream hegemonic world order.

The fifth chapter has attempted to unravel the uncanny structure of power which seems to be omnipresent with its roots in knowledge and the process of subjectivity. It begins the basic philosophy of power structure which expels the dispossessed, powerless, isolated, and destitute to the brink of margin by confining them into a marginal space. The marginal space in Naylor's *Bailey's Café* contains a Hegelian dialectics in itself with the perpetuation of the subalterns who dwell there and its potentiality of resistance. The antinomy of power does not only allow the characters to explore their space in the world but it also allows the characters to be trapped into the eminence of power. This entrapment of the characters into the vortex of power at the marginal place inculcates a rebellious tendency in them. Gloria Naylor through her subaltern and marginalized characters in the novel explicates and delineates the entire process of objectification and subjetification in which her characters experience the odor of repressive, oppressive and exploitative nature of power. This allows the characters of the novel to play with the aporatic nature of marginal space. Further, the novel also proposes the fact that female subjectivity may find full play at Eve's boarding house, the marginal space in the mainstream world. The place provides ample space for the female bonding where the female may share common experiences and the world view. However, Naylor provides her characters with the place of Eve, only as sojourn where they may recollect enough energy so that they may fight against the power of patriarch and may continue their search into the dismal yet eliminating space where they may find their subjectivity, ideology, or the world view.

Chapter six presents the sublime object of ideology and the formation of subjects. It explores the entire process of subject formation and acculturation of the individuals through the unavoidable, complex web of power structure. In the synchronic study of power structure the place of the black men is exemplified as oppressed on the one hand and oppressor on the other. The chapter expounds, through the portrayal of male characters, the concept of Hegelian dialectics in which each anti-thesis tries to reach to a synthesis because each order resists the order itself. Further, it also explains the fact that the men at Brewster Place share the same marginal space as the women of Brewster have shared at the same place which reiterates the fact that the men, despite their sexist behavior, are their compatriot in their struggle against the hegemonic power structure which subjects the African Americans alike irrespective of their gender. The odyssey of the men towards Brewster Place is replete with the experiences of suffering and pain which have been a result of their rebellion against the order of the power structure which is, for instance, evident in the case of revealing homosexuality by Eugene. Finally, the chapter also exemplifies the dialectic inherent in the characters themselves as they explicitly or implicitly experience the process of subjectivization but perpetuate the same process of social constructionism on their counterparts. Thus, the chapter successfully sums up its subject, the formation of subjectivity through the process of subjectivization.

The aforementioned deliberation summarizes the whole discourse and discussion carried on the location of marginal space with its perpetuation of repression and potentiality of resistance of African American men and women in the novels of Gloria Naylor along with their mechanism of bonding against resistance and role of the marginal positionality in enabling and offering them with the opportunity to resist. The historical and political construction of marginal space and its diverse realization in each novel has also been discussed above.

Works Cited

ade-Gayles, Gloria. *No Crystal Stair: Visions of Race and Sex in Black Women's Fiction.* New York: The Pilgrim Press, 1984. Print.

Althusser, Louis. "The Ideology and the Ideological State Apparatuses." Trans. Ben Brewster. *Lenin and Philosophy and Other Essays.* Ed. Louis Althusser. New York: Monthly Review Press, 1971. 127-86. Print.

Andrews, Larry. "Black Sisterhood in Gloria Naylor's Novels." *Gloria Naylor: Critical Perspectives Past and Present.* Eds. Henry Louis Gates, Jr. and K.A. Appiah. New York: Amistad, 1993. 285-301. Print.

Armstrong, Aurelia. "Beyond Resistance: A Response to Žižek's Critique of Foucault's Subject of Freedom." *Parrhesia* 5 (2008): 19-31. Print.

Awkward, Michael. "Authorial Dreams of Wholeness: (Dis)Unity, (Literary) Parentage, and *The Women of Brewster Place.*" *Gloria Naylor: Critical Perspectives Past and Present.* Eds. Gates, Henry Louis, Jr. and K.A. Appiah. New York: Amistad, 1993. 37-70. Print.

Basu, Tapan Kumar. "Beyond the National Question: Shifting Agendas of African-American Resistance." *Economic and Political Weekly* 29.7 (1994): 377-85. Web. 14 April 2012.

Beal, Francis M. "Double Jeopardy: To be Black and Female." *Sisterhood is Powerful.* Ed. Robin Morgan. New York: Random, 1970. Print.

Beauvoir, Simone de. *The Second Sex.* New York: Vintage Books, 1973. Print.

Berg, Christine G. "Light from a Hill of Carbon Paper Dolls": Gloria Naylor's "Linden Hills" and Dante's "Inferno". *Modern Language Studies* 29.2 (1999): 1-19. Web. 13 March 2011.

Bharati, Megha and L.M. Joshi. "Race, Class and Gender Bias as Reflected in Toni Morrison's First Novel *The Bluest Eye.*" *Journal of Literature, Culture and Media Studies* 1 (2009): 37-45. Print.

Billingslea-Brown, Alma Jean. "Yearning for the Homeland: The "Return to the Source" in Contemporary African-American Women's Fiction and Visual Art." *The Contemporary West* 14.2 (1997): 1-7. Web. 12 January. 2012.

Blyn, Robert. "The Ethnographer's Story: "Mama Day" and the Specter of Relativism." *Twentieth Century Literature* 48.3 (2002): 239-63. Web. 12 October 2010.

Bobo, Jacqueline and Ellen Seiter. "Black Feminism and Media Criticism: *The Women of Brewster Place*." *The Critical Response to Gloria Naylor*. Eds. Sharon Felton and Michelle C. Loris. Westport, Connecticut: Greenwood Press, 1997. 26-41. Print.

Bouvier, Luke. "Reading in Black and White: Space and Race in *Linden Hills.*" *Gloria Naylor: Critical Perspectives Past and Present.* Eds. Gates, Henry Louis, Jr. and K.A. Appiah. New York: Amistad, 1993. 140-51. Print.

Boyd, Nellie. "Dominion and Proprietorship in Gloria Naylor's *Mama Day* and *Linden Hills.*" *Critical Response to Gloria Naylor.* Eds. Sharon Felton and Michelle C. Loris. Westport, Connecticut: Greenwood Press, 1997. 76-80. Print.

Bozeman, Terry Sinclair. "The Good Cut: The Barbershop in the African American Literary Tradition" (2009). English Dissertations. Paper 49. Web. 12 February 2012. http://digitalarchive.gsu.edu/english_diss/49

Brantley, Jennifer. "Women's Screams and Women's Laughter: Connections and Creations in Gloria Naylor's Novels." *Gloria Naylor's Early Novels*. Ed. Margot Anne Kelley. Gainesville: University of Florida, 1999. 21-38. Print.

Branzburg, Judith V. "Seven Women and a Wall." *Callaloo* 21 (1984): 116-19. Web. 28 April. 2011.

Brooks, Dwight E. and Lisa P. Hebert. "Gender, Race, and Media Representation." *The SAGE Handbook of Gender and Communication.* Eds. Bonnie J. Dow and Julia T. Wood. London: Sage Publication, 2006. 297-317. Print.

Carabi, Angela. "An Interview with Gloria Naylor." *Conversations with Gloria Naylor.* Ed. Maxine Lavon Montgomery. Jackson: University of Mississippi, 2004: 111-22. Print.

Carmichael, Stokely, "Black Power." *Black Power: The Politics of Liberation in America.* Ed. Charles V. Hamilton. New York: Random House, 1967. 44-56. Print.

Cash, Floris Barnett. "Kinship and Quilting: An Examination of an African-American Tradition." *The Journal of Negro History* 80.1 (1995): 30-41. Web. 24 March 2010.

Chatterjee, Srirupa and G. Neelkantan. "Woman as Survivor in Oates' *Rape: A Love Story.*" *Notes on Contemporary Literature* 39.4 (2009): 4-6. Print.

Christian, Barbara. "Naylor's Geography: Community, Class and Patriarchy in *The Women of Brewster Place* and *Linden Hills.*" *Gloria Naylor: Critical Perspectives Past and Present.* Eds. Henry Louis Gates, Jr. and K.A. Appiah. New York: Amistad, 1993: 106-25. Print.

——. *Black Feminist Criticism: Perspectives on Black Women Writers.* New York: Pergamon Press, 1985. Print.

Cixous, Helen. "The Laugh of Medusa." Trans. Keith Cohen and Paula Cohen. *The Sign Reader: Women, Gender, and Scholarship.* Eds. Elizabeth Abel and Emily K. Abel. Chicago and London: University of Chicago Press, 1983. Print.

Clarke, Cheryl. "The Failure to Transform: Homophobia in the Black Community." *Home Girls: A Black Feminist Anthology.* Ed. Barbara Smith. New York: Women of Color Press, 1983. 195-217. Print.

Collins, Patricia Hill. "Intersecting Oppressions". February 12, 2012. Web. http://www.uk.sagepub.com/upm-data/13299_Chapter_16_Web_Byte_Patricia_Hill_Collins.pdf

——. "The Social Construction of Black Feminist Thought." *Sings* 14.4 (1989): 745-73. Web. 26 August 2011.

——. *Black Feminist Thought: Knowledge, Consciousness, and the Politics of Empowerment.* New York: Routledge, 2000. Print.

——. *Black Sexual Politics: African Americans, Gender, and the New Racism.* New York and London: Routledge, 2004. Print.

——. "Shifting the Centre: Race, Class, and Feminist Theorizing about Motherhood." *Mothering: Ideology, Experience and Agency.* Eds. Evelyn Nakano Glenn, Grace Chang, and Linda Forcey. New York: Routledge, 1994. 45-65. Print.

Costino, Kimberly A. "'Weapons Against Women': Compulsory Heterosexuality and Capitalism in *Linden Hills.*" *Gloria Naylor's Early Novels.* Ed. Margot Anne Kelley. Gainesville: University of Florida, 1999. 39-54. Print.

Crenshaw, Kimberle. "Mapping the Margins: Intersectionality, Identity Politics, and Violence Against Women of Color." *Stanford Law Review* 43 (1991): 1241-99. Web. 14 December 2011.

Delgado, R. and J. Stefancic. "Minority Men, Misery, and the Marketplace of Ideas." *Constructing Masculinity.* Eds. M. Berger, B. Wallis and S. Watson. New York: Routledge. 1995. 211-20. Print.

Dill, Bonnie Thornton. "Race, Class, and Gender: Prospects for an All-inclusive Sisterhood." *Feminist Studies* 9.1 (1983): 131-50. Web. 23 March 2010.

Eckard, Paula Gallant. "The Prismatic Past in Oral History and Mama Day." *MELUS* 20.3 (1995): 121-35. Web. 23 March 2010.

Eko, Ebele. "Beyond the Myth of Confrontation: A Comparative Study of African and African American Female Protagonists." *The Critical Response to Gloria Naylor*. Eds. Sharon Felton and Michelle C. Loris. Westport, Connecticut: Greenwood Press, 1997. 13-22. Print.

Erickson, Peter. ""Shakespeare's Black?": The Role of Shakespeare in Naylor's Novels." *Gloria Naylor: Critical Perspectives Past and Present*. Eds. Henry Louis Gates, Jr. and K.A. Appiah. New York: Amistad, 1993. 231-48. Print.

Felton, Sharon and Michelle C. Loris. "The Human Spirit is a Kick-Ass Thing." *Conversations with Gloria Naylor.* Ed. Maxine Lavon Montgomery. Jackson: University of Mississippi, 2004. 138-49. Print.

——. *The Critical Response to Gloria Naylor.* Westport, Connecticut. London: Greenwood Press, 1997. Print.

Foucault, Michel. *The History of Sexuality: An Introduction Volume 1*. New York: Vintage Books, 1990. Print.

Foust Vinson, Sarah Katherine, "Storied Memories: Memory as Resistance in Contemporary Women's Literature" (2010). *Dissertations* Paper 176. Web. February 15, 2012. http://ecommons.luc.edu/luc_diss/176

Fowler, Virginia C. "A Conversation with Gloria Naylor." *Conversations with Gloria Naylor.* Ed. Maxine Lavon Montgomery. Jackson: University of Mississippi, 2004. 123-37. Print.

——. *Gloria Naylor: In Search of Sanctuary.* New York: Simon and Schuster Macmillan, 1996. Print.

Fraser, Celeste. "Stealing B(l)ack Voices: The Myth of the Black Matriarchy and *The Women of Brewster Place.*" *Gloria Naylor: Critical Perspectives Past and Present*. Eds. Henry Louis Gates, Jr. and K.A. Appiah. New York: Amistad, 1993. 90-105. Print.

Friedan, Betty. *The Feminist Mystique*. Harmondsworth: Penguin, 1963. Print.

Goddu, Teresa. "Reconstructing History in *Linden Hills.*" *Gloria Naylor: Critical Perspectives Past and Present*. Eds. Henry Louis, Gates Jr. and K.A. Appiah. New York: Amistad, 1993: 215-30. Print.

Gramsci, Antonio. *Selections from Political Writings*. Trans. J. Mathews. Ed. Q. Hoare. New York: International Publishers, 1977. Print.

Habib, M.A.R. *Modern Literary Criticism and Theory.* New Delhi: Wiley India (P) Ltd, 2008. Print.

Harris, Trudier. "African American Protest Poetry." Freedom's Story, Teacher Serve©. National Humanities Center. Web. February 4, 2012. http://nationalhumanitiescenter.org/tserve/freedom/1917beyond/essays/aaprotestpoetry.htm

Henderson, Mae G. "Speaking in Tongues: Dialogic, Dialectics, and the Black Women Writer's Literary Tradition" 3.3 & 4.1. *The Scholar & Feminist. XXX: Past Controversies, Present Challenges, Future Feminisms* Document Archive. Web. February 10, 2011.

Higginbotham, Evelyn Brooks. "African American Women's History and the Metalanguage of Race." *Sign: Journal of Women in Culture and Society* 17.2 (1992): 251-74. Web. March 12, 2012.

Homans, Margaret. "The Woman in the Cave: Recent Feminist Fictions and the Classical Underworld." *Gloria Naylor: Critical Perspectives Past and Present.* Eds. Henry Louis Gates, Jr. and K.A. Appiah. New York: Amistad, 1993. 152-81. Print.

Hooks, bell and Tanya McKinnon. "Sisterhood: Beyond Public and Private." *Signs* 21.4 (1996): Web. 24 April, 2011.

Hooks, bell. "Choosing the Margin as a Space of Radical Openness." *Yearning: Race, Gender and Cultural Politics.* Ed. bell hooks. Boston: South End Press, 1990. 145-53. Print.

——. "Homespace (a site of resistance)." *Yearning: Race, Gender, and Cultural Politics.* Ed. Bell hooks. Boston: South End Press, 1990. 41-49. Print.

——. "The Oppositional Gaze: Black Female Spectators." *Black Looks: Race and Representation.* Ed. Bell hooks. Boston: South End Press, 1992. 115-31. Print.

——. "Understanding Patriarchy." Web. March 1, 2012, http://tribar.net/jemma/bellhooks-understandingpatriarchy.pdf

——. *Ain't I a Woman: Black Women and Feminism.* Boston: South and Press, 1981. Print.

——. *Black Looks: Race and Representation.* Boston: South End Press. 1992. Print.

——. *Feminism is for Everybody: Passionate Politics.* Cambridge, MA: South End Press, 2000. Print.

——. *Feminist Theory: From Margin to Center.* Boston: South End Press, 1984. Print.

——. *Feminist Theory: From Margin to Center.* Cambridge, MA: South End Press. 2000. Print.

——. *Yearning: Race, Gender, and Cultural Politics.* Boston: South End Press, 1990. Print.

Ivey, Adriane L. "Beyond Sacrifice: Gloria Naylor Rewrites the Passion." *MELUS* 30.1 (2005): 85-108. Web. 23 April 2011.

Jackson, Edward M. *Images of Black Men in Black Women Writers 1950-1990.* Indiana: Wyndham Hall Press, 1992. Print.

Jewell, K. Sue. *From Mammy to Miss America and Beyond: Cultural Images and the Shaping of US Social Policy.* New York: Routledge, 1993. Print.

Johnson, C., and McCluskey, Jr., J. *Black Men Speaking*. Bloomington: Indiana University Press, 1997. Print.

Kelley, Margot Anne (ed.). *Gloria Naylor's Early Novels*. Gainesville: University Press of Florida, 1999. Print.

——. "Framing the Possibilities: Collective Agency and the Novels of Gloria Naylor." *Gloria Naylor's Early Novels*. Ed. Margot Anne Kelley. Gainesville: University of Florida, 1999. 133-54. Print.

Khay, Renee. "The Ties that Bind: Female Relationships in the Works of Gloria Naylor." Yahoo! Contributor Network Web. 6 December 2006. www.associatedocument.com

Kovel, Joel. *White Racism: A Psychohistory.* New York: Columbia University Press, 1984. Print.

Kriesteva, Julia. *Revolution in Poetic Language*. Trans. Margaret Waller. New York: Columbia University Press, 1984. Print.

Kristeva, Julia, Alice Jardine, and Harry Blake. "Women's Time." *Signs* 7.1 (1981): 13-35. Web. 07 February 2010.

Kubitschek, Missy Dehn. "Toward a New Order: Shakespeare, Morrison, and Gloria Naylor's Mama Day." *MELUS* 19.3 (1994): 75-90. Web. 13 October 2011.

Lacan, Jacques. *Écrits*. Paris: Seuil, 1966. Print.

Lamothe, Daphne. "Gloria Naylor's "Mama Day": Bridging Roots and Routes." *African American Review* 39.1/2 (2005): 155-69. Web. 17 March. 2011.

Lerner, Gerda. *Black Women in White America*. New York: Pantheon, 1972. Print.

Levin, Amy K. "Metaphor and Maternity in *Mama Day*." *Gloria Naylor's Early Novels*. Ed. Margot Anne Kelley. Gainesville: University of Florida, 1999. 70-88. Print.

Littlefield, Marci Bounds. "Black Women, Mothering, and Protest in 19th Century American Society." *The Journal of Pan African Studies* 2.1 (2007): 53-61. Web. 17 March, 2011.

Marshall, Paule. "From The Poets In the Kitchen." *Merle: A Novella and Other Stories*. Ed. Paule Marshall. New York: The Feminist Press, 1983. 1-12. Web. 24 October, 2011.

Matus, Jill L. "Dream, Deferral, and Closure in *The Women of Brewster Place.*" *Black American Literature Forum* 24.1 (1990): 49-64. Web. 18 October 2011.

Meisenhelder, Susan. ""The Whole Picture" in Gloria Naylor's Mama Day." *African American Review* 27.3 (1993): 405-19. Web. 13 December 2011.

Montgomery, Maxine Lavon, ed. *Conversations with Gloria Naylor.* Jackson: University Press of Mississippi, 2004. Print.

——. "Good Housekeeping: Domestic Ritual in Gloria Naylor's Fiction." *Gloria Naylor's Early Novels.* Ed. Margot Anne Kelley. Gainesville: University of Florida, 1999. 55-69. Print.

——. "Authority, Multivocality, and the New World Order in Gloria Naylor's *Bailey's Café.*" *The Critical Response to Gloria Naylor.* Eds. Felton, Sharon and Michelle C. Loris. Westport, Connecticut. London: Greenwood Press, 1997. 187-93. Print.

——. "The Fathomless Dream: Gloria Naylor's Use of the Descent Motif in *The Women of Brewster Place.*" *The Critical Response to Gloria Naylor.* Eds. Sharon Felton and Michelle C. Loris, Westport, Connecticut: Greenwood Press, 1997: 42-47. Print.

——. "The Men of Brewster Place. - Review - book review." March 10, 1012. http://findarticles.com/p/articles/mi_m2838/is_1_34/ai_62258924/

——. *The Apocalypse in African American Fiction.* Gainesville: University of Florida, 1996. Print.

——. *The Fiction of Gloria Naylor: Houses and Spaces of Resistance.* Knoxville: The University of Tennessee Press, 2010. Print.

Moore, John Noell. "Myth, Fairy Tale, Epic, and Romance: Narrative as Re-Vision in Linden Hills." *Callaloo* 23.4 (2000): 1410-29. Web. October 13, 2010.

Naylor, Gloria and Toni Morrison. "A Conversation." *Southern Review* 21 (1985): 567-93. Print.

——. *Bailey's Café.* New York: Harcourt Brace Jovanovich, 1992. Print.

——. *Linden Hills.* New York: Ticknor & Fields, 1985. Print.

——. *Mama Day.* New York: Ticker & Fields, 1988. Print.

——. *The Men of Brewster Place.* New York: Hyperion, 1998. Print.

——. *The Women of Brewster Place.* New York: Penguin, 1982. Print.

——. *1996.* Chicago: Third World Press, 2005. Print.

O'Connor, Maurice. "Writing From Memory: The Diasporic Discourse of Abdulrazak Gurnah and Ben Okri." *Afroeuropeo: revista de afroeuropeos* 1.2 (2007): 1-9. Web. http://journal.afroeuropa.eu/index.php/afroeuropa/issue/view/2

Okonkwo, Christopher N. "Suicide or Messianic Self-Sacrifice?: Exhuming Willa's Body in Gloria Naylor's Linden Hills." *African American Review* 35.1 (2001): 117-31. Web. 13 March 2011.

Pandey, Surya Nath. *Writing in a Post-colonial Space*. New Delhi: Atlantic Publishers and Distributors, 1999. Print.

Perry, Donna. "Gloria Naylor." *Conversations with Gloria Naylor*. Ed. Maxine Lavon Montgomery. Jackson: University of Mississippi, 2004. 76-104. Print.

Pickett, Brent L. "Foucault and the Politics of Resistance." *Polity* 28.4 (1996): 445-66. Web. 13 March 2011.

Plakkoottam, Alphy J. "Racial and Gender Discrimination in Fiction by Afro-American Women." *Indian Journal of American Studies* 20.1 (1990): 11-19. Print.

Puhr, Kathleen M. "Healers in Gloria Naylor's Fiction." *Twentieth Century Literature* 40.4 (1994): 518-27. Web. 15 March 2011.

Ray, Suranjita. "Understanding Patriarchy." *Human Rights, Gender & Patriarchy*. 14 March 2012. Web. http://www.du.ac.in/fileadmin/DU/Academics/course_material/hrge_06.pdf

Rowell, Charles. "An Interview with Gloria Naylor." *Conversations with Gloria Naylor*. Ed. Maxine Lavon Montgomery. Jackson: University of Mississippi, 2004. 151-61. Print.

Schneider, Karen. "Gloria Naylor's Poetics of Emancipation: (E)merging (Im)possibilities in *Bailey's Café*." *Gloria Naylor's Early Novels*. Ed. Margot Anne Kelley. Gainesville: University of Florida, 1999. Print.

Shukla, A.K. "The Image of a Black in the Poetry of Langston Hughes." *Points of View* 11.2 (2004): 49-58. Print.

Simpson, G.E and J.M. Yinger. *Racial and Cultural Minorities*. New York: Harper & Row, 1965. Web. 14 March 2011.

Smith, Valerie, Lea Bachiler and A. Walton Litz (eds). *African American Writers Profiles of Their Lives and Works—From the 1700s to the Present*. Collier Books. MacMillan Pub. Co. NY. 1993. Print.

Spivak, Gayatri Chakraborty. "Feminism and Critical Theory". *Modern Criticism and Theory: A Reader*. Eds. David Lodge and Nigel Wood. India: Dorling Kindersley, 2007. Print.

Stoddart, Mark C.J. "Ideology, Hegemony, Discourse: A Critical Review of Theories of Knowledge and Power." *Social Thought & Research* 28 (2007): 191-225. Web. 14 March 2011.

Tanner, Laura E. "Reading Rape." *Gloria Naylor: Critical Perspectives Past and Present*. Eds. Henry Louis Gates, Jr. and K.A. Appiah. New York: Amistad, 1993. 71-89. Print.

Thomas, Jackie. *The Men Of Brewster Place.* - Review - book reviews. July 15, 2007. Web. http://diverseeducation.com/article/8694c2/the-men-of-brewster-place-review-book-reviews.html

Thompson, Dorothy Perry. "Africana Womanist Revision in Gloria Naylor's *Mama Day* and *Bailey's Café.*" *Gloria Naylor's Early Novels.* Ed. Margot Anne Kelley. Gainesville: University of Florida, 1999. 89-111. Print.

Walker, Alice. *In Love & Trouble: Stories of Black Women.* San Diego: Harvest Books, 2003. Print.

Wall, Cheryl A. "Extending the Line: From "Sula" to "Mama Day."" *Callaloo* 23.4 (2000): 1449-63. Web. 15 March 2011.

Webb, Claudia Lawrence et al. "African American Intergender Relationships: A Theoretical Exploration of Roles, Patriarchy and Love." *Journal of Black Studies* 34.5 (2004): 623-39. Web. 15 March 2011.

White, J.L. and Cones, III, J.H. *Black Man Emerging: Facing the Past and Seizing a Future in America.* New York: Routledge, 1999. Print.

Whitsitt, Sam. "In Spite of It All: A Reading of Alice Walker's "Everyday Use."" *African American Review* 34.3 (2000): 443-59. Web. 16 March. 2011.

Whitt, Margaret Earley. *Understanding Gloria Naylor.* Columbia: University of South Carolina Press, 1999. Print.

Williams, Raymond. "Base and Superstructure in Marxist Cultural Theory." Web. March 12, 2012. http://www.extrememediastudies.org/extreme_media/2_mobiles/pdf/capsules_williams_base_super.pdf

Wilson Jr., Charles E. *Gloria Naylor: A Critical Companion.* Westport, Connecticut: Greenwood Press, 2001. Print.